APARTHEID — The Closing Phases?

Stellenbosch University, situated in the three
hundred year old and beautiful city of
Stellenbosch, was founded as an education centre
and cultural focal point for the Afrikaner. Six of
South Africa's eight Prime Ministers were once its
students.

In August 1978, the author, a citizen and
former Supreme Court Judge of Sri Lanka and
presently a Law Professor in Australia, received an
invitation from the Faculty of Law of the
University. The invitation suggested a visit of
approximately six weeks, and offered a range of
subjects as the subject-matter of the courses to be
taught by him during his stay. The subjects
offered included Jurisprudence, Constitutional
Law and the Sociology of Law.

The author, who has worked and written in
the human rights field, made two conditions
regarding his acceptance of the invitation. He
indicated categorically that he would not be
prepared to accept the status of 'honorary white'
which is sometimes conferred on non-white invited
visitors to South Africa. He also stipulated that he
would teach jurisprudence with a strong human
rights content and that he should have complete
freedom regarding his manner of presentation. The
author was reassured on these two points.

In pursuance of this invitation, the author
visited Stellenbosch University as a Visiting
Professor from August 11 to September 10 1979.
He also visited and delivered lectures at the
Universities of Cape Town, the Western Cape,
Durban-Westville and the University of South
Africa. He was also hosted both formally and
informally by members of the Supreme Court and
the Bar in South Africa.

The author's previous publications include
two volumes on the Roman-Dutch law of Contract,
which are used in South Africa, *The Law in Crisis*
which had been the subject of a detailed review in
the Stellenbosch Law Journal and *Equality and
Freedom*, a study of equality and freedom
problems of the Third World. The author is a
Doctor of Laws of the University of London and a
member of the United Nations University's Task
Force on Human Rights.

APARTHEID
The closing phases?

C.G. Weeramantry

LANTANA
Melbourne

First Published 1980
Typesetting: Jurik Stationery Co.
156 Francis Street, Yarraville, 3013
Artwork & Layout: Abb-typesetting Pty. Ltd.,
83-85 Little Oxford Street, Collingwood, Victoria, 3066
Printed by: Vitesse Printing Pty. Ltd.,
24 Lincoln Street, East Brunswick, 3057
Cover Design & Artwork: Chris Gentle
Publisher: Lantana Books,
18 Ash Grove, South Caulfield, 3162

ISBN 0 908265 02 6

I DEDICATE
THIS WORK
TO
THE PEOPLE
OF
SOUTH AFRICA

*"With confidence we lay
our case before the whole
world. Whether we win or
die. freedom will rise in
Africa like the sun from
the morning clouds."
— President Kruger*

(Words inscribed on the
base of his statue in the
courthouse in Pretoria)

TABLE OF CONTENTS

PREFACE

I have returned from South Africa after a brief academic visit, gratified that I have visited South Africa, but saddened by what I have seen and heard. I visited that country in response to an invitation, the circumstances of which are detailed elsewhere in this book. Having long been interested in legal protections of the human personality, I was concerned to see, from within, one of the global storm centres in this field. I am glad of my visit, and believe it can be of value in ways which the ensuing pages will explain. There was, on many sides, an intense confirmation that man's inhumanity to man, of a starkness which words cannot convey, can be perpetrated with invocations of moral righteousness if not scriptural justification. True, there are many signs, on both sides of the colour line, of a selflessness, heroism and dedication to the cause of change, which shine like beacons on a darkened landscape. True, there are some rays of hope, which I shall describe. But the overall tragedy of South Africa, enacted in the name of the loftiest principles formulated by God or man, stands as a monument to lack of human understanding and communication.

Nor is the fault entirely one way. The Afrikaner is not alone to blame for the tragedy. Many have helped to kindle this fire in the past and many are self-interestedly fanning the flames to this day, while pointing the finger of guilt at the Afrikaner alone. All men of goodwill need to put their heads and hearts together to quell these flames, which may else not merely engulf South Africa but also spread damage throughout the African continent and the world.

Little is gained by attitudes of blanket condemnation, recrimination, resignation or incitement to violence. It is easy to make abstract pronouncements of equality, to tar all South Africans with the same brush and to suggest civil disobedience from the comfort of a distant armchair. There are many realitites which show how hollow and empty are these attitudes, which to a large extent the external world has thus far adopted. There is also much double-dealing and double-talk which feign an attitude of concern, while being prepared to make unholy profit of the human miseries involved. We are dealing here with human dignity and all those values which mankind has struggled through twenty tortuous centuries to achieve. We are dealing with the stark realities of fear and squalor and homelesness and separation of families and forcible dispossession and imprisonment without trial and solitary confinement. We are dealing above all with human lives, which, if the situation be permitted to move out of control, may have to be sacrificed on a scale dwarfing some of the great conflagations of the recent past.

The world must not let this happen. There is yet hope. It is only by moving actively towards communication and understanding and action, that any result can be achieved. However slender the chance, let us move towards this possibility, exploring every avenue, lest we should regret our inaction for all future time. Even at five minutes to midnight every possible means of avoiding conflict must be explored.

Readers both within and without South Africa will find much in these pages to trouble their conscience. Complacency as well as armchair criticism are not merely negative, but generate positive harm. It is hoped that readers within South Africa will take these observations as those of an observer who came to South Africa to attempt to understand and communicate, not to prejudge or condemn. I hope this book will reach large numbers of white persons in South Africa. If it can stir some of them out of their sense of complacency, and some non-South Africans out of their sense of resignation, it will have achieved its purpose.

Readers outside South Africa will find in it a rebuttal of one of the constant arguments of those who defend the South African system. The latter tend to condemn criticism from outside, and constantly challenge the outsider to visit South Africa and see how much better the reality is than the allegedly biased descriptions carried by the world media.

A useful purpose served by visits to South Africa is to afford an informed answer to comments such as these, which too often succeed in temporarily side-tracking the issue.

It is hoped this short account will stimulate interest in, and generate a sense of urgency concerning, the South African problem. It needs to be seen at first hand to be understood: and since so few see it, a heavy obligation rests upon those few to communicate to others what they have seen. This work has been undertaken in discharge of this obligation and it is hoped will clear some old cobwebs and provide some new perspectives. The South African scene is changing from year to year and these observations will have some value also as recording the position as an academic observer saw it in the latter half of 1979. To the extent it is critical, it is hoped that it will make more immediate to South Africans the extent of the divergence between their thinking and that of the outside world, and the need for urgent attention to this problem. To the extent it is constructive, it will indicate ways in which persons of good will everywhere can assist to make South Africa a more accepted member of the international community which needs her so much.

While it is true that the South African problem has important military and economic facets, an aspect no less important is the legal. Legal aspects underpin nearly every South African problem, and without reference to them any presentation of South Africa is incomplete. Necessary legal material in easily assimilable form will therefore be found throughout this narrative.

These observations are subject to all the fallibilities attendant on an attempt to view and assess a colossal problem with the information and the contacts available on a short visit. Yet I have attempted to study the problem as intensively as I could within the short time at my disposal. I have also attempted to be as fair as possible, though I must admit that my personal attitudes towards the South African situation must seep through these pages unconsciously, for there is no such thing as a totally dispassionate and value-free judgment on a great social issue.

With these reservations, I release these observations, hopeful that they will stimulate interest and discussion of one of those global problems for the resolution of which time is fast running out.

If I have visited South Africa and concluded that the reality was worse than the expectation, it was not for want of sympathy or of an effort to understand. If I now challenge complacencies both within and without South Africa, it is not without that first hand knowledge which no amount of reading can confer. I offer observations, not surmises; action, not resignation; hope, not despair.

I trust this book will serve a useful purpose.

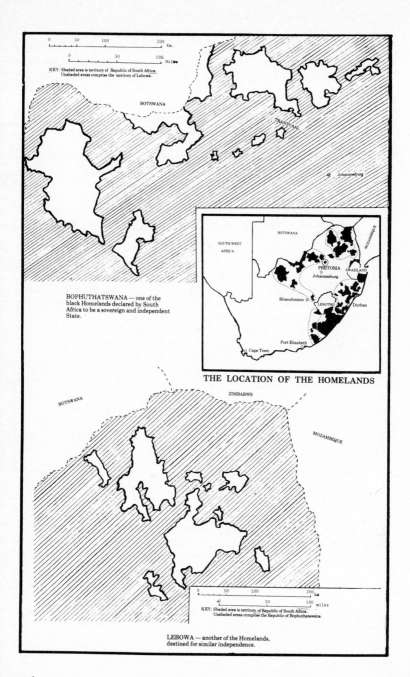

KEY: Shaded area is territory of Republic of South Africa.
Unshaded areas comprise the territory of Lebowa.

BOTSWANA

TRANSVAAL

○ Johannesburg

BOPHUTHATSWANA — one of the
black Homelands declared by South
Africa to be a sovereign and independent
State.

SOUTH WEST
AFRICA

BOTSWANA

MOZAMBIQUE

PRETORIA
○
Johannesburg

SWAZILAND

Bloemfontein ○

LESOTHO

Durban

Port Elizabeth

○ Cape Town

THE LOCATION OF THE HOMELANDS

BOTSWANA

ZIMBABWE

MOZAMBIQUE

KEY: Shaded area is territory of Republic of South Africa.
Unshaded areas comprise the Republic of Bophuthatswana.

LEBOWA — another of the Homelands,
destined for similar independence.

ACKNOWLEDGEMENTS

I must place on record my warm appreciation of the kindness of the Law Faculty of Stellenbosch University and of the immense pains they took both collectively as a Faculty and individually as friends to make my visit to South Africa pleasant, interesting and fruitful.

Not merely did they go far beyond what was needful to make my stay physically comfortable. They went out of their way to arrange for me the maximum opportunities, within the limitations of the time available, to see as many places and meet as many people as possible, so as to add to my understanding of the total South African picture. In doing this they allowed me the maximum freedom to sample as many cross-sections of opinion as possible and arranged for me a series of interviews with persons I might have been unable to reach on my own.

To them I give my hearfelt thanks. Perhaps without disrespect to other universities I may add that Stellenbosch is among the most influential and most beautiful of South African Universities and it was a memorable experience to have been a Visiting Professor of this institution.

I must also thank a host of friends for arranging for me a series of official, social and informal meetings without which my trip would not have been a rounded experience. David Dallas, presently of Melbourne and formerly of Cape Town, gave me a number of invaluable introductions to persons in Stellenbosch, Cape Town, Durban, Johannesburg and Pretoria. The authorities of the Universities of Cape Town, the Western Cape, Natal, Durban-Westville and the University of South Africa, afforded me opportunities to address their staff and students. The Judge President and the bar at Cape Town, many judges of the Supreme Court and members of the bar in various other jurisdictions, Judge Steyn of the Urban Foundation, Dr. van Slabbert the leader of the opposition — all these went out of their way to spare time to receive me and give me a better understanding of the South African scene.

I have had a rare privilege of seeing from within many varied aspects of South African life and society ranging from the peaks of privilege to the depths of degradation. I have in the process had the opportunity of speaking to and attempting to understand the thoughts and attitudes of a varied cross section of South African citizens — ministers and theologians of the Dutch Reformed Church, members of the ruling party and of the opposition, rectors of universities, professors and large numbers of students, doctors, Supreme Court judges, advocates and attorneys, leaders of the Indian, coloured and black communities, social workers, banned persons and members of the rank and file of the black community. I have seen perhaps more places in South Africa than many an average resident, black or white. These range again from centres of opulent living to the black ghettoes, from the museums to the gold mines, from white students' hostels to black workers' dormitories. My period of observation was short but it took in as much as was physically possible during that period.

I have also had the privilege of meeting many persons of all communities. I have visited Crossroads, Soweto, Alexandra and other centres where the disadvantaged live. I have visited many centres of service for the poor and the indigent such as the offices of Black Sash and Dependants Conference.

I must not fail to express my thanks also to Professor Gerard Nash, Dean of the Faculty of Law of Monash University, for the unqualified encouragement he gave me in undertaking this assignment. In the midst of contradictory counsels on the wisdom of a visit to South Africa, the clarity of his analysis of the implications and possibilities of my visit was to me of the utmost assistance.

My visit to South Africa has afforded me an opportunity which no amount of book reading could have yielded of seeing some of the true dimensions of the South African problem. I hope others will follow and report back to the world impartially and fairly what they have seen in South Africa. This is an important means for stimulating South African and world conscience in this area. It should not be neglected.

To all who have afforded me this opportunity, I am grateful.

I must finally thank my secretary, Miss Lynette Cook, for her indefatigable and unstinting labours in the production of an intelligible manuscript from a mass of disordered notes. If this work has seen the light of day with some measure of speed, she is largely responsible for this result.

CHAPTER 1

Vignettes

In the heart of Cape Town's residential district, an expanse the size of a soccer stadium lies knee deep in rubble. Once populous, and inter-racial for generations, District 6 remains as the bulldozers left it, destroyed under the Group Areas Act to separate racial groups that once lived there in amity. Not merely a physical scar on the face of Cape Town, but a moral, intellectual, emotional scar, still raw and uncovered. Hundreds of habitable houses destroyed in the midst of a paucity of housing, hundreds of inter-racial friendships destroyed in the midst of a paucity of goodwill. The site raises memories of war-torn Berlin — Berlin destroyed by military action in conditions of war, District 6 by civilian decree in conditions of peace: Berlin destroyed to entrench human rights and overthrow racism, District 6 destroyed to overthrow human rights and entrench racism. As a mute witness to the heavy hand of apartheid, District 6 must be seen to be believed.

☆

A winery proud of the excellence of its products, is host to selected guests. A spacious Dutch farm house, high-ceilinged, chandeliered, graciously furnished, provides the setting. The elegant dining table sparkles with crystal and silver. Guests work their way through four elaborate courses cooked by expert black chefs, served by trained black waiters, washed down with fastidiously selected wines. Conversation centres on the exquisite foods and wines of South Africa and the world. The farm house is the venue of regular musical evenings for invited guests, and life glows warmly with all the charm and elegance of affluence and privilege.

1

Soweto at night. Largest city of an immensely affluent nation. Dirt roads, unlit, unpaved, nameless, numberless, shrouded in darkness and smog. An occasional overloaded sewer discharging its filth on the road. Decrepit cars, driving through pot-holes and slush, bespattering pedestrians. Black figures hurrying home, weary from a day of fuelling white industry seventeen miles away in Jo'burg. Weary from discriminations at the work place, weary from travel on the crowded black train, weary from protecting person and property against knifing, assault and murder, especially on pay night. Hurrying to homes which the law of their own country ensures they can never own. Hundreds of thousands illegally sheltering in makeshift shacks, tin shelters or empty drums. Children picking morsels of food from refuse bins, instinctive checking in pockets for passbooks, the black man's only passport to a life outside the white man's prison. Lives lived in fear of the midnight knock and the one-way trip to prison and torture. Memories of hundreds of children killed by police action three years ago. Hundreds more still missing from their homes. A life of toil, squalor, rightlessness and fear.

☆

A church flower show. Formerly a church with a mixed congregation. Now, after the Group Areas Act, a white church. Flowers exquisitely arranged in the church hall in thirty tableaux, each as large as a double window, depicting thirty scenes from scripture — The Ascension, Saul's Persecution of the Church, The Road to Damascus. Masses of flowers arranged with hours of loving labour, in imaginative combinations of superb artistry and infinite patience. An act of worship, through the medium of flowers, betokening wealth and leisure, culture and refinement, concern for the hereafter and obliviousness of the present. Solemn, still, beauty — an oasis of peace in a troubled world.

☆

A young bride from the Transkei, brought 700 miles to Cape Town to see her young groom, a political prisoner on Robben Island, taken into custody within a month of their marriage. Brought 700 miles by Dependants' Conference, a group of dedicated white people who alleviate the misery of dependants by financing one visit per family each year. Bright eyed, she savours in advance every moment of the anticipated meeting. Kind ladies warn her she will have no contact with her husband, not hold his hands or kiss his cheeks, but will speak to him through a bullet-proof partition.   The warning does not pierce the rapture of anticipation and falls on deaf ears. She returns after the meeting, crestfallen, angry that throughout her half hour interview she could not once hold his hand or touch him.   She will wait patiently another year for another half hour of white mercy and black frustration.

☆

A university professor, expert in criminal and constitutional law, makes an analysis of death sentences meted out by the Supreme Court.   He finds a disproportionate number of blacks among those convicted, and embodies his research in a paper.   He is noticed to show cause why he should not be convicted of contempt of court.

☆

A unisex dormitory in Durban.   Thousands of men, fuelling the industries of Durban, living crowded together eight to a room in three storeyed warrens. Row upon row of rooms dark enough to require candles by day.   Eight beds, many rented out illegally while the rightful occupant is at work, thus totalling sixteen occupants to many a room. Men washing their underwear at taps and hanging them out to dry in unending rows.   Not a female or child to be seen, for that would be against the law.   In the words of one administrator, the city needs units of labour, not appendages of labour units.   The place for the latter is in the homelands.   An occasional woman enters the 'lines' in disguise, huddled under a man's overcoat and assuming a man's gait.   She leaves after two or three days having slept on many beds, and having collected many coins.

☆

A white businessman, acutely conscious that he must do all he can to end the iniquities of apartheid within his sphere of influence.   A devout Christian, he seeks to practise his faith in his social life and at his place of work. He invites non-white employees to frequent social meetings at his home, plans church activities jointly with them and abolishes petty apartheid in the canteens and toilets of his modest business operation.   He feels pangs of conscience at having to use amenities which by law are separate for whites and non-whites and which by judgment of the Supreme Court do not have to be equal.   He boycotts all restaurants and theatres which cater for whites only but has no alternative but to use facilities such as buses and trains and toilets, which are for whites only.   He is perturbed at the lack of similar delicacy of conscience on the part of most other whites. He tries to teach his children that they must see all humans as equal, but the separate education system catering for them prevents them from seeing black children except as social inferiors. Whether the children will respond to parental teaching or experiential learning is yet to be seen.

☆

A shanty town in kwaZulu on the outskirts of Durban. A population of thirty thousand, served by one tap, sends its womenfolk in long queues to collect their pails of water. Queues commence before midnight and each woman, patiently awaiting her turn, chats pleasantly with her companions. Dirt roads, heavily scarred with ruts and pot-holes, disfigured with litter and refuse. Makeshift lean-to's, four sticks and a piece of zinc, holes in the ground, any shelter wherein a human can lay his head is acceptable. By the decrees of grand apartheid the homelands are where the blacks should live, however impoverished and unable to support their population.

☆

A white social service worker is under a banning order. He cannot leave his home between 6 p.m. and 6 a.m. He cannot publish his work. He cannot meet more than one person at a time, apart from normal contacts at his workplace. He pays a visit to a friend. The friend's brother is with him. The brother must leave to enable the banned person to come in. If he should be found talking to two persons at the same time he becomes liable to a term of three years' rigorous imprisonment. He does not know who watches him or when or how. His friends now avoid him, for it is dangerous to be seen too often with a banned person. He becomes a lonely man. How long he will have to live alone with his thoughts depends on the Minister's discretion. The Minister can quite lawfully pronounce this sentence for life, without inquiry, without charges framed, without trial. And be accountable to none.

☆

Ndolu lives in a black spot — a piece of land occupied by blacks in white territory. It is good pastoral land he and his ancestors have long occupied. The black spot needs to be cleaned up and he has been served with notice to move off with his family into a homeland three hundred miles away. He has no assurance of owning land in his new home where he and his family will be strangers and will have no employment. He will need to persuade the chief, if he can, to give him a strip of land, which will probably be arid and waterless. But this is too much to hope for and in all probability he will be looking for work, waiting patiently till the white recruiting officer comes on his annual visit. He must not miss the date and must take his place in the queue or he may miss out and his family starve for a year. The terms offered, however poor, will seem dazzling to him. Once accepted, Ndolu will be committed to leaving his family, wife and children for a year, returning every fifty weeks to see them, perhaps at a cost of fifty dollars rail fare per visit. His children will grow up without knowing their father, his mother will pass away without the comfort of her son's society, his wife will wilt in the loneliness of separation. The expense of the trip and the new relationships of the new environment will loosen family ties and perhaps Ndolu may become a stranger to his family. Scriptural justifications of parallel development, decreed with all the panoply of a General Synod, will break up the unity of a Christian family.

☆

Conversation at the white breakfast table turns upon the instability of the social order and on the eventual shooting match which many whites fear. The conversation warms up and, forgetful of the presence of children, each participant suggests his own scenario of the violence that is ahead. The children watch wide-eyed, not comprehending, but imbibing fear. Too late, the error is realised and they are asked to leave the table and go out and play. Their parents know it in their bones that the haven they have built for themselves will not protect their children. They still keep building for themselves a world of hopeless hope.

☆

An Indian resident and his family, forced out of their house by the Group Areas Act, find no accommodation available for them in the Indian areas. Houses occupied by Indians in inappropriate areas are being demolished while in the areas appropriate for Indians there are no houses. The Indian prevails upon a white landlord who owns many unoccupied flats in a white area to permit him to occupy one of them. He is prosecuted by the police for living where he ought not to live. He pleads the defence of necessity. The law has moved far, for the plea is considered as a possible defence. The court rules, however, that his plea must fail, for he has not eliminated the possibility of staying in a hotel.

A medical practitioner's waiting room in Soweto. Packed with patients waiting their turn, as in any consulting rooms anywhere. Some suckling their babies, infants yelling, old women being helped in. No different from waiting rooms anywhere, except for memories, for the floor of this same room some years ago was packed close with the bodies of dead and dying children and adolescents. As the bullet wounds of each set were attended to and they were carried away the floor was hosed down and another set brought in. Again and again and again. Unpleasant memories, but they cling.

☆

On the verandah of his Transvaal farmhouse an Afrikaner patriarch is talking to his son back home from the University for his holidays. The boy talks of the rights of blacks, the need for a sharing of power and the eventual evolution of a one-man-one-vote political framework. The father cannot understand this new fangled thinking. "I fought for the Afrikaner cause, my father fought for the Afrikaner cause, we fought whites and blacks and established ourselves in this country. We were a persecuted people and after centuries of struggle we have risen out of persecution. You want to throw away all that we have achieved. They will try to liquidate us. They will take our farms. They do not know how to rule, and there will be chaos. It is not merely I, your father, who says so. Your church says so. Your ancestors say so. Can my own son be so disloyal?" ·Mother joins in to support father's viewpoint. " You do not know this country, my son. My mother was born on the open veldt in front of the advancing British troops. Her home had been burnt down and pregnant though she was she was thrown out. My aunts and cousins were confined in a concentration camp by Kitchener, and 15,000 like them died. We have fought hard to regain our position and when we have succeeded, others will persuade us to throw away our achievement. Do not be deceived." The other children are divided, but the majority view is with the parents. Lest the family be sundered the boy abandons the topic.

☆

Six young blacks, out camping in the bush have assembled around a log fire. They sing songs, some of them modern, some of them about their storied past. The police swoop in on them, for they are an unlawful assembly, too close in spirit to the concept of black independence to be at large. They are charged under the Terrorism Act, with all the burdens of proof reversed. The prosecution does not have to prove they are guilty. The accused must prove beyond reasonable doubt that they are innocent of a dozen possible 'guilty' intentions specified by the Act. They are unable to discharge this almost impossible legal burden. Potential leadership material, they are convicted and sentenced to long terms of hard labour. They will live out their manhood and their spirit of independence on Robben Island, prison of maximum security, surrounded by armed guards and sharks.

☆

A brightly lit Johannesburg hotel. Men and women in woollens and satins, wining and dining by candlelight to the strains of Viennese waltzes. Not a black face in sight except to serve the food, to sweep the floors, to dust the furniture, to lay out the linen. Rich hotel shops displaying merchandise from all over the globe. An elderly white chatting to the white girl at the counter. "Have you heard the news? Another girl stabbed at the security gate. Two stabbings every night on the Kaffir train. This is what the people in England do not understand when they talk of equality. These people are in the stone age. Uncivilised. Still hanging by one arm from the trees".

☆

Dr. Ntshuntasha is detained under the Terrorism Act. His wife is refused permission to see him. Within a month it is reported that he has been found dead in the police cells. The head of the security police says he has torn a vest into strips and hanged himself. The widow waits for the body to be released by the police for burial. The doctor commissioned by the family to represent its interests at the post mortem refuses to perform the post mortem because he finds major incisions already made on the body. He finds a major incision from throat to groin and another from ear to ear across the top of the skull. He says this is "contrary to all recognised practice in mortuaries and infinitely more so in case of unnatural death." The Minister of Justice says in the Assembly that the incisions had been made by an experienced mortuary assistant, and that "incisions are made without explicit authority following a practice that has apparently developed in some mortuaries". He admits that standing instructions require that incisions should be made only under the supervision of a pathologist or district surgeon. The final police report says Dr. Ntshuntasha was questioned on two occasions and returned to his cell, and that on the following day "he was found dead, hanging by his vest in his cell". The doctor is buried in the presence of 3,000 mourners, and a student leader pays tribute to him as one who worked for the liberation of the oppressed. The incident occurred two years ago. The memory is fresh and raw. Some still go in alive under the Terrorism Act and come out dead. This has happened even after the death in detention of Steve Biko and the protests and publicity in its wake. They are often the cream of their community.

☆

Magistrate to accused in Pass Law Case: "Why have you not given the police your fingerprints?"
Accused: "But they did not tell me why my fingerprints were required".

Magistrate: "What do you mean by 'they'?"
Accused: "I mean the police".

Magistrate: "Did I not tell you to give your fingerprints when this case was called last Thursday?"
Accused: (No answer)

Magistrate: "I will tell you why your fingerprints were wanted. The prosecution was wanting to look into the question whether your defence that you were born in Cape Town could be sustained. It would have helped if you had given your fingerprints because in that event it might have been possible for the prosecution to have given you the evidence that you needed to establish your case. Are you satisfied now?"
Accused: (No answer)

Magistrate: "Do you realise that your conduct now verges on contempt of court?"
Accused: (No answer)

Magistrate: "You stated that you did not know why your fingerprints were required and I was good enough to give you the reason. Will you now be so good as to tell me why you do not want to give your fingerprints?"
Accused: (No answer)

Magistrate: "Your behaviour verges on contempt of court. In any event I will give you a further opportunity to re-consider this matter. Let this case be called in two weeks' time. In the meantime, I order you to give your finger-prints".

Accused committed to another two weeks of custody, making a total of three weeks before his trial even commences. If he now does not give his fingerprints he will be in contempt of court — that is, if the police are prepared to suffer his obstinacy without intimidation and torture.

☆

A young black athlete of world class has an offer of a scholarship at an American university, with all expenses paid. It is the first step in a dazzling career. He applies for a passport. He is told that he has not yet obtained citizenship of one of the homelands, which would be his appropriate citizenship. This is a precondition, he is told. The correspondence swings to and fro. The scholarship offer runs out.

☆

A white social worker. Intensely aware of the injustice of the system and dedicated to minimising its human suffering. Exposing herself to surveillance, ostracism, possible imprisonment. Dedicated to her work even to the extent of depriving her family of her company. Moving around the ghettoes, attending Black Sash meetings, interviewing blacks in hardship, writing leaflets, collecting evidence, trying to stir up world opinion, standing in protest before bull-dozers. Boycotted by the outside world because she is South African. Boycotted at home because she is liberal. Keeping her enthusiasm glowing despite frustration. Hoping that such endeavours will avoid the holocaust which else seems certain.

☆

A sports club has taken its first black member. He practises with the team. He uses designated rooms of the club. He travels to practice in a different bus from his team mates. He cannot enter areas of the club where liquor is served. For this purpose he requires to be signed in. At club dances he may not dance with a white lady. He is a member all the same, an equal member of the club.

☆

Students at an Afrikaner university. Cream of the youth of their racial group. Bred to adulthood in a regime of rigid apartheid — studying apart, thinking apart, living apart in all-white hostels. Liberal, well meaning, anxious for change, but knowing little of the habits or conditions of living or ways of thought of their counterparts in the coloured university a few miles away. Future leaders of their community, growing up on a social and intellectual island without intra-mural or extra-mural contact with the future leaders of the other communities, in the other universities of their land. As remote from each other as people on different continents. Aware that their way of life will not survive their life span but not knowing when or how the end will come. Aware that compulsory military service may compel them to kill their black countrymen who may one day fight for no less than their just due. Aware that the system of privilege of which they are the beneficiaries is grounded in injustice, but vague and uncertain regarding their moral duties and the clash of loyalties involved.

☆

The Minister of Police is holding a press conference to answer questions regarding deaths in detention. "Why is there apparently so little supervision that detainees are able to jump to their deaths down stairwells and out of buildings?" The charge of "little supervision" is denied. "There are numerous standing orders and precautions for the protection of prisoners. Bars are fitted to all offices where interrogations take place, but owing to the number of detainees following the bombing and subversive activities in Johannesburg, the interview had to be conducted in offices where bars are not yet fitted".[2] The Minister refuses to appoint a full scale judicial commission of inquiry into deaths in detention. He is considering other methods to prevent suicides such as the use of leg irons, straitjackets and clothes which cannot be torn and used as ropes.[3]

☆

Prime Minister Botha addresses a political meeting, saying change is inevitable and the alternative is to perish. The first Prime Minister ever to make such a statement. He is heckled by antagonists from the extreme right. A heckler shouts that all blacks should be sent to the homelands. The Prime Ministerial rejoinder: "If all blacks were in the homelands, who would bring you your coffee in the morning?... and you probably need someone to change your nappy as well." The Prime Minister also displays unusual courage in reiterating from a public platform his revolutionary and unorthodox view that mixed marriages are indeed no sin.

Extract from a booklet issued to white immigrants[4] who become naturalised South African citizens.

TO:
JOHN BROWN

With the compliments of the Department of the Interior on the occasion of your acquisition of South African citizenship.

"You have this day received a precious gift from South Africa — her citizenship. On behalf of the Government and people of South Africa I welcome you as a member of the South African community.

"To transfer one's allegiance from one country to another involves a decision of no mean import. For this reason you did not lightly apply for citizenship, nor was it lightly conferred upon you.

"It is my sincere wish that you will avail yourself wisely of the privilege of South African citizenship and that it will bring you and your descendants peace, happiness and prosperity..."

Message from the State President.

Extract from a temporary permit issued to a black South African who is now in the homelands but was born in South Africa and whose ancestors for generations were born and lived in South Africa.

This permit is granted to the abovementioned holder — to enter and reside in the district or districts described, in the Province mentioned, for the purpose of undertaking unskilled or domestic labour and is issued subject to the following conditions and to the provisions of the Admission of Persons to the Republic Regulation Act, 1972 .

Conditions:
1. That the holder enter into a contract of service with the undermentioned employer.
2. That the permit is valid for a period of six months from the date of issue and the holder shall leave the Province, without expenses to the Government on or before...
3. In the event of the holder not leaving the Province on or before the date specified herein, the deposit will be forfeitable and the holder will render himself liable to be dealt with further according to law...
4. Not to be employed without special permission under Section 12 of Act No. 25 of 1945 or Section 28 (1) of Act 15 of 1911.

I/We agree to the above conditions...

Extract from *Human Relations and the South African Scene in the Light of Scripture*, official translation of a report approved and accepted by the General Synod of the Dutch Reformed Church Oct 1974, representing official doctrine of the Dutch Reformed Church[5] most powerful church in the country, and only alterable by another General Synod, not to be held till 1982:

Article 13.6: In specific circumstances and under specific conditions the New Testament makes provision for the regulation on the basis of separate development of the co-existence of various peoples in one country.

From the fact that the existence of a diversity of peoples is accepted as a relative, but nevertheless real, premise, one may infer that the New Testament allows for the possibility that a given country may decide to regulate its inter-people relationships on the basis of separate development — considering its own peculiar circumstances, with due respect for the basic norms which the Bible prescribes for the regulation of social relations (cf. proposition 3.2.8) and after careful consideration of all possible solutions offered. When such a country honestly comes to the conclusion that the ethical norms for ordering social relationships, i.e. love of one's neighbour and social justice, can best be realized on the basis of parallel development, and if such a conviction is based on factual reasoning, the choice of parallel development can be justified in the light of what the Bible teaches (RES, Grand Rapids, p.32 and 225, RES Lunteren, p.340 and RES, Sydney, p.330).

FOOTNOTES

1. See pp. 89-90 below.
2. Report dated 28/1/77 issued by the Institute of Race Relations, pp. 63-4.
3. Ibid. p.67.
4. Interior Minister Alwyn Schlebusch, said in a statement issued on 30 January 1980 that as from 1 April 1980 up to eighty per cent of an intending immigrant's fare would be paid for him by the South African government in a bid to attract more immigrants.
5. Dutch Reformed Church Publishers, Cape Town-Pretoria, ISBN O 86991 158 9.

The South African Landscape

Brave New World

The traveller recently returned from South Africa is inevitably asked at every turn for his impressions of the country. In some respects his answer will probably be that he encountered conditions better than he had been led to expect. For example, he has seen, especially in the English press, a sharper and more overt criticism of apartheid and of government policies than he probably expected. He has observed a fair amount of academic freedom and of judicial criticism of some aspects of apartheid. He has seen many white persons genuinely dedicated to change and sacrificing their own interests for it. He has seen the different racial groups mixing with apparent unconcern in the shops and in the public areas of the city.

On the other hand, his observations on the spot have turned out in many respects to be worse than his anticipations. The hardships of the blacks under the pass laws, the conditions in the black ghettoes and dormitories, the separation of families, the displacement of populations and the billions wastefully spent on maintaining the apparatus of apartheid do not make their impact so forcefully as when one observes them in reality. But most lasting of all is the impression, unreal to the outside observer, of colour becoming the badge of one's station in life. If a visitor travels (not along the super highway) from Cape Town to Stellenbosch, he will be struck by the stark and coldly calculated segregation of the races. He will pass through suburbs of affluent whites, middle class whites, middle class coloureds, poorer coloureds, and blacks, in a sequence of ordered diminution of human comforts. The visual impact of this graded inequality is far more telling than any impression one gathers from current literature.

It is true that economic differentials in any society often decree such an ordered descent from one social stratum to another, but it is rarely preserved with that sharpness of definition that one sees here. Whole areas, where formerly whites and non-whites lived together, have been callously razed to the ground to provide buffer zones in a manner reminiscent of the devastations of war. Generations of happy memories and of togetherness between racial groups were wiped out in District 6 at one stroke of the legislator's pen and wistful former inhabitants still repair to the site to indulge in nostalgia for a neighbourhood, flattened by the government bulldozer. The heartlessness of such actions seems to generate little remorse in the legislative or administrative mind, for to this day the land lies in rubble. Continuing demolition of good residential accommodation in the name of apartheid is a symbol of the blunting of the South African conscience to destructive conduct classifiable by ordinary standards as criminal.

As one proceeds from the areas of the affluent to those of the impoverished, one is in general terms proceeding from the white to the black. The occasional wealthy or educated exception, well able to hold his own at any level of society, must perforce live in an area determined by the colour of his skin, and work in an appropriate capacity. If one sees men working at a distance in any menial capacity, one does not need to approach close enough to see the colour of their skin. It is a safe assumption that they are black. The alphas and the epsilons of Huxley's Brave New World, pre-ordained to a station in life from which no effort can remove them, come alive every day on the roads of South Africa.

This chapter will proceed to set out some of the principal features of the rather peculiar landscape against which this unusual human phenomenon occurs.

The Unhappy Country

South Africa as all the world knows is a country most highly blessed by nature. Natural beauty, fertility, mineral wealth, wild life, human resources — all these abound to give it more plenty and potential than are given to most nations upon the face of the earth.

But nature's kindness is offset by the unkindness of man. This most highly blessed country is one of the earth's unhappiest. Rulers and ruled are in constant fear, inequality flourishes, injustice is enthroned. Those who enjoy disproportionately the wealth of this disproportionately wealthy country know they cannot retain this position of privilege indefinitely. They know also that in order to extend the term of their privilege they will need to compromise with their conscience — to imprison and to deny basic rights and to kill if need be on a massive scale. They train for it through compulsory army service and they train their children for it. They know that conscientious objection, however commendable, is incompatible with the retention of privilege and that the conscientious objector however genuine must be crushed — beaten and ostracised and gaoled. They suffer guilt feelings in regard to the people they keep outside the pale but by continued practice of discrimination their conscience is blunted and their sensitivity dulled. The ethnic groups, physically separated from all save formal business intercourse, are different nations living within one border, as remote from each other as Brazilian from Chinese. The remoteness will grow as a whole generation reaches maturity in separate cantonments.

When the writer asked one of his students at Stellenbosch to consider what it was to live in his country if he had a black skin, the latter's reply was, "I'd be a revolutionary". It must be hard on the conscience of a young white to realise this and at the same time to be obliged by law to kill the young black who reacts the way he himself would.

In short, the sorrow of the ruling classes is not merely fear, but — what is even more corrosive of human personality — a compromise with conscience on a massive scale.

Those of the ruling groups whose conscience remains sensitive — and this is one of South Africa's happiest features which the world rarely acknowledges — are unhappy, obsessed by a feeling that their obstacles are insuperable and their struggles are in vain. They keep up the struggle, exposing themselves to personal danger and ostracism in one of the great sagas of courage of our time. Yet they feel deep within their bones that they are condemned to ineffectiveness, not for lack of internal resolve but for lack of external understanding. Rejection by South Africa they can understand, but rejection by the world community under its blanket condemnation of all South Africans deprives them of moral sustenance and cross fertilisation of ideas. What good they can achieve is negatived by the world's well-meaning but thoughtless condemnation, and the yeast in the dough, which alone can lift it, is prevented from fermenting. To use another metaphor, a ready-made fifth column against racial oppression is spurned and neglected by a world desperately needing this very ally.

The sufferings and denigrations of the human personality among the non-whites need no documentation here. They have been elaborated upon in thousands of books and articles but they need to be seen and heard to be understood. One needs to move around in the squalor of the black settlement and to knock at the make-shift doors behind every one of which lurk a dozen tales of oppression, of denials of legal rights, of intimidations and insults. One needs to speak to coloured and black students at the Universities and feel their smouldering sense of bitterness with South Africa and the world, to speak to wives separated from husbands and fathers separated from children, not by some quirk of fate but by the deliberately planned law of a Christian country. Yet one can only glimpse but never plumb the depths of black South Africa's degradation. Of course these things sometimes happen elsewhere in the world and sometimes with greater intensity. South Africans justifying the system are often fond of pointing out iniquities elsewhere and lamenting what they believe to be an unjust concentration on South Africa as an object of world condemnation. But two wrongs never make a right and no amount of injustice elsewhere can excuse the nationwide perpetration of human misery by legislative plan.

The story is best told in the words of a woman at Crossroads met by the author when he visited there in the company of a group of friends. The women had just concluded a women's meeting, and one of them said:

"Before the white man came here we lived our lives in happiness.

"They have come here and they want land. All the time they want more and more land.

"We were driven further and further away and now in our own land we have no land.

"Germans, Dutch, Italians, French, Indians — anybody can come into our land and go anywhere, but not we.

"That is not all. They are now trying to separate husband and wife, they are trying to interfere with love, they are trying to interfere with God's law.

"A man has to be away from his family for 50 weeks. He goes back for 2 weeks. His family does not know him. His children do not know their father. He lives away and may come to know other women. We do not blame him.

"We want to live with our husbands. We want to live as a family. We believe in God. God will help us.

"It costs R18 each way by bus, R20 by train. When a man goes home he has to go with sufficient money in his pocket to come back to work. He has to take something for his family. How often can he do this trip? How much can he save? The cost of living is rising every day.

"The government wants us to live separate from our men. God tells us to live together as a family. If we obey God's law and try to live together we are punished. If we obey man's law we disobey God's law. As between man's law and God's law, we will obey God's law. God will help us. The white man can live as God tells us but not we. Why is this? Why should it be so in our very own country where we were once happy?

"When we are together at night they come even at midnight and arrest us. They break into our houses. They arrest us on the streets. We have to carry our passes with us and are fined if we do not have them. We are sent to jail or to places hundreds of miles away, places which were never our homes and we are strangers and beggars there. We must then come back to the cities in search of employment and then we get arrested again.

"This is great suffering, but we believe in God. God will help us. We will wait. God will help us.

"You gentlemen please, please, please tell the world about us...".

And as we left they came after us with the words, "Please, please, please, tell the world".

Racial Divisions

The population of South Africa according to the mid-1977 figures was as follows:

White	4,365,000
Coloured	2,432,000
Asian	765,000
African	16,950,000
	24,512,000[1]

These figures do not include the Transkei's 2,434,000 people of whom 14,500 are white and coloured and 2,419,500 are African.

The white population divides into Afrikaner and English. The Afrikaners form approximately sixty per cent of the white population. There is a smouldering tension

17

between these groups, the legacy of the bitterness engendered by long years of colonialism and by the Boer war.

The English tend to be more liberal in their views concerning racial equality and power sharing, but the majority of them seem content to enjoy the privilege that apartheid brings them, while decrying it in principle.

The coloured[2] population are the African counterpart of those who in Asia would be described as Eurasians. They are the mixed European-African race that has emerged during more than three centuries of European occupation.

The Asians, mainly Indian, have come to South Africa partly as indentured labour and partly as traders and have been there so long as to have few if any ties with India. Some South African born Indians brought brides over from their respective communities in India, a practice which came under a government ban. The ban was partially relaxed in 1978 when permission was granted for 100 Indian women and children to enter the country.

The African population breaks down into the following ethnic groups:

Xhosa	2,994,000
Zulu	5,140,000
Swazi	606,000
Sepedi	2,066,000
Tswana	2,161,000
Seshoeshoe	1,672,000
Shangaan	836,000
Venda	461,000
Other	631,000
Foreign Africans	383,000
	16,950,000

The four main population groups are in many matters such as education, residence and the pass laws governed by legislation specially framed for their racial group. Neither in legislation nor in common parlance is there any reticence in describing a person as a member of any particular group. People will talk of blacks, whites and coloureds with the same lack of inhibition as in other countries one speaks of Americans, Germans or Chinese. A business organisation will for example subdivide its personnel section into 'black' and 'white' departments and announce this with no apparent chagrin to a foreign visitor taken on a tour of its establishment — as for example in the conducted tours offered for selected visitors to the goldmines.

With rigid divisions between the various population groups there needs to be an apparatus for settling the status of persons who are apparently on the borderline between one group and the other — especially between coloured and white.   For this purpose Race Classification Boards are given jurisdiction to entertain appeals from classifications that have been made by officials.   In 1978 the race classifications of 98 persons were altered, 44 of them being from coloured to white.   The Population Registration Act of 1950 defines a white person as meaning a person who —

a) in appearance obviously is a white person and who is generally not accepted as a coloured person: or

b) is generally accepted as a white person and is not in appearance obviously not a white person.

In deciding applications made to courts on these matters physiologists and anthropologists are called in evidence, apart from such other evidence as the parties may place before the court.   A judgment indicating the process of judicial reasoning on such an application is appended in Appendix D.

From a political point of view the two principal racial groups are the Afrikaners and the blacks.   It is in the tussle between these two groups that the future of South Africa will be determined.   English, Coloured and Asian can at best make a contribution by supporting one side or the other, but they are not principals in the drama.

The Disintegration of Apartheid

In the year 1945 the world heaved a sigh of relief at having thrown off the yoke of a regime based upon the superiority of race and the predestiny of others from birth to serve the master race.   That regime lasted twelve years and cost millions of lives and untold suffering to overturn.   It was a regime which condemned to inferiority and trampled underfoot a vital minority that had for centuries formed an important constituent element of that society.

Three years later, in 1948, there commenced another regime based upon the superiority of race and the predestiny of others from birth to serve the master race.   It differed from the previous regime in that it was not a tyranny of a majority over a minority group but of a minority group over the vast majority of the country's people.   It has now lasted thirty one years and caused untold suffering.   Ironically, it has received active support from many who made great sacrifices to throw off the earlier regime. It is practised by those deeply committed to Christianity. It has even received the blessing of the country's most important Christian church. It is one of the great anomalies of our time, recreating in these closing years of the twentieth century the serfdoms of man's dim and distant past. An entire generation has now grown up on both sides of the frontiers of privilege, which knows no other way of life.

This regime looks upon itself as a part of the 'free world' and in fact openly describes itself as such. The 'free world' itself gives it active support, often assisting covertly while condemning overtly. It invests considerably in the exploitation of the fund of cheap labour available in this nearly union-less reservoir. It provides military assistance for the maintenance of the regime. In fact it looks upon this bastion of inequality as one of the bastions of the free world, for while the present regime holds in South Africa the sea routes to the Indian Ocean are assured.

There is however a streak of hope, for the winds of change are blowing over South Africa — not fast enough or widely enough, but the still air is stirring. It is submitted in this work that apartheid has reached and passed its peak. There is no mistaking the signs that the entire apparatus of apartheid is falling apart. Ideologically it is no longer seriously accepted. Practically, it has sprung considerable leaks.

The ideological plank has so far fallen away that few indeed, save some old stalwarts of the Dutch Reformed Church, dare to support it from a moral or scriptural standpoint. The daughter churches, or substantial sections of them, are in open revolt against the traditional doctrinal stance. The resort to the semantics of 'parallel development' rather than 'apartheid' is itself an admission that the doctrinal supports have collapsed.

The practical base has collapsed with the realisation of the total inability of the state to move the ten million urban blacks back to the homelands. This same fact proves that the grand dream of apartheid — the total transfer of the blacks into the black homelands — was a grand misconception. The ultimate admission that apartheid is an impracticable notion will be the relaxation of the legislative prohibition of sex across the colour line — which the Prime Minister has said his government will consider. If people of different groups can consort sexually, there is little sense in lesser prohibitions. They will inevitably collapse.

The simultaneous weakening of the moral and practical

base has dealt a blow to apartheid from which it is unlikely to recover.

In the result, apartheid tends to rest for support on its military arm.   But a purely military support, unbacked by moral authority, cannot, according to the lessons of history, maintain a regime indefinitely.   The army of the Shah, the world's fifth most powerful, was ill-equipped to fight the forces of a people's uprising when the moral authority of the regime had crumbled — a lesson not lost on South Africa's rulers.   The lesson of Iran must indubitably reflect itself on any practical thinking underlying the attempt of four million people to keep twenty million under subjection with no vestiges of political rights.

If armed force alone, unsupported by moral authority, can never be a stable basis for power, this becomes doubly so in the context of the crumbling of the buffer states that have hitherto protected South Africa from immediate border problems.   One by one, Angola, Namibia, Zimbabwe and Mozambique have passed out of white control. Many disaffected black South Africans have already crossed the borders and are under training or under arms.   No one has the figures but some estimates place the figure at 10,000 or more.   Should the negotiated London settlement on Zimbabwe fail in its implementation, a vast tap will be opened on the borders, from which a flow of military forces into South Africa will begin.

The South African army, excellently equipped, is probably more than adequate to contain such an inflow, but it certainly has not the resources to fight both an external and an internal war.   If simultaneously with such an incursion there should be an internal uprising or massive civil disobedience, the army has, according to rumours currently circulating in South Africa, warned the government that it will not be equal to the task.   This is perhaps one of the reasons underlying the unprecendented statement of the Prime Minister that South Africa must change if it is to avoid revolution.

These pages will reflect various thoughts and observations, some of them apparently suggestive of a continuance of the present ordering of society, some of them suggestive of change.   However strong the former, they must be viewed against the incontrovertible background that the moral basis of apartheid which once it enjoyed with its supporters, has perished — and with it that the great initial momentum of the movement is spent.

When and how the eventual collapse will occur, no observer can tell.   There can be little doubt however that

21

whether through violent or peaceful change, this abberration on the statute books of mankind will inevitably pass into the realm of historical curiosities, to be studied with wonder and disbelief by later generations. Its passing can be painful but, hopefully, will not be long delayed. Its continuance is too deeply contrary to the self-respect of the majority of mankind for armies however powerful and however supported from abroad, to invest it with longevity.

The Rationale of Apartheid

The observer outside South Africa tends to wonder what manner of justification can possibly be made out by its exponents for so extraordinary a doctrine as that of apartheid. Afrikaner theorists have at various stages offered explanations. Whether one agrees with them or not, they need to be known.

1. *The traditionalist argument.* Apartheid is said to be traditional ever since the white man came to South Africa. It is no invention of the Afrikaners but only a continuation of the process which even British rulership endorsed as appropriate for South Africa. With limitations, such as that coloureds in the Cape had the vote, this is substantially correct historically, but to use one piece of wrongdoing as a justification for another makes no sense.

2. *The historical argument.* This argument has it that historically it was the whites who arrived first in much of the territory of South Africa and that therefore by right of first occupation the land is theirs to do with it as they please. The basis of the claim is the contention that the whites arrived over three centuries ago in the Cape and that at that time the tribes from Central Africa were just coming down along the East Coast and crossing the Limpopo River.

One often hears this argument in South Africa. The contrary view, however, carefully researched by Professor Monica Wilson, is that in much of the land which is under white control, it was the Africans who arrived and settled first. Professor Wilson[3] shows that the first stated view is a misconception and a myth created to bolster up apartheid.

Even conceding the historical facts as contended for by the supporters of apartheid, racial discrimination on the statute book of a country can never be justified on the basis of prior arrival of a component element of a country's population. Every nation is made up of different groups some of whom arrived in the national territory after others. The late-comers, once accepted as citizens, can never on the basis of late arrival be deprived of equal treatment before the law.

3. *The theological argument.*   The Dutch Reformed Church has sought to justify 'separate development' in the light of scripture.   This argument is dealt with elsewhere[4] and very little needs to be stated in this day and age to support a submission that this contention is undeserving of serious consideration.

4. *The separationist argument.*   Theoreticians of apartheid draw a sharp distinction between separation, which they submit is justifiable, and segregation, which is not.   Separation aims at establishing distinct racial societies, whereupon the multiracial society is ended and one has a series of separate societies each functioning according to its own ethos and traditions without any discriminations within it. Segregation on the other hand establishes a caste-like hierarchy within a society, which is discriminatory.[5] Apartheid, it is said, aims at separation and eventually will separate out the black from the white, when the homelands policy is fully implemented.   There will then be a series of separate and independent societies functioning free of discrimination.

   The futility of the homelands policy is dealt with elsewhere.[6] Until the manifestly unattainable stage of complete separation is reached, there can be no doubt whatever that there will be discrimination within the segregated groups that are marked out for eventual separation.   The distinction seems therefore to be a verbal one. Even if total separation should eventually be achieved, the independence of the states to which the blacks will be confined will never be a real independence as elsewhere explained,[7] and consequently there will never be equality between the white South African citizen and the black 'homelands' citizen.

5. *The argument of pluriformity.*   It is said by the advocates of this contention that the various racial groups in South Africa can best benefit from the presence of each other in the same country if each of them should preserve its integrity and culture intact without dilution or contamination by the other. That way each group can make its richest contribution to the diversity of South African life, and at the same time develop its ethnic and cultural back-

ground without interference. This argument forms a part of the theological justification set out earlier.

The argument overlooks the fact that the pluriformity thus promoted cannot include also a graded plurality of political, social and economic levels such as the South Afrcan situation engenders.

6. *The argument of ethnic incompatibility.* The various groups are said to be so diverse that they cannot achieve any harmonious mix — physically, culturally or socially. African tribalism and European sophistication, like oil and water, must always remain separate. The arrogance and ignorance implicit in this argument need no refutation. Governor Van der Stel, a hero of Afrikaner culture, was himself the product of a mixed marriage.[8]

7. *The racial purity argument.* This argument, not articulated so often nowadays but still implicit in the attitudes of many whites, negates commonsense and experience. No race is pure and here one soberly recalls the history of the Nazi philosophy which sought to base itself upon such a theory.

The Afrikaner is thought by some anthropologists to have an admixture of Hottentot blood. The three million coloureds are not the only instances of white/black mixture, and scattered through white society there are undoubtedly tens of thousands of mixed persons. The very fact that courts are required to decide the question whether a person is white or coloured[9] shows the prevalence of numerous borderline cases.

8. *The paternalistic argument.* The white man, superior in talent, accomplishment and the arts of government, has a paternalistic role placed on him of leading the non-whites towards the level of understanding which will enable them to govern themselves. That stage is still far removed, but till then social and political rights must be withheld from them. The mission is thought by many to be a God-given one, for it was part of the divine plan by which the heathen was to be led towards salvation.

South Africa's coloured and black lawyers and doctors, competent to handle the affairs of any citizen but deemed not to possess an understanding sufficient to vote wisely, must rank as one of the world's strange political phenomena.

9. *The Homelands argument.*   For many years supporters of apartheid, guilt stricken inwardly by its injustices, were casting around for some practical basis on which they could claim the system in fact gave the black man fair status and opportunity.   In 1951 a commission under the chairmanship of Professor F.R. Tomlinson was appointed to report on the 'Socio-economic development of the Bantu areas within the Union of South Africa'.   Its report, presented in 1954 provides the blueprint of the homelands policy.   Here there would be large tracts of land which the blacks would look upon as their home, where they could govern themselves, trade freely, enter any profession, develop their industries and flower as separate nations.

The report provided the answer apartheid supporters were awaiting and they greeted it enthusiastically.   It was a positive plan for the upliftment of the blacks and as a sop to white conscience, the white government was to spend hundreds of millions of dollars on implementing it.   This was a new vision of positive apartheid, keeping the races separate while yet doing positive good to the blacks.

The flaws in the scheme have already been discussed. Thirteen per cent of the land — and not the best land either — for more than eighty per cent of the people is a division with no claims to fairness.   Nor is the deprivation of a South African's South African citizenship against his volition fair either.   Nor does industry flourish in the homelands when by deliberate government policy the industries serviced by homelands labour are located on the peripheries of the homelands but within white territory.

10. *The development argument.*   By this argument, the whites are the developers of South Africa and the creators of its wealth.   They must therefore enjoy the products of their initiative.   The blacks will be given a just reward for their labour but that is the limit of their entitlement.   The mere fact of their presence in the same nation cannot entitle them to equal rights.   One recalls similar arguments at one time in the US in a period of history which the US and the rest of the world have long left behind.

11. *The domino argument.*   The proponents of this view contend that the slightest concession made in the rigidity of current apartheid must lead to more concessions till one by one the privileges — and the property — of whites fall.   The only way to prevent this process is to stop the initial step.   Many *verkramptes* hold strongly to this view.

25

12. The argument of self-preservation.   This is closely related to the previous argument.   It underlines many white South African attitudes.   The fear is a fear that if the blacks win power they will deal with the whites as the whites dealt with the blacks.   A similar fear underlay US attitudes at the time of the emancipation of the slaves, and did not materialise.   Nearly all whites in South Africa have a measure of fear of black power though, in fairness, only some use it as an argument for legitimising the present position.

    The argument applies not merely to life but to property and employment as well.   There is also a lurking fear that if blacks are admitted to positions of expertise and responsibility they will prove more attractive to employers, both local and foreign, than the whites.

13. The argument of despair.   The whites have no place else in the world to which they can go.   South Africa is their only home.   There is no way in which South Africa can continue to be a home for them unless they build walls of privilege around themselves.   It is not through wickedness that the blacks are kept apart but because there is no other known way of continuing to keep South Africa as their home.

14. The argument of superiority.   This is not commonly articulated today but there are many who feel it.   In fact there is evidence that this attitude is still inculcated in young minds at school.

    One of the most explicit and unabashed formulations of it was that by Chief Justice Lord de Villiers, scion of a distinguished Afrikaner family (originally Huguenot) who said in 1911:

    "As a matter of public history we know that the first civilised legislators in South Africa came from Holland and regarded the aboriginal natives of the country as belonging to an inferior race, whom the Dutch, as Europeans, were entitled to rule over, and whom they refused to admit to social or political equality...these prepossessions, or as many might term them, these prejudices, have never died out, and are not less deeply rooted at the present day among the Europeans in South Africa, whether of Dutch or English or French descent.   We cannot as judges, when called upon to construe an act of Parliament, ignore the reasons which must have induced the legislature to adopt the policy of separate education for European and non-European children."[10]

15. *The argument of compatibility between separation and equality.*   It was said till the doctrine was judicially exploded some years ago that there was no derogation of the concept of equality inherent in the concept of separation. One could provide separate facilities for different racial groups without in any way suggesting inequality between the groups or in the facilities offered. Apartheid and separate facilities were therefore valid and reasonable — a view judicially endorsed.

Unfortunately for the theory, in the same way as it was judicially supported, it was also judicially rejected when the Supreme Court held that separate facilities did not necessarily have to be equal.[11]

16. *The economic argument.*   The blacks living under apartheid in South Africa are economically better off per capita than any blacks in any of the black African countries. Therefore government by the white man under apartheid laws is best for the blacks.   Implicit in this argument is the concept of inequality between the black citizen and the white citizen in his own country.   As Nelson Mandela said of this argument at his trial on April 20 1964, the argument is irrelevant.   "Our complaint is not that we are poor by comparison with people in other countries, but that we are poor by comparison with the white people in our own country, and that we are prevented by legislation from altering this imbalance."

17. *The elimination-of-friction argument.*   An argument of great antiquity and authority in South Africa is that if you separate races you diminish the points at which friction between them may occur, and hence ensure good relations. Bram Fischer, Q.C. at his trial under the Sabotage Act referred to this reason and said the answer was the essence of simplicity.   "If you place the races of one country in two camps . . . and cut off contact between them, those in each camp begin to forget that those in the other are ordinary human beings, that each lives and laughs in the same way, that each experiences joy or sorrow, pride or humiliation for the same reasons.   Thereby each becomes suspicious of the other and each eventually fears the other, which is the basis of all racialism."

18. *The misgovernment argument.*　　Every African country since attainment of black rule has lurched from one crisis to another. If power should be given to the blacks in South Africa a similar fate would overtake that country. The blacks must therefore be kept away from controlling the government. The only way to achieve this is by preserving political power for the whites. This preservation of political power becomes impossible once equality in other matters is conceded. Hence the need for apartheid.

　　Not every African country has been ill governed. Some of the best governed from the standpoint of black interests may be ill governed from the standpoint of white interests.　Where unrest and chaos have resulted, this has often been due in large measure to the delay in recognising black political demands and the consistent attempt to keep the blacks out of positions of responsibility.　If the outstanding black leadership of South Africa had not been crushed, and if it does not continue to be crushed, South Africa has outstanding leadership potential sufficient to administer the government in collaboration with the white population.　The high road to chaos and misgovernment is in fact the process of delaying the transfer of power, rather than the handing over of power.

19.　*The White Nationalistic argument.* German *volksgeist* theory held that the *volk* (the people) had a spirit and a history characteristic of themselves — *Volksgeist*. This was a manifestation of God.　German nationalism, according to some philosophers such as Fichte was the purest because German *volksgeist* was the purest.

　　With this theory there is mixed also, in the Afrikaner mind, the myth of the chosen people, giving rise to pronouncements such as D.F. Malan's statement, "The history of the Afrikaner reveals a determination and a definiteness of purpose which make one feel that Afrikanerdom is not the work of man, but a creation of God.　We have a divine right to be Afrikaners.　Our history is the highest work of art of the Architect of the centuries"[12] Pursuing this thinking further General C. de Wet has observed, "Providence had drawn the line between black and white and we must make that clear to the Natives and not instil into their minds false ideas of equality"[13]

20.　*The argument of sub-humanness.* In the introductory chapter the reader will recall the vignette recounting a conversation the author heard in a hotel shop — "Still hanging by one arm from the trees". It is regrettable that in a study of South Africa in 1979, reference has to be made to this sort of argument, which, it is to be hoped, humanity has outlived, but one needs to be true to reality and to paint the picture whole. While perhaps only the most insignificant and uneducated of the whites still articulate this belief, what is significant is that there still are such. These beliefs were much more generally held in the past and were an influential factor in the formation of apartheid attitudes. As in the days of slavery in the US where whites were 'persons' and blacks were 'niggers' and articles of property, or in Australia where aborigines were not counted as 'persons' for census purposes, so also in South Africa the black did not rank as a 'person'. In 1910 when the truck was replacing the horse drawn wagon, whites commonly asserted that "the native will never be able to drive mechanical vehicles".[14] Ignorance and isolation from the main stream of world affairs helped shape this outlook. The author has met South Africans who say that some school teachers still tend to foster it.

These are in short some of the arguments one reads or hears. There is probably some degree of overlap among them and the supporters of apartheid draw upon a vague and varied mix of these arguments, some attaching importance to some arguments and not to others. The inability of these arguments to stand the test of reason or of modern conditions is all too apparent to so many South Africans that it may fairly be said that although apartheid still commands some measure of reasoned support its rationale has broken down. It was indeed true that one or other of these arguments might have commended itself to the majority of South Africa's white population at an earlier stage, but this is no longer the case. Try as it may, apartheid has run out of moral and intellectual props. It is only the military prop that remains.

The Cost of Apartheid

An account sheet of the cost of apartheid, if such could be even remotely attempted, might run somewhat as shown below. An explanatory note in regard to each item is appended at the end of the table. In compiling this table, I have had considerable assistance from Joyce Harris' article on the Cost of Apartheid in the May 1979 issue of the Black Sash Magazine.[15] I have indicated which figures from this assessment I have adopted. I have added some items, and, where my estimate differs from those figures, have so indicated in the explanatory notes. The figures are at best rough and probably in some instances overlapping, but they give a general idea of the enormous cost of apartheid.

Balance Sheet

Capital Expenditure	Cost in Millions
1. Cost of land aquisition for the homelands policy and of housing migrants.	1,200
2. Ten million Reference Books @ R.10 each.	100
3. Demolition of Crossroads and other habitable housing throughout the country.	20
4. Migrant Hostels	150
5. Unnecessary duplication of University facilities (arbitrary figure)	20
6. Resettlement of Indian Traders	200
7. Resettlement of Displaced Persons	100
8. Necessary infrastructure for the homelands.	200
9. Loss of foreign investment.	? x 1000
Total	**? x 1000 + 1990**

Recurrent Direct Expenditure

10. New Reference Books	4
11. Keeping Reference Books up-to-date	20
12. Quarter million pass laws prosecutions annually @ R.20 per prosecution (time of police, prosecutors, magistrates, clerks, paperwork, transport of accused persons)	5
13. Cost of imprisonment	18.7
14. Cost of patrolling and policing the system	11.5
15. Loss of man-days of work of people arrested (Quarter million x 8 = 2 million man-days = 16 million man hours)	16
16. Operation of Labour Bureaux	12
17. Contract labour documents	35
18. Conducting unnecessary duplicate University faculties (arbitrary figure)	4
19. Apartheid-induced extra expenditure for defence	500
20. Internal Security	200
21. The human costs.	∞
22. Loss of foreign investment	? x 100
Total	**? x 100 + ∞ + 826.2**

Notes to Items in Balance Sheet

1. In 1979 Dr. Hartzenburg, Deputy Minister of Plural Relations, estimated the land still to be bought at R.400-700 million. To this must be added the cost of housing migrants, estimated by Joyce Harris at R.3 billion. I have taken only a token R.500 million out of this figure.

2. Joyce Harris' figures, 1979 May *Sash,* p.1.

3. The *Financial Mail* of 23 March, 1978 estimated the demolition of existing family housing in Alexandra alone at one million Rand.

4. For Alexandra alone the complex of eight hostels, with 2000 - 3000 beds in each was estimated in the Financial Mail of 23 March 1978 to cost R.2,300 per bed, i.e. a total of 57.5 million Rand.
   Spouses' accommodation, since it must be provided for even occasional visits, could cost up to one tenth of this.

5. See note 18 below.

6. The removal of Indian traders from shopping areas where they had traded for generations, as in Johannesburg, into trading areas specially created with a view to their segregation, e.g. the Oriental Plaza. Mr. Abram Meyet of the Indian Reform Party, as reported in *Sash* at p.3, estimated that the government had up to June 1976 spent more than 29 million rand on the construction of 852 new Indian shopping units.
   1300 Indian traders were resettled in shopping complexes such as the Oriental Plaza, Fordsberg, and the Orient Bazaar, Pretoria, at a cost of R.31.5 million. The government was planning to spend another R.29.5 million to move 398 Indian traders in Natal and the Transvaal between 1976 and 1982. Mr. Meyet said, "We have estimated that it is going to cost the taxpayer more than R.200 million by 1980 to resettle all the Indian people." See also the similar figures of Mr. Marais Steyn as reported in the *Star* of 29 June 1977.

7. The resettlement of people under the Homelands scheme and the Group Areas Act is one of the most gigantic population re-locations undertaken by a government in modern times. Up to May 1979, 2,115,000 people had been moved (all but 7,000 of them black). Another 1,727,000 have yet to be moved. Even on the figures of 3,842,000 at the meagre cost of R.30 per head this represents R.100 million.

8. The homelands into which vast numbers of blacks are transported and to be transported have no resources to support these populations. Basic amenities such as water supply and transport need to be provided. The provision of these would require a minimum of R.200 million, which could more usefully be spent elsewhere. See Leo Marquard, *The Peoples and Policies of South Africa,* 4th ed. p.38.

9. This figure is speculative.

10. and 11. The figures come from Joyce Harris' estimates, May 1979, *Sash* 1.

12.   Mrs. Harris estimates the cost of half a million prosecutions at R1.5 million, i.e. R.3 per prosecution. I believe the cost of prosecutors, magistrates, police, clerks, paperwork and transport would be nearer R.20 — at best an arbitrary figure.

13.   Joyce Harris, *ibid.*

14.   Joyce Harris, *ibid.*

15.   Harris: estimate is R.7.7 million on the basis of 12.3 million man hours. I have estimated the man-hour loss at 16 million man hours.

16.   Joyce Harris, *ibid.*

17.   Joyce Harris, *ibid.*

18.   This is based on unnecessary duplication of facilities, e.g. law. For a few black students a whole faculty is created in close proximity to a white university law faculty which can easily absorb these students. The same would apply presumably, to other faculties.

19.   Defence expenditure in 1977/78 ran to 1,700,082,000 Rand. Every country needs a defence force but South Africa's intense unpopularity in consequence of apartheid, as well as her military incursions into neighbouring countries, greatly heighten the necessary military expenditure. A conservative arbitrary assessment of these additional needs is one third. If South Africa had had a democratically elected government based on one-man-one-vote a good proportion of its heavy military establishment could be dismantled.

20.   Similar comments to 19, except that a greater proportion of internal security expenditure is attributable to apartheid — the Bureau of State Security, the Security Police, the Prisons, the supervision of banned persons, riot control, commissions of inquiry such as the Cillie commission into the 1976 riots, payments to common informers, a substantial proportion of the time of the ordinary police force (e.g. on raids under the Mixed Marriages Acts and checking passes on the streets).

21.   Broken families, uprooting from traditional homes, resettlement as strangers in new areas often hundreds of miles away, unemployment, dependence on migratory labour, humiliation, loss of self respect, imprisonment, insecurity, loss of life in riots, fear. Every black person in South Africa is affected by one or other or many of these. The catalogue is unending and the cost is infinite.

22.   Similar comments to 19 and 20. The cost in terms of withdrawal of investment and non-investment is incalculable. See further pp.233-7.

It will be seen from this most skeletal of balance sheets that the capital cost, apart from loss of foreign investment, is in the region of two billion dollars, while the recurrent cost, apart from that item and the human costs, approaches a billion dollars. These are figures even the economy of South Africa cannot sustain.

This table does not in any way take account of the loss of productivity caused to the economy by apartheid. The unhappiness and discontent of the labour force, and the way in which technical and managerial skills have been withheld from it must cost the South African economy several times the figures outlined. On February 28, 1979, Mr. A. Widman, M.P. estimated the cost of apartheid at R.18,795 million annually.[16]   Another survey quotes the cost at R.13,000 million a year,[17]   and an estimate by a South African financier assesses that the 1976 gross national product would have been R.38,800 million rather than R.26,700 million as it was — a cost of R.12,100 million.[18]

These figures, again, are only rough estimates but highlight the colossal waste involved.

To waste these resources on establishing and maintaining a system of discrimination in a world of poverty and shortages of earth resources must, by the established principles of international law, rank as a crime against humanity — a crime altogether separate and distinct from the crime of apartheid *per se*. It is difficult to see how the responsibility for this can be avoided by any white South African who participates in the benefits of the system without working actively for its reform.

Obstacles to Black Equality

What has just been said regarding the end of apartheid is not intended in any way to minimise the problem. It has numerous facets which need to be noted. The factors that stand in the way of an equalisation of the economic, social and political position of the blacks in South Africa are too numerous to list comprehensively.

Some of the factors enumerated below would constitute important items upon such a list if indeed such a list could be attempted.

a) The Western world's strategic dependence on the white South African regime.

b) The Western world's de facto support of the white South African regime.

c) The desire of white South Africans to continue in the enjoyment of privileges which make them one of the world's most privileged communities.

d) The unjustifiability of the political, social and economic privileges enjoyed by the whites and the consequent impossibility of maintaining these under any regime based on justice and equality.

e) The blunting of the white South African conscience by continued years of unjust privilege.

f) The enormous natural wealth of South Africa which political power sharing will take out of the control of the whites.

g) The Afrikaners' long history of oppression, their fortuitous advent to power and the desire to retain what has so long eluded them.

h) The failure of nearly all proposed sanctions against South Africa.

i) Lack of communication and contact between freedom workers inside South Africa and those in the external world.

j) The lack of a free flow of information both ways, between South Africa and the world. Recent revelations of South African government attempts to buy up news media in the Western world to propagate a false view of itself underscore this point.

k) Misguidance by the Dutch Reformed Church on scriptural teaching regarding apartheid.

l) Failure by the churches generally to take a positive stand against the system.

m) The habit of describing all movements for social reform as communist-inspired, and thus condemning and stifling them.

n) The activities of the Broederbond.

o) Attitudes of racism on the part of the white population.

p) Attitudes of complacency on the part of the white population.

q) Attitudes of ignorance on the part of the white population regarding African potential, achievements and culture.

r) A consuming fear on the part of the white population that any surrender of power to the blacks is fraught with physical danger to the entire white population.

s) Total lack of communication between the various component elements of the South African population, increased substantially by the isolations induced by the Group Areas Act.

t) The Pass Laws.

u) The Homelands Policy, inspiring a misguided hope that the blacks could eventually be relegated to a defined territorial area, leaving the bulk of South Africa as white territory.

v)   The lack of an effective opposition.

w)   The incarceration and suppression of the flower of black leadership.

x)   Security Legislation.

y)   Disunity and lack of common leadership among black groups.

z)   The inability of blacks to compete economically on equal terms with whites due to a variety of discriminatory laws — e.g. the requirement that they should trade only in their own areas — with consequent inability of the blacks to become an economic force.

aa)   The payment of inadequate wages to blacks — often not adequate to support a household — even by established foreign companies such as Firestone, Kellogs, McGraw-Hill, Colgate Palmolive and Gillette.   Their emergence as an economic force is therefore beyond black ability in all but the most exceptional cases.

bb)   The lack of black technical expertise, directly caused by the failure over a long term of years to impart such expertise to blacks.

cc)   The lack of recognition of African unions.   According to the 1978 Race Relations Survey, no U.S. firm either recognised or negotiated with one.

dd)   State control of media.

ee)   The differential education system.

The ensuing pages will contain many references to these aspects, all of which in combination present a formidable obstacle to reform.   If the apparatus of apartheid is to be dismantled every one of these points will need concerted attention.

The Lack of an Effective Opposition

One of the principal obstacles to change in South Africa is the Nationalist Party's enjoyment of power for a continuous period of 31 years.   In the course of this period the opposition has been reduced to such ineffectiveness that there is a virtually monolithic power structure in the state. In the 1977 elections the ruling Nationalist Party, with 134 M.P.s in a house of 165, faced an official opposition of seventeen members of the Progressive Federal Party, and a New Republic Party (successors to the disbanded United Party) of only ten M.P.'s.

Even though those in power feel urgently the need for reform, it becomes difficult in this context for the leaders to acknowledge that there has been any fundamental error in the policies that have led the present ruling party to the present position. So to acknowledge would be to require an admission that the founding fathers of apartheid, its great high priests and prophets, have failed their people and led them in the wrong direction. No ruling party can admit that its prophets were wrong and it is necessary therefore for face-saving formulae to be devised. These formulae are necessary to enable a withdrawal from some basic positions without an apparent acknowledgement that those positions were taken up in error. This perhaps explains the need for semantics in South African politics. One speaks not of 'apartheid' but of 'parallel development', not of the 'Department of Bantu Administration and Development' but of the 'Department of Plural Relations', not of 'discrimination' but of 'differentiation', not of 'equality' but of 'equal opportunity'. These verbal formulae are meant to appease radical blacks as well as conservative whites, but it is not difficult for either group to rip through these semantic disguises.

The problem in South Africa has affinities with the problem that arose in India, where Congress was in power without a break for well over a generation. The lack of an effective and organised opposition drove all reformers into one of two alternative positions. They needed to align themselves with the opposition which to a large extent did not enjoy a reputation for responsibility in public affairs — or at any rate was portrayed as being so — or alternatively to resort to intrigue within the ranks of the government party. There was no other way in which change could be effected. For this reason any effective ventilation of opposition views was rendered impossible under the Indian system. South Africa is not very different in this regard, though poles apart in general policies. Whoever is outside the government party tends to be an outcast from the establishment and is not infrequently the object of a smear campaign. He is condemned as a reformist and a communist. Indeed whoever talks of basic change in South Africa however sincerely motivated is at once identified with communism and with the enemies of South Africa. This is no healthy constitutional position.

The parliamentary opposition sees itself as not likely to offer a viable opposition to the enormous strength that government commands in parliament, but rather as a catalyst. It hopes to a large extent to achieve the objectives of an opposition in South Africa by sowing the seeds of new ideas in the minds of government members and by causing them to have doubts regarding the basic stands of their party.

Another difficulty which organised opposition confronts in South Africa is the disunity of black leadership. Black leadership varies from a readiness to acquiesce in the present dispensation and to take as much benefit as possible out of it, to the opposite extreme of revolution. There are many shades of opinion between these extremes. Rich rewards await the black leader who is prepared to have truck with the government. The extreme example of this is to be found in the homelands where a Prime Minister would enjoy such perks of office as a lavish official residence, a fleet of cars, a cabinet and a pension for life. All these trappings of office are attractive and exceed the price some leaders are prepared to pay for their principles. There are other leaders who, while not prepared to accept handouts in this fashion, are for pragmatic reasons reconciled to having truck with the establishment with a view to gaining for their people the maximum possible advantage.

On the other hand, there are leaders who say that they will have no discussion whatsoever with the establishment until the policy of one man, one vote receives complete official endorsement.

Among these varied shades of opinion it becomes extremely difficult for the opposition to line up a phalanx of black opposition in support of its policies. Whatever views it might express in regard to the needs of the blacks can be contradicted by contrary opinions cited by the government from the mouth of a black leader.

Apart from the leadership level there is also a lack of unity among the black people at grass roots level. There will always be informers prepared to carry to the government news of any activity that might be antagonistic to government policies even though it is not necessarily subversive of the government. Here too rewards await the informer and the task of organisers of opposition from among the rank and file of the blacks becomes extremely difficult. There is no doubt a great deal of antagonism towards the 'Uncle Toms' or the 'sellouts' as these people are called. But still the facts of life are grim and in a situation of extreme privation it becomes a rewarding attitude to curry favour with the government.

Current black leadership is dealt with later.[20]

Breakdown of Communication

South Africa is a society in a state of polarisation.

The different racial groups have now withdrawn within themselves and such interrelationships as might have existed in the past seem no longer to exist.

With calculated thoroughness all available channels of communication have one by one been closed. Any flicker of protest is snuffed out, any semblance of dialogue discouraged. Censorship, incarceration of leaders, separation of communities, segregation in education — all these have over the years taken their toll of such understanding and goodwill as once existed.

If one were deliberately attempting to place South African whites in a position of isolation which they could never expect to hold indefinitely, one could not have performed the task with greater success. One is reminded of the proverbial woodcutter hacking at the branch on which he is perched. With complete separation from the main trunk his destruction is assured. The South African white is not far from this self-created fate.

Students at universities, the potential leadership of their respective racial groups, have no contact with each other even if their universities are in the same city. To expect them to live in peace and understanding when they assume leadership is almost fantasy unless their isolation can now be broken down. The political leadership of all but the white communities is behind bars, leaving few with authority to speak for these groups. There is consequently no one to hold discussions with, should this be necessary. Non-white viewpoints are not allowed to mature through discussion and most remain raw and radical. The hand of the censor falls with special severity on the non-white press.

A strange South African phenomenon is the law that mixed political parties cannot exist. The division of the country being avowedly on the basis of colour, blacks, coloureds, Indians or whites of the same political persuasion cannot work together. They must form their own political parties. Consequently political parties which contained a combination of racial groups in their composition were required to disband and form their own separate groups.

Political leaders of coloured and white parties recount with sorrow the break-up of their common political party into splinter groups based on race. Some fellow members went out of politics altogether. Others formed their own new political parties.

South Africa is now a series of islands. Where the bridge builders should have been building their piers, the gunners are taking up their posts, eyes fixed on their adversaries. Before the guns swivel finally into position communication must be restored.

Education

The statute book provides expressly for four different systems of education — for whites, Indians, coloureds and blacks. This education is conducted at four different levels and there is no possibility of a person of one group opting into another or of being transferred into another, however excellent may be his educational attainments.

Strangely enough, this has been achieved under what has been described as a University Extension Act, the purpose of which is to restrict each particular racial group to its own appropriate university. It means that a person of one group has no right to attend a university of another group however appropriate it may be that he should follow a course at that University, unless he can prove that his own University does not offer the course which he desires to follow. If the education authorities can on this basis be persuaded to issue a permit, a person can enter a University which is not of his appropriate racial group. This has resulted in a nominal relaxation of the exclusiveness of the white universities. Stellenbosch for example had in 1978 25 coloured, 1 Indian, 2 Chinese and 7 African students out of its student body of 11,206; Cape Town, more liberal in this respect, has 652 coloured, 143 Indian, 19 Chinese and 33 African students out of a student body of 9,778; Potchefstroom, 2 coloured, 2 Indian, and 6 African out of a student body of 6,649; Pretoria and Rand Afrikaans had no non-whites out of student totals of 17,378 and 3,957 respectively. Perhaps the most liberal was Witwatersrand with 75 coloured, 433 Indian, 188 Chinese and 101 African of a total of 11,749 students.[21] It is interesting to note also that in 1978, 650 applications for entry into other universities were received from Africans, of which only 189 were granted, and that 745 of 899 Indian applications were granted.[22]

The general principle still holds good that each racial group has its own appropriate university and the State is prepared to go to any expense in order to keep up an appearance of availability of educational services for all the racial groups. One of the best examples is the University of Durban-Westville. A most impressive campus has been built at a cost of several millions of rand to emphasise that educational facilities for Indians are available right through to tertiary and postgraduate level. Often this is done at the cost of duplication of faculties, at tremendous expense. For example, some black law faculties have few students but are nevertheless maintained at great public expense merely in order to provide some of the apparatus necessary to keep apartheid working. For example the University of kwaZulu maintains a law faculty quite unnecessarily, when these facilities are available in close proximity in other universities. The black universities, Fort Hare in the Ciskei, the University of Umtata in the Transkei, the University of kwaZulu, and The University of the North in Lebowa, have all been established at very great expense, often with similar unnecessary duplication of facilities.

The extent of discrimination in secondary education will be appreciated when it is pointed out that in 1975/1976 the education of each white child cost 644 rand, each coloured child 140 rand, each Asian child 190 rand and each African child 42 rand. Nor is the education that is available to blacks anything like what it is in the white schools. One of the reasons for this is the lack of black trained school teachers, 48 percent of whom have only the junior certificate or its equivalent. Furthermore, a great anomaly which was recently erased from the statute book was the requirement that although white children had their textbooks and stationery free, two-thirds of black school children still had to pay for them. Another source of basic difference was that black children did not have compulsory education until a year ago when an announcement was made that Bantu education would be compulsory up to 12 years.

All this accords well with Dr. Verwoerd's speech in Parliament in 1953 when he introduced the Bantu Education Bill:

"My department's policy is that education should stand with both feet in the reserves and have its roots in the spirit and being of Bantu society. There, Bantu education must be able to give itself complete expression and there it will be called upon to perform its real service...There is no place for him in the European community above the level of certain forms of labour...For that reason it is of no avail for him to receive a training which has as its aim, absorption in the European community...Until now he has been subject to a school system which drew him away from his own country and misled him by showing him the green pastures of European society in which he is not allowed to graze...I will reform (Bantu education) so that natives will be taught from childhood to realize that equality with

Europeans is not for them.   Race relations cannot improve
if the wrong type of education is given to natives".

Resources

As everyone knows, South Africa is most richly en-
dowed with mineral wealth. This has to a large extent determined her strange history. It makes possible the immense
waste of resources which supports the apparatus of apartheid. It accounts in large measure for the British desire to
annex the Afrikaner republics — which led to the Boer War.
It accounts for the desire of the Western world to preserve
stability in South Africa, for its wealth has attracted immense
investments which need to be safeguarded.

But one gap in all this natural wealth is oil. South
Africa, which provides the world with the bulk of its gold
and diamonds, must in the world market be a suppliant for
oil.   Industrialisation is important to it to keep its black
workforce from labour unrest, but industrialisation cannot
be pursued without oil and hence without the goodwill of
the external world.   Especially when the oil producing
Middle East is antagonistic to South Africa, this becomes a
thorny problem for South African rulers. Iran till recently
was the source which largely supplied this need, but that
too has been cut off.

In anticipation of these situations South Africa has
taken three steps which can help it out of the difficulty.
The first is the stockpiling of oil, which is commonly
thought to have built up a store sufficient for five years.

The second is a pioneering of oil production from
coal, for which the South African formula, used in the
SASOL I and SASOL II plants has been keenly sought
by other industrial countries. It is expected that these
plants will produce upwards of 30 per cent of South
Africa's energy requirements by 1981.

The third is the development of nuclear power. South
Africa's nuclear plants have top priority in a government programme which will make use of South African uranium and is
calculated to take the pressure off the oil shortage in a very
substantial measure. Even more importantly this step introduces South Africa to nuclear technology in a manner
which has grave military implications, and many believe
that South Africa has nuclear weapons capability as well.

Despite these steps, South Africa's dependence on oil
is still great, for stock piles will run out, SASOL meets only

41

part of her needs, nuclear power has its problems, and the demands of industry keep growing.

Oil is therefore the Achilles' heel of the South African economy. The deposition of the Shah and the loss of the principal single source of supply, Iran (which provided 20 per cent of her recent needs) must gravely complicate the issue. In the growing climate of anti-South African feeling substitute sources will be difficult to tap.

Oil is an important factor in understanding South Africa's relations with the external world.

Foreign Investment

Despite her affluence, South Africa needs foreign investment. A withdrawal of foreign capital necessarily means higher unemployment and possibly civil unrest, a situation the South African government does not want on its hands.

Foreign companies investing in South Africa are led by the U.K. with an investment of over five billion pounds spread through a significant shareholding in over 1,000 companies. The United States with nearly two billion dollars spread over 300 companies and West Germany with three hundred million dollars spread over 300 companies are the other major investors. Other significant shareholdings are:

France	50 companies
Australia	35 companies
Belgium	20 companies
Netherlands	20 companies
Italy	21 companies
Switzerland	12 companies
Sweden	11 companies
Spain	6 companies
Canada	5 companies [23]

In addition over one hundred United States banks have lent over two billion rand to South Africa.

Countries as openly committed to human rights as these investors are quite obviously one of the most powerful sources of potential international influence on South Africa. Whether this opportunity has been used in a manner matching their professed interest in human rights is a question to which the answer, as observed by blacks within South Africa, is quite clearly in the negative.

The absence of trade union protections, the laws relating to racial segregation, the separation of the worker from his family, differential wage scales, the practice of apartheid in the workplace — all these are taken advantage of for the extraction of profit from the investment, in a manner which must cause moral qualms in the receivers of dividends from these ventures. It is little to the point that these practices generally prevail in the country. The truth is that every one of these human rights denials becomes transmuted into dollars and cents, for each of them means so much extra profit in the company till. Every ten dollars drawn in dividends must, on a costing, include some dollars at least which flow directly from such human rights denials. Whether churches, trusts, universities and well meaning small investors can conscientiously receive this money is one of the moral problems over which there hovers a large question mark. Any investor who sees the unisex dormitories described elsewhere in this book and realises that his dividend dollar includes profit from this practice, will not, it is submitted, be able to keep his dollar and retain his peace with himself. He keeps his dollar and retains his peace only because he has not seen or has not been told of or does not believe this reality. Those who have seen it fail in their duty if they do not communicate this reality to the outside world.

What, then, is the consequence of such a line of thought? Does it mean total disinvestment or sanctions of a limited nature? What are the alternatives that present themselves? These are discussed in Chapter 8.

The Importance to the West of Peaceful Change in South Africa.

The global configuration of power has so altered in recent months that South Africa has become of even greater importance than ever before to the Western world. South Africa controls sea routes vital to the West especially in the context of an uncertain Suez Canal controlled by the Middle East. If South Africa should turn unfriendly to the Western world, the latter's global influence is cut by half.

If the West desires any long term continuance of its access to Eastern waters, as it undoubtedly does, it therefore needs a South Africa that will not close its sea routes. A black South Africa taking over through violence will almost certainly do this.

It is a major premise of this work that a white South Africa cannot much longer continue in power on the basis of repression. Since change must come, it is of vital importance to the Western world to ensure that such change is

43

peaceful. Self interest if nothing else, must therefore cause the West to bend its energies to a peaceful resolution of the South African problem. The means of achieving this is still within the control of the West if it will address itself more realistically to the problem. If it pursues its current self-centred, ambivalent and complacent policies it will be cutting the ground under its feet, speaking in global terms.

It seems strange, if one views South Africa in the context of global strategy, that this aspect has not thus far struck the policy makers of the Western world. They are pursuing the short term advantage of continuing to derive maximum profits from South Africa to the detriment of their long term global influence.

Thus far it is only West Germany that has made a clear public statement of the goals towards which it thinks South Africa should move — including full political participation by all. Other Western governments, though condemning South Africa from time to time, are still content to leave change to the processes that operate within South Africa itself.[24] It is perhaps time for a clearer commitment.

Some Home Truths Concerning South Africa.

Some home truths regarding South Africa, however obvious they may be, will bear repetition.

In the first place the prospect of the external world bringing South Africa to her knees by sheer physical force without great damage to itself seems remote. South Africa has armed strength enough to inflict severe damage on her attackers and can hold out for a very considerable period. However undesirable her racial policies, she will still have covert and overt support from many countries who profess to be opponents of the system. The prospect of a power vacuum in South Africa is one which none of the great powers can permit and they will all rush in. An international confrontation between the great powers can result not out of concern for human rights but out of concern for themselves and their financial and military interests. The possibility must also be very seriously considered of South Africa having nuclear capabilities which can in a desperate situation be used. A sizeable number of informed South Africans believe South Africa has or will shortly have this capability.

In the second place internal unrest, civil disobedience and open revolt are unlikely to succeed except after a massive expenditure of life and an amount of suffering which will make the sufferings of the past pale into insignificance.

South Africa watchers are often quite content to deliver themselves of the opinion that nothing short of an explosion can solve South Africa's problems, and, having made this observation, shrug off responsibility for any further personal commitments. This, rather conveniently, passes all responsibility to the black South African, to whom it means courting imprisonment, torture, death, loss of children or parents, scattering of families and shooting on the streets on a scale of tens if not hundreds of thousands. That black South Africans are now steeled to face this possibility is no excuse for complacency and inaction. In any event it does not serve the human rights cause either, for it will leave the people so exhausted and embittered that further strife is inevitable even if the old order is overthrown.

It may well be that massive internal unrest spread throughout the country is something the government may find it difficult to control. Indeed rumour in South Africa has it that the army has warned the Prime Minister of the very real dangers involved in suppressing such general unrest and at the same time fighting the commando units on South Africa's vast borders.

Still, the ability of the South African government to throw a ring of steel in an instant around the black and coloured settlements must be clearly understood. The Group Areas Act was framed not only with racial but also with military considerations in mind. Furthermore, Soweto, which perhaps caught the government unprepared, has taught its military lessons and it is idle to think that contingency plans have not been made for exactly this kind of situation on a greatly magnified scale.

Black and coloured South Africans can of course bring the South African economy to a grinding halt by an organised boycott, but the loss of income and the starvation involved are such that very severe hardship will be imposed upon millions. When one adds to this the police and military oppression which will surely be involved, the suffering will reach proportions of total war and this will leave impoverishment and chaos in its wake. Even if the war is won, the prospect will be one of a continuing downward slide in the economy and in law and order and South Africa will be a repetition on a colossal scale of the Angolan strife.

There is often talk in the outside world of massive civil disobedience, invoking the example of Gandhi in India.

45

This loses sight of some basic differences between the Indian and the South African situations. The Indian civil resister was perhaps more docile and quiet than his South African counterpart. In any event he was not such an embittered man, with pent up emotions resulting from cruel suppression and an open legal and legislative framework pronouncing him inferior. Consequently, the chances of a spark of violence here or there are infinitely greater in the South African situation and can, with the pent up sense of grievance all over the country, escalate in a trice into violence of serious proportions. It is to be remembered also that the government the Indian resister faced was one which, though it was indeed guilty of oppression and shooting on the streets, was not one which denied its allegiance to the Rule of Law. If challenged in the courts or elsewhere, it could articulate its stand only in terms of a fundamental acceptance of the Rule of Law and an attempted justification within that framework. The South African resister faces a government openly and blatantly rejecting those principles. It will consequently have no compunction in putting down any disobedience movement with an extremely heavy hand. Nor is its police and military machine inadequate for this purpose. Soweto was easily quelled by the police alone without the need for military intervention.

Another factor to be borne in mind is that South Africa has not one but many black leaders. Its millions will not march or desist from doing so at the command of one, as the Indians were prepared to do under Gandhi. No one of them can therefore hold all resisting blacks upon a leash.

For all these reasons the success of the Indian movement holds no promise of similar success in South Africa. Indeed it would be a fair inference that if Gandhi himself had led a movement on identical principles in the South Africa of today, it would have been doomed to an early failure.

It seems immoral, in the light of all these difficulties, to abandon to the black South African the task of curing South Africa of the disease of apartheid. The disease is not of his creation. Created by white South Africa, it has progressed to achieve its present stranglehold through the complacency and self interestedness of a world which could have cured it at the outset had it acted consistently with its professions. A world which marshalled its resources to eliminate racism in World War II allowed those same resources to fuel the world's major postwar phenomenon of racism. The problem is, in other words, the responsibility of the world and cannot morally be left to inadequate black resources alone. There is much the world can do. Whether such action will achieve success or not, the responsibility lying upon the external world is clear. Left to themselves the only way open to the blacks in South Africa is violent action on a scale involving monumental suffering. With concerted and informed assistance from the outside world alone is there the slightest chance of a peaceful solution. The outside world cannot shirk this responsibility, so long as action is still possible, however slender the apparent chances of success.

One final consideration. The Marxist scare is often invoked in discussions on the future of South Africa. If the present regime should collapse, the Marxists will take over — so runs the argument. Therefore, do all in your power — you the citizens of South Africa — to stem this tide. From the standpoint of the average black South African this argument can have no meaning so long as he is subject to a regime which in many ways is worse than Marxism. The denials of equality in his own country, the racial discrimination, the humiliations and insults, the arrogation of the lion's share of the national wealth to serve the needs of a small minority in his country, the total denial of even the semblance of participation in the government of his country — these are worse than would be his lot under any Marxist regime. And if Marxism holds fears also of torture and the midnight knock, so does his own government. If white South Africa desires black South Africa to reject Marxism it must make it reasonably possible for the black citizen to say that his system of government gives more dignity to the individual than does Marxism.

South African speakers and apologists often call for a clear commitment of South Africans to the western cause if the whole South Atlantic and Indian Ocean theatre were not to become ideologically threatened or militarily imperilled. If a Marxist belt were established right across Southern Africa from Angola to Mozambique, through Zimbabwe falling to Marxist-dominated groups, South Africa would be effectively sealed off.

"So what?" may well be the black South African's reply, so long as the present dispensation lasts. The Western world's only hope of averting such a result is not its pronouncements regarding the preservation of freedom or its invocation of the fears of Marxism, but a considered and sincere attempt to remove the yoke which the black South

African has long and silently borne, beyond the limits of human endurance.

FOOTNOTES

1. 1978 *Survey of Race Relations* p.49 based on Bulletin of Statistics Vol.12 No.3 Sept.1978 Table 1—1.
2. 1978 *Survey of Race Relations,* p.49.
3. *African Studies,* Vol.18, No.4, 1959.
4. See pp.88-90.
5. RFA Hoernle, *South African Native Policy and the Liberal Spirit* p.158. See also Rhoodie and Venter, *Apartheid* p.148.
6. See pp.131-7.
7. See pp.131-7.
8. It is generally accepted in South Africa that his maternal grandmother was Sinhalese.
9. See Appendix D.
10. 1911 AD at 643-4.
11. *Minister of Posts* v *Rasool* 1939 AD 167.
12. E. Robbins, *This Man Malan,* Cape Town, 1953, p.7.
13. L.M. Thompson, *The Unification of South Africa,* London, 1960, p.219.
14. Munger, *Afrikaner and African Nationalism,* p.34.
15. 1979 (21) *Sash,* p.1.
16. *Star,* 28 Feb. 1979.
17. *Sash,* op.cit. p.2.
18. *Ibid.*
19. 1978 *Survey of Race Relations.* p.141.
20. See Chapter 5.
21. 1978 *Survey of Race Relations.* p.451.
22. *Ibid.*
23. 1978 *Survey of Race Relations,* p.140.
24. See Christopher Hill, *South Africa Seen from the West,* (1979) 235 *Contemporary Review* 113 at 115-6.

3

The Building of the Edifice

The beginnings

In 1652 the Dutch East India Company (established 50 years earlier, and already rich and powerful through its trade with the East) sent Jan van Riebeeck to the Cape to establish a refreshment station to provide ships to the East with fresh vegetables and meat. This led to the establishment of the Cape Colony. From a victualling station for ships on their way to the East Indies, this colony grew to one of considerable size and affluence. The colonists, deeply influenced by Calvinism which had taken firm hold in Holland, had "a strong church and a strong creed, certain educational ideas and social institutions which must long remain powers in the land."[1] They had fought hard to become masters of the fertile country they acquired and their Calvinism gave them a sense of being God's agents in carrying out His Divine plan in the Promised Land of the African Continent.

The settlers had come in contact with Hottentots who were loosely organised and nomadic. Their pasture lands in the vicinity of Cape Town's Table Mountain were progressively taken over by the settlers as the operations of the market garden expanded, and two brief wars were necessary for their subjugation. Thereafter they provided, along with slaves imported from the East Coast and Madagascar, a source of cheap labour for the farms.

Van Riebeeck's successor, Simon Van der Stel, was the first administrator to have a vision of a greater future for the colony. He founded Stellenbosch, the first city to be established outside Cape Town, where he saw the possibilities of expanding the colony to more than a victualling station. He urged the East India Company to send more settlers, thus bringing in small numbers of Dutch, German and French immigrants. Ample farm land, ample labour and ample freedom gave to the members of the growing settlement a lifestyle of affluence, leisure and independence which left its stamp upon the settlers even when in later years they pro-- ceeded northwards. Calvinism gave them also an individual- istic stamp as well as a doctrinal justification for the feeling of racial superiority and exclusiveness which, over the years built itself into their character.

There followed the British occupation of the Cape in 1806, a consequence of the need to preserve Britain's eastern sea route under the threat of the Napoleonic wars. Waves of British migration following the end of these wars — especially a wave of settlement in 1820 — brought a strong British influence into the Cape. With the settlers there came also British institutions and concepts such as trial by jury, freedom of the press, the abolition of slavery and legislative represen- tation, thus providing another of the strands which make up the complex web of South African society. The dual character of European influence — the Dutch Calvinistic tradition and the British liberal democratic — are to be seen in uneasy juxtaposition everywhere and in every problem in South Africa.

By 1837, British control was established in Cape Colony and the Great Trek commenced in protest against British rule and the enthroning of English as the only official language. The descendants of the Dutch settlers trekked northwards and established the northern republics of the Orange Free State and the Transvaal, the independence of which the British recognised. A few years later, in 1843, the British established a colony in Natal and the Boers in that area as well trekked to the northern states.

The Trek northwards of the Boers was one of the sig- nificant population movements in history and has left such a lasting impression on South Africa that its implications need some special examination. Apartheid cannot be under- stood apart from the Great Trek.

The independent republic which was the Trekkers' dream was to be based on the Afrikaner's concept of justice and religion and racial inequality. The blacks were to be well looked after but by no means sharers in political power. These republics treasured their independence and when ex- panding British power and interests threatened them the great war started which has been variously described as the Boer war by the British, the English war by the Afrikaners and the Anglo-Boer war by middle-of-the-roaders. The significance of this war for modern South Africa is, like that of the Great Trek, so immense, as to require consideration in a separate section.

The defeat of the Afrikaner in the Boer war laid the foundation for many trends and policies which characterise the life of modern South Africa.

The Great Trek

The traveller approaching Pretoria from Johannesburg cannot miss the magnificent *Voortrekker* monument which, from its commanding hilltop, proclaims the power and dominance of the Afrikaner. The monument, at once a shrine, a museum and a political showpiece, is a constant reminder to Afrikanerdom of the difficulties experienced by the trekker and of the togetherness in adversity which has been the Afrikaner's constant strength. Its architect built it 'to last a thousand years'. Its perimeter, depicting the *laager's* circle of ox wagons, encloses a central monument containing a gigantic marble frieze of the great trek. The shrine is holy and the site of regular religious services. On the hillsides the faithful camp out on the holy days of the Afrikaner. The memories of the trek are so interwoven into the current ethos of Afrikanerdom that the monument has become its holiest shrine.

In the decade between 1836 and 1846 nearly 10,000 men, women and children commenced the trek away from British authority and towards Afrikaner freedom. They carried with them their brand of Christianity and of individualism. They shared a stubborn determination that, whatever the cost, they would find themselves the promised land which they would rule free of external authority and internal dissension. They knew they were leaving behind them the achievements of nearly two centuries of pioneering toil and that they were venturing into the unknown with only their own resources and no metropolitan power to back them. They were severing their links with Europe once and for all and trusting that God would find them a land which they could call their own. They were anti-colonialists courageously seeking escape from the spreading reach of British colonialism and imbued with all the fervour of the righteous revolutionary — an aspect of Afrikaner history unfortunately forgotten both by the Afrinkaner turned ruler and by the world turned Afrikaner-critic.

Their women and children, their household belongings and farm implements, their independence, their Christianity and their memories, all packed tightly in 12-foot long ox-wagons, moved northwards into the territory of Zulu and wild animal in one of the great sagas of modern times. At night the wagons formed a circle within which the women and children found protection, sheltered by the guns of the nightwatchmen and the prayers of the community. The circle or *laager* thus formed (and on which the entire *Voortrekker* monument is designed) gives to Afrikaners the bond of fellow feeling and inward orientation which some modern writers describe as South Africa's *laager* mentality. The powder horn of the early *Voortrekkers* gives the ruling Nationalist Party its dominant emblem. To this day the Great Trek provides the focal point of Afrikaner nationalism and of Afrikaner social, political and religious life.

The *Voortrekkers* came in contact with the martial, disciplined and numerous Zulu, very unlike the Bushmen and the Hottentots they had encountered at the Cape. Dingaan, the Zulu King, unhappy at the territorial designs of the *Voortrekkers* upon his land, slew seventy of them and ordered the killings of more. The Battle of Blood River, December 16, 1838, resulted in the defeat of the Zulu and the annexation of their country, the modern Natal.

This victory is often claimed by the Afrikaner to have been the result of a pact made directly with God. Its anniversary, December 16, is the Day of the Covenant, the holiest day in the Afrikaner calendar, and perpetual reminder of God's graces to the Afrikaner. It is also looked on as a symbol of white supremacy over the blacks and this latter aspect tends for many to be the predominant one. It is significant that on December 16, 1979, Prime Minister Botha sought to shift the emphasis back to the religious aspect. He emphasised that the day was not a symbol of Afrikaner superiority or a triumph of white over black, but of the willingness of the Afrikaner to kneel before God. On the same day, Dr. Treurnicht, regarded as an Afrikaner hardliner, emphasised that the day should be treated as a religious festival rather than the celebration of a victory. The need for both these leaders to direct attention away from the supremacy angle shows how deep-seated that aspect is in the Afrikaner consciousness.

British officialdom, watching from Cape Town, cast eyes on this new rich territory of Natal and annexed it in 1843. The trekkers proclaimed their freedom in the areas now occupied by the Free State and the Transvaal. What attitude imperial Britain should take to these sparks of independence was for some time undecided until by the Sand River Convention of 1852 and the Bloemfontain Convention of 1854, Britain withdrew her claims to sovereignty. The Orange Free State and the South African Republic (The Transvaal) thus became independent of British control.

As with the Athenian states which practised the completest democracy within the context of slavery, so the Boer republics were complete democracies so far as concerned the settlers. There was no question of equal rights as between settlers and blacks. The blacks were deprived of territorial rights in vast areas although some reserves were left in their possession. Christian principles of government, as understood by the settlers, were enthroned and the mission of leadership over the heathen seriously assumed.

The Great Trek helps explain the configuration of power in South Africa today. The Cape and the Transvaal, the two political power bases of modern South Africa, are entirely different in character. The English military dominance of the Cape area, followed by the withdrawal to the north of a substantial proportion of the Dutch population, left the Dutch at the Cape weakened and isolated from their independent kinsmen. They continued to live uninterruptedly under British rule, governed by British institutions, surrounded by British concepts and British commerce. The Transvaal, principal home of Afrikaner independence, throbbed to a different heart-beat — the slower, patriarchal, simpler, Old Testament lifestyle under which the Chosen People fulfilled their God-given mission in accordance with their reading of the Holy Book. If one were to ask, to this day, where, geographically, lies the heart of Afrikanerdom, the answer must therefore be the Transvaal, although the Cape settlement was nearly two centuries older. All successive Prime Ministers of South Africa hail from this power base with the sole exception of the present Prime Minister, Dr. Botha.

The later discovery of gold in the Transvaal added greatly to this importance, an importance that needs to be traced through the aberrations of the influence of Cecil Rhodes and of the Boer war.

Cecil Rhodes

A visitor to Cape Town cannot avoid hearing the name and seeing the relics of Cecil Rhodes' connection with the area. The Rhodes Monument, which a visitor is invariably taken to see, is an extravaganza of egoism and vanity, created in terms of Rhodes' last will and sited so as to command an imperial view of the countryside for miles around. A plaque informs the visitor that the soul of Rhodes is the soul of Africa. A greater-than-life equestrian statue of Rhodes flanked by lions induces a greater-than-life impression of the work and importance of its egotistical donor. An imperious gesture of the God-like figure urges the young man on into the hinterland. The memorial is symptomatic of the cult of empire which in Rhodes' age was taking its hold over the British people and imposing its vice-like grip over a large sector of the globe.

Cecil Rhodes, self-made millionaire and apostle of British expansionism, was anxious to extend British influence northwards from the Cape. For this purpose he organised an incursion into African territory west of the Transvaal and after inducing numerous conflicts with the Matabele and other tribes, extended British influence through Bechuanaland into the territory which later came to be known as the Rhodesias. Indeed he planned the annexation of Rhodesia in secret so as to be able to offer it on a platter as a birthday present to Queen Victoria.

Such extensions of British influence in territory adjacent to the Transvaal caused concern in Pretoria. The settlers who had fled from British imperialism found themselves almost surrounded by it, and feared for the future.

That their fears were not without foundation was proved very shortly when Rhodes organised the Jameson raid. The plan, which Colonial Secretary Chamberlain is thought to have known, aimed at fomenting an uprising in Johannesburg and a simultaneous incursion by Jameson on the pretext of 'restoring order'. The entire concept was both immoral and illegal and when the raid failed and the raiders were captured, Rhodes was constrained to resign his position as Prime Minister of the Cape Colony and a Parliamentary Committee of Inquiry sat at Westminster to inquire how such patently illegal conduct could have been pursued at such a high level. Interestingly, some important cases on illegality in the law of contract decided by the English courts arise from the illegal hiring of mercenaries for the Jameson raid.

The raid had the natural effect of turning all Dutch settlers, including those at the Cape, against Britain and her imperial plans. Relations were embittered and the foundations laid for the Boer war.

The role of Cecil Rhodes in South Africa is not an

honoured one, but it is important as giving a direction to South African affairs which heightened tensions, fostered racial inequality and left a legacy of bitterness which persists to this day.

The Boer War

It is not possible to spend many days in South Africa without hearing a great deal about the bitterness left by the Boer war. Eight decades have passed but the bitterness that remains is strong enough to stamp into Afrikaner consciousness a determination to cling to power, which is one of the principal obstacles to a resolution of the South African problem.

The full story of the Boer war has yet to be written. The foreigner in South Africa soon realises that the world in general has heard only the British version, as presented in the history books meant for consumption in the former British Empire. That there is another version emerges not merely from inquiries in South Africa but also from recent disinterested research. A major recent work, Thomas Pakenham's *The Boer War*,[2] sets out a version very close to what one hears from the Afrikaners in South Africa.[3]

The 'promised land' found by the wandering Boers was found to be a treasure chest. In the Orange Free State a rich diamond pipe was found and in the Witwatersrand an immense reef of gold. British empire builders saw in these another stimulus to the growth of Empire. According to Pakenham, a surviving Tommy told him, "It was all for the gold mines" — a view to some extent supported by Kitchener's conduct when Parliament voted him a 50,000 pound victory purse. He cabled his brokers to invest it in South African gold mining stocks.[4]

Pakenham's research reveals the Boer war as one engineered in the interests of the grandiose concept of Empire prevalent in Britain at the turn of the century. Alfred Milner, British governor of the Cape and Natal, wanted in his own words to "knock the bottom out of 'the great Afrikander nation' for ever and ever, Amen". He is recorded as having said to Lord Roberts that he precipitated the crisis, which was inevitable, before it was too late.

The grand dream was of a white English republic of South Africa which along with the white English governments of Canada, Australia, New Zealand and Britain would form an imperial Parliament in London. "The ultimate end is a self-governing White Community supported by well treated and justly governed black labour from Cape Town to the Zambesi". In the words of Neal Ascherson, commenting on this book in the New York Review of Books[5] and describing Milner as a British leader who deserved comparison with Adolf Hitler, "Both looked forward to world domination by their own tribe of the white race; both engineered and provoked war to bring that vision nearer".

This view accords also with the views of Empire then prevalent in England.[6] Joseph Chamberlain voiced these sentiments in a speech at the Imperial Institute, in 1895, when he proclaimed his belief that "the British race is the greatest of governing races the world has ever seen".[7] This was the age of Rhodes and Kipling and Curzon, an age whose spirit of self-righteous expansionism we find it difficult now to recapture.

It is little wonder that the fiercely independent Afrikaner sensed this feeling and resented the possibilities. He loved his culture and valued his independence. Unlike most other victims of the colonialism he had the firepower, the resources and the knowledge of European military tactics with which to withstand the threatened assault on his liberty. He was able to stretch British resources to their limits and defeat the British forces on three main fronts. The privations he suffered steeled his resolve to continue his fight for the emancipation of his people. These sufferings included the razing of houses and farmsteads to the ground, the death of 26,000 of women and children in the concentration camps set up by the British, and the exile to distant countries such as Ceylon of the flower of Boer manhood. The scar on the Afrikaner memory left by the war is a very real reason for his stubborn and resolute clinging to power when it was once obtained and for his reluctance to share or imperil it in any way.

When eventually the British forced a capitulation by the Boers it was on a promise to recognise the equality of the Dutch language and to grant responsible government when the ravages of war were repaired. The Treaty of Vereeniging, 31 May 1902, brought the war to a close. The way in which responsible government was eventually granted without any consultation whatsoever with the blacks who formed the majority of the population is a dark chapter in the history of apartheid which yet needs to be explored.

One other dark chapter needs to be noted. The Boer war was not one involving suffering and sacrifices for the white people alone. The blacks participated — some 80,000 of them — as non-combatants. Their sufferings were worse than those of their employers. Their pay was less. The gratitude they had from it all was nil. When the war was over Englishman and Boer united to put the African black in his place. "The blacks who had cheered and burned their passes when Roberts entered Johannesburg were sent back to their locations and had their wages cut".[8]

The Boer war, tragic while it was being waged, was thus more tragic still in its ending. The peace signed between Englishman and Afrikaner laid the scene for the trampling underfoot of black liberty for all succeeding time until this day. The peace treaty contained a clause reserving a decision on the vote for blacks until after self-government was achieved, thus sweeping away even the rights which the blacks already enjoyed, under the liberal laws of the Cape Colony. The eventual result is nothing to be surprised at. It was of a piece with British policy from the very commencement. We find the key to it in a minute of Sir Alfred Milner written in 1897: "I personally could win over the Dutch in the (Cape) Colony and indeed in all of the South African Dominions in my term of office...without offending the British. You only have to sacrifice the 'nigger' absolutely, and the game is easy".[9]

The game of sacrificing the 'nigger' proved all too easy, as we shall see[10] largely owing to the gentleness in negotiation and the trust in good faith displayed by African leaders in the years between the Boer war and World War 11.

From Boer War to Afrikaner Supremacy

The governing party in South Africa is the National Party. This is the party formed in 1914 as the protector of Afrikaner nationalism and the restorer of Afrikaner morale after the sufferings of the Boer war. It came to power in 1948 and has since been in full control of South Africa.

It was not without a long struggle that the Afrikaner came to power in South Africa. The story of his advent to power will help explain some of the bitterness which lies behind his authoritarian and racial attitudes. Even at the risk of covering ground familiar to some readers, a brief background sketch is attempted.

By the Treaty of Vereeniging, 1902, the Boers, after their defeat in the Boer war accepted British sovereignty over the Orange Free State and Transvaal. Although the Boers gave so good an account of themselves as to stretch to its limits the might of the till then invincible British Empire, the war damaged Afrikaner interests and morale so significantly as to place in peril the survival of the Afrikaner ethos. The Afrikaner emerged from the war impoverished, his spirit nearly broken.

The terms of the treaty, however, provided hope, for the equality of the Dutch language with English was recognised, Britain promised to grant responsible government when the ravages of war were overcome and Britain offered its help in the reconstruction of the country. In 1909 the South Africa Act was passed in Westminster and on May 31, 1910 the Union of South Africa was established.

In apportioning the blame for apartheid, Britain's share in the initial guilt is often overlooked. Blacks were not consulted on the form of the Union Constitution and indeed their protests were disregarded by the British Parliament. Power was handed over exclusively to the whites with a nominal exception in the Cape Province where black voting rights were confirmed with the reservation that they could be changed by a two-thirds majority in the South African Parliament — a result which, not unpredictably, ensued in 1936 when Africans were removed from the common voters' roll by the Representation of Natives Act, passed with the requisite two-thirds majority. Britain, in a position of trusteeship for all the races under her dominion, passed on power to a white minority in the midst of a large, already exploited, black majority and must have known full well what consequences would ensue from this unilateral handing over of power. While one condemns the Afrikaner for the injustices of apartheid one cannot lose sight of the fact that the foundation for this structure of iniquity was laid with the full participation and approval of the government of Great Britain.

Three times at least Britain betrayed the trust reposed in her by black African leadership, and rejected outright appeals made to her for the use of her influence on the side of justice and fair play.

The first occasion was when, before the South Africa Act, a delegation of five African leaders interviewed the colonial Secretary on the question of the denial of political rights to blacks, and received short shrift. Cape lawyer, W.P. Schreiner, accompanied them and helped in procuring the interview, but all to no effect.

The second appeal to Britain occurred when in 1913 the Land Act was passed, limiting African landownership to

73 per cent of the land and imposing on blacks who remained on white property a feudal requirement of working ninety days a year for the landowner. The alternative was to return to the Reserves or to seek employment in the mines or in the towns. A deputation of five left again for Britain to interview the Colonial Secretary, only to be told that this was an internal South African affair and no concern of His Majesty's government in Great Britain.

The third opportunity for Britain to use her good offices to forestall apartheid offered itself in 1919. The 1917 Native Administration Bill proposed a separate set of institutions for African legal, administrative and legislative business, and also foreshadowed the abolition of the Cape franchise. The Bill did not pass into law but contained warnings enough of the shape of things to come. The Africans saw this, demanded an extension of parliamentary representation, and sent a third deputation to London in 1919. Lloyd George promised no more — and that not too clearly — than that he would forward their views to General Smuts — a postal service which the African delegates need not have come all the way to London to obtain.[11]

To see all these events in proper perspective one must view them against the trustful attitude of John Dube, first president of the African National Congress. He expressed a "hopeful reliance on the sense of common justice and the love of freedom, so innate in the British character".[12]

General Botha, an outstanding hero of the Boer war, was the first Prime Minister. His policy was one of conciliation between English and Afrikaners — an attitude resented by many Afrikaners in the Free State and the Transvaal. Afrikaner opponents of conciliation gathered around another of the Boer war generals, who began to form the Nationalist Party. The feeling grew that the interests of South Africa should take priority over those of the British Empire. In Hertzog's words, delivered in a speech on December 28, 1912, he would rather live with his own people on a dunghill than stay in the palaces of the British Empire.

The outbreak of the World War in 1914 and Botha's proclaimed intention of supporting the Empire brought to a head this clash of priorities. In January 1914, Hertzog called a special congress of his followers and the National Party was formed. In the general elections of 1915, Botha failed to obtain an absolute majority, the distribution of seats being 54 for Botha's South African Party, 27 for Hertzog's Nationalists and 40 for the intermediate Unionist

Party on which Botha had to depend. The National Party thus formed the effective opposition.

Through the war years Afrikaners continued to divide into two streams rendering them culturally confused if not demoralised by the end of the war. The Broederbond grew up and made its appearance in these circumstances and developed Afrikaner consciousness in a manner dealt with elsewhere.[13]

Hertzog became Prime Minister in 1924, first in coalition with the Labour Party, and then for three years with an absolute majority. From 1933 he held power in coalition and later in fusion with Smuts' South Africa Party. The Hertzog-Smuts coalition was responsible for many significant advances on the road to racial segregation. This period was also marked by the Status of the Union Act 1934 by which South Africa passed from a dominion under the British Crown to the status of a "sovereign independent state" within the British Empire.

The outbreak of the second World War in 1939 brought about a split between Hertzog and Smuts on the question of South Africa's entry into the war against Germany. Smuts became Prime Minister, led South Africa to victory through the war years and forced a General Election in 1948 when the Nationalist-Afrikaner bloc opposed to Smuts based their electoral campaign on apartheid. They succeeded in winning a majority of seats in the lower House of Parliament although Smuts won a larger popular vote. Dr. Malan became Prime Minister and held office until November 1954.

The Consolidation of Afrikaner Supremacy

The year 1948 marks the inauguration of the official policy of apartheid. For the first time since Union a purely Afrikaans speaking party was now in power, and the Afrikaner, after long generations of oppression and suffering, was at last in control of the promised land. The Nationalist and Afrikaner parties were strengthened in 1951 by their merger under the name of the Nationalist party. The resulting entrenchment of Afrikaner power manifested itself in a series of legislative measures aimed at consolidating their rule. No time was lost in implementing the policies of apartheid.

From 1948 the contours of contemporary South Africa took shape with increasing boldness on the part of the landscaper and increasing ruthlessness in eradicating every feature that stood in the way of the grand plan. The grand plan was to consolidate the tenuous hold on power which the vagaries of the representative system had placed in the hands of the government. Danger lay not only in the white opposition parties but also in the white parliamentarians who represented African and coloured voters. It was necessary therefore to deprive the non-white groups of any form of representation.

On September 30, 1948 the first step was taken, of abolishing the Indian franchise which had been granted in 1848. Indeed the government went further and announced that its intention was to repatriate all Indians. In 1950 three significant Acts were passed — the Population Registration Act (June 9) requiring a register to be compiled in accordance with racial groups, the Group Areas Act (June 23) providing for the zoning of the country into separate areas for the occupation of the different racial groups and the Suppression of Communism Act (June 23). The next year saw the removal of Cape Coloured from the common electoral roll by the Separate Representation of Voters Act.

A constitutional crisis resulted, for the Act was passed by simple majorities in both Houses of Parliament whereas the South Africa Act 1909 required a two-thirds majority of both Houses sitting together. In 1952 the Appellate Division of the Supreme Court declared the Act unconstitutional whereupon the unprecedented step was taken of enabling Parliament, by the High Court of Parliament Act, to establish a High Court of Parliament with a right to review judicial decisions. This was a total departure from established principles of the Rule of Law, as it arrogated to the legislative branch of government, power to review decisions of the judicial branch. Parliament proceeded to use this unprecedented power and sitting as a High Court overruled the Supreme Court decision which had invalidated the Act. The drama continued with a decision by the Cape Provincial Division the very next day (August 29, 1952) invalidating the High Court of Parliament Act. An appeal by the Government to the Appellate Division was unsuccessful and this aberration on the Statute Book ceased to exist.

In the General Elections of 1953, Dr. Malan's Nationalist Party won a majority of seats although the vote for the opposition was again greater. In 1954, Advocate Strijdom succeeded Dr. Malan. In 1956, the South Africa Act Amendment Act gave the force of law to the Separate Representation of Voters Act 1951 and strictly limited the circumstances in which courts could pronounce upon the validity of laws passed by Parliament. Parliament had prepared the way for the constitutional struggle with the judiciary by increasing the number of judges on the Appellate Division from six to eleven when sitting on constitutional cases. The expected challenge of the Act came before the Appellate Division in 1956 and the Appellate Division upheld the South Africa Act Amendment Act. The process of erosion of judicial authority first seriously commenced in 1951 was thus carried significantly forward. The stage was set for even bolder erosions of judicial authority, and it became increasingly difficult for the judiciary, having once yielded, to set up a front of resistance to further encroachments on the Rule of Law.

Within a month of the Appellate Division's decision, 137 South Africans of all races were arrested at dawn on December 5, 1956 on charges of treason, with more arrests following in the course of the week.

The entrenchment of the Nationalist Party in power was reflected at the next General Election, in 1958, when it won 103 out of 163 seats in the House of Assembly. The resulting monolithic power structure rendered opposition a purely nominal exercise. A few months later on the death of Prime Minister Strijdom, Dr. Verwoerd assumed power. In 1959 a new political party, the Progressive Party, was formed with a nucleus of fifteen defecting United Party members. The same year saw the total elimination of any form of African representation in Parliament. Till then Africans throughout South Africa were able to elect four white representatives to the Senate. This minimal representation was abolished with the Promotion of Bantu Self-Government Act which established territorial, regional and tribal authorities in the African "homelands" and, by giving the blacks a share in the government of "black South Africa", furnished a spurious justification for depriving Africans of even the minimal and indirect participation they enjoyed in the government of "white South Africa".

The year 1960 was eventful. In February British Prime Minister, Harold Macmillan, addressing a joint session of the South African Parliament said the "winds of change" were blowing over South Africa; in March a crowd of unarmed Africans demonstrating at Sharpeville against the restrictive pass laws were fired on by the police, resulting in sixty nine deaths and sending a shock wave through South Africa and the world; in April the Unlawful Organisations Act was passed and the African National Congress and the Pan African Congress were banned for a year; in October a referendum on the question whether South Africa should become a republic received an affirmative answer, thus realising one of the great dreams of Afrikanerdom. South Africa left the Commonwealth, severing its last remaining links with Great Britain. In this referendum only the white population was consulted.

The ensuing years were troubled and marked by violence. Unlawful organisations went underground and reappeared under new names such as Pogo and the African Resistance Movement; serious riots took place in 1962 at Paarl. In 1963 an underground movement, Spear of the Nation, was found to have extensive plans for sabotage, guerilla warfare and revolution; in the same year Nelson Mandela and other national black leaders were sentenced to life imprisonment following the "Rivonia Trial" where Mandela's indictment of the principles and practice of apartheid gained worldwide publicity; in 1964 a bomb was left to explode in a Johannesburg railway station; in 1966 Mr. Abram Fischer, Q.C. of Johannesburg who had defended many accused found guilty of political crimes was found guilty of furthering the aims of communism and imprisoned for life; and by the end of that year thousands of persons were arrested on charges of sabotage and membership of unlawful organisations. The apparatus of repression was being perfected, tension was intensifying and South Africa becoming steadily more totalitarian. The blacks were becoming a beleaguered people in their own country.

The Terrorism Act and After

Against this background there appeared in 1967 the Terrorism Act No.839 of 1967, made retrospective to 1962, which created the new offence of 'terrorism — defined as any activity likely to endanger the maintenance of law and order. Activities which produced any of twelve enumerated results fell within the description of terrorism. These included obstruction to the free movement of any traffic on land, at sea or in the air, embarrassment to the administration of the affairs of the State, the achievement of any political aim including the bringing about of any social or economic change by violent or forcible means and causing financial loss to any person or the State.

The Act reversed the traditional burden of proof regarding intent. Accused were presumed to have acted with the specified intent unless they could demonstrate beyond reasonable doubt that they did not intend their action to have any of the stipulated results. Not only was the traditional burden of proof thus shifted from prosecution to accused. The accused had to discharge that burden by the very high standard of "proof beyond reasonable doubt", the high standard the law traditionally laid upon the prosecution in a criminal case. It is notorious that in many cases of crime the criminal goes free under ordinary criminal law because the prosecution, with all the resources of the State at its disposal, cannot prove guilt by this very high standard of proof beyond reasonable doubt. The accused, often ignorant and resourceless, are placed by the Act under this burden and should they fail in a true defence, as the prosecution often fails in a true accusation, they take the penalty. This single statutory provision is more eloquent than any book that can be written about repression in South Africa.

The penalties which an accused person incurs under the Act range from a mandatory minimum of five years' imprisonment to the death penalty. Nor is this all. The Act authorises any police officer of or above the rank of lieutenant colonel to arrest without warrant or charge anyone suspected of being a "terrorist" or of possessing information relating to terrorists or terrorist offences. The Commissioner of Police has power to hold such persons incommunicado until they reply "satisfactorily" to all questions put to them by their interrogators. There is no appeal to any court from the decision to take a person into such custody or in regard to the conditions under which he is held.

The Internal Security Act No.79 of 1976 superseded the Suppression of Communism Act of 1950. The Minister of Justice was empowered to serve banning orders on any person who in his opinion "engages in activities which endanger or are calculated to endanger the security of the State or the maintenance of public order". The Suppression of Communism Act was narrower in its terms in that it was directed at those who were "furthering the aims of communism", whereas there were many categories of persons such as members of the black consciousness and other anti-apartheid movements whom it was now desired to take into the net. The scope of banning orders is dealt with elsewhere.[14]

Four other episodes call for mention in a review of this period — the Soweto riots, the Biko episode, the banning order on Rev. Beyers Naude, and the Muldergate Scandal.

The Soweto riots are too well known internationally to need detailed description. On 16 June 1976 police killings on an unprecedented scale startled South Africa and the world. Lists of the dead were not issued by the police but independent inquiries such as by the *Rand Daily Mail* and the American magazine *Newsday* revealed several hundred deaths. Local opinion in Soweto puts the death toll at thousands rather than hundreds. Evidence recorded by Amnesty International describes police vehicles packed full of injured people and corpses of the dead. The dead bodies were stacked in one corner of Orlando police station while seriously injured people "were made to lie flat on their stomachs and the police walked on them with their heavy boots until they were dead".[15]

In January 1977 an Indemnity Bill was introduced by the Minister of Justice under the terms of which the State and its servants were indemnified against civil or criminal prosecution of any kind for acts committed, "in good faith with the intent of suppressing or terminating internal disorder". The indemnity was given retroactive effect taking it back to 16 June 1976, the date of the riots.

The Cillie Commission, appointed by the government to investigate the Soweto riots, has, quite extraordinarily, failed to produce a report up to the time of writing.

The Biko episode, dealt with elsewhere,[16] resulted from the arrest on 6 September 1977 of Steve Biko, described by Donald Woods who wrote a book on Biko[17] as the greatest man, quite literally, that he ever had the privilege to know. Biko, a man of quite unique charisma and leadership, of intellect and integrity and courage, "was taken by the Security Police to Room 619 of the Sanlam Building in Strand Street, Port Elizabeth, handcuffed, put into leg-irons, chained to a grille and subjected to twenty two hours of interrogation, torture and beating. He received between two and four blows to the head, fatally damaging his brain. He died six days later. No charges were pressed against his captors".[18] The South African government in belated recognition of the culpability of its officials has settled suits brought against it by the dependents of Biko, by payment of a sum of 65,000 rand.

The Biko incident had grave political repercussions. Minister of Police Kruger, was indiscreet enough to anger world opinion by the remark that Biko's death "left him cold". Within a month heavy censorship had to be clamped down. Eighteen organisations, both white and black were banned, several individuals detained, three publications suppressed.

South Africa was taken to task internationally both in the United Nations and by individual action from countries that mattered greatly to South Africa. In the United Nations a mandatory arms embargo on South Africa was passed.

Prime Minister Vorster felt the pressures very shortly after Biko's death and announced a general election. The
criticism South Africa had received internationally probably
produced an impact on the voting in that it gave an election
point to the Nationalists — that the world was attempting to
dictate to South Africa. The party increased its support in
a house of 165 from 117 to 134.

Beyers Naude typifies another aspect of the South
African scene. Rev. Naude, Director of the Christian Institute of Southern Africa, son of a founder of the Broederbond
who was also a minister of the Dutch Reformed Church,
Moderator of the Southern Transvaal Synod of the Church,
was brought to trial for having refused to give evidence to a
Commission set up "to inquire into certain organizations".
He was prepared, he said to face any allegations about the
role of the Christian Institute in open court where all the
facilities of justice were available. The issues raised were of
the very greatest importance for Christians in all countries.[19]
Dr. Naude's case again attracted world publicity and Dr.
Naude — of whom Archbishop Ramsey of Canterbury says
(in his preface to the book regarding the trial): "When I
think of the men who have shown me what it means to be a
Christian, my thoughts will always go quickly to Beyers
Naude" — remains a banned person in the country of his
birth.

The Muldergate scandal brought to world attention
the manner in which the agencies of the South African government secretly spent state funds both at home and abroad
in activities illegitimate by all accepted moral standards, for
the entrenchment of the regime. The purchase of newspapers abroad, whitewashing and cover up operations of all
sorts, bribes, misappropriations and undercover activities
which had seemed unthinkable in a Christianity-professing
administration, showed South Africans and the world that
the mantle of self-righteousness which South African governments had customarily worn bore certain resemblances
to the Emperor's new clothes.

The reverberations of Muldergate will long be felt in
the power politics of South Africa. It has set in motion a
process of self-scrutiny which can do nothing but lasting
good.

With these broad sketches of background events the
stage is set for the observations and discussions that ensue.
The picture we have painted is necessarily incomplete but no
more can be attempted in a work of this size.

FOOTNOTES

1.   Lord Tweedsmuir, *The African Colony: Studies in Recon-struction,* Edinburgh, Blackwood, 1903.
2.   Random House, 1979.
3.   The other major works on the Boer War which have appeared in the last twenty years are, Rayne Kruger's *Good Bye Dolly Gray* (1959) and Byron Farwell's *The Great Anglo-Boer War* (1976).   The former is strong on military action, the latter on the emotional and mental wreckage resulting from the war.
4.   See the review of Pakenham's *Boer War* in *Time,* Nov.26, 1979.
5.   Dec.6, 1979, p.12.
6.   On these justifications see the present author's *Equality and Freedom,* Hansa Publishers, Colombo 1976, pp.39-40.
7.   Bennetts, ed. *The Concept of Empire,* A & C. Black, London, 315.
8.   Neil Ascherson, op.cit.p.13.
9.   Sash, the Black Sash magazine, Feb. 1979, p.16.
10.   See pp.151-2. Page no's to be changed.
11.   For these facts see Tom Lodge,"Black Opposition: A Historical Perspective" *Sash*, Feb. 1979, pp.16-17.
12.   *Ibid.*
13.   See pp.80-82.
14.   See pp.179-81.
15.   Amnesty International Report on Political Imprisonment in South Africa, 1978, p.99.
16.   See p.71.
17.   Donald Woods, *Biko,* Random House, 1978, p.60.
18.   From the dust jacket of Donald Woods, *Biko.*
19.   See the International Commission of Jurists *Report on the Trial of Beyers Naude,* Search Press, London, 1975.

CHAPTER 4

White South Africa

The Gilded Cocoon

If you are white and South African and not particularly tender of conscience you could not have it better in
this or any other age. Every institution — social, political,
industrial, religious — is tailor-made for your maximum comfort. You will enjoy industrial privilege without industrial
responsibility, a disproportionate share of the wealth of a
disproportionately wealthy country, feudal service combined
with late twentieth century technology, the reservation for
you of the country's choicest land, privileged medical services. There will be opulence for your minority in the midst
of squalor for the majority, leisure for your minority in the
midst of toil for the majority, power for your minority in
the midst of serfdom for the majority. The slave wealth
of colonial America, the mineral wealth of Ophir and
Tarshish, the territorial wealth of the last days of Empire
— all come together to give you a lifestyle you will not willingly
surrender.

You live in pleasant surroundings, with affluent
whites all around you, you travel in separate transport,
study in separate universities, dine in separate restaurants,
play in separate fields, relax in separate clubs, worship in
separate churches. You pass your life in a gilded cocoon.
May be, as you drift from one gilded cocoon to another,
you catch a fleeting glimpse of the darkness and desolation
between — but the vision is too fleeting to be meaningful.

The difficulties encountered by the vast majority,
the squalor of the shanty towns, the homelessness, the
forced separation of husband and wife, the unemployment,

that inaccessibility of the legal system — all these are unpleasant and distant aspects of a different world. One is aware of them in the same way that one is aware of the squalor and poverty that may prevail in India or Peru.

These are however only the less obnoxious features of the system. The midnight knock and sudden police entry, the demand for one's pass along the public road, the surliness and superciliousness of the petty official, the brooding omnipresence of discrimination owing to the colour of one's skin, the consciousness that one cannot move about freely in one's own country — all these are constant and grim realities in the life of the average black, which, being less seen, penetrate even less into the white consciousness. They cut more bitingly than poverty or petty apartheid.

Unless one is specially concerned, these unpleasant features on the periphery of one's world do not unduly trouble one. In fact the policy of segregation which keeps these citizens of the same country in worlds which are physically apart encourages a lotus-eating sense of general satisfaction with one's lot. Even in universities one does not have to study the racial problem or to see its sordid realities unless one happens to be a law student, and needs to study their enshrinements upon the statute book. Indeed even this is not necessarily the case, for many courses on constitutional or criminal law skirt around such enormities of the statute book as the Terrorism Act. It is only the concerned teacher of these subjects who introduces these to his students and causes in them a feeling of shocked concern. For years many courses in these subject have successfully avoided these issues till in recent years the pioneering work of professors such as Barend van Niekerk, Tony Mathews and John Dugard have forced these to the surface.

The white man's world in South Africa is not very different from the view of South Africa presented in the glossy tourist and guide books the visitor picks up on arrival.

"Introducing Cape Town" for example is a glossy guide book with seascapes, historic buildings, scenic views of Table Mountain, the skyline of the modern city, the Houses of Parliament — all as grand as one could find them anywhere in the world. There is not a word about the squatters' towns, the shacks, the sordid dormitories. That is not Cape Town as the white sees it. A picture of a sunlit beach will announce: "Paddling, swimming, sun-bathing or surfing — one can do all of these at Fish Hoek's beach". It is necessary to read in the qualification "if one is white". That does not appear on the guidebook. One takes it for granted. There is so much the white takes for granted in South Africa that he ceases even to be conscious of his own thought processes.

It requires a special effort of the will for a white South African to look beyond his gilded cocoon into the sad realities of his country.

The Blunting of the White South African Conscience

The constant enjoyment of discriminatory privilege causes most white South Africans to accept such discrimination without any marked feelings of moral revulsion. One learns from even concerned white South Africans that they require time, after a trip abroad, to readjust to the South African situation. Every trip abroad, however brief, calls for a renewed period of readjustment. However, to judge from their reactions, most whites do settle down to the comfort of the old complacencies and the pricks of conscience soon die away. So also, in regard to the severe measures on the statute book, which were introduced initially as emergency measures, time has blunted the public sensitivity to their unjustifiable harshness. This was emphasised recently by Dr. David de Villiers in his L.C. Steyn Commemoration Lecture, in which he drew attention to the fact that many of the repressive measures on the statute books were initially introduced by the government under plea of urgent necessity and emergency. Fifteen years have passed, he said, since such emergency was pleaded as justification and both the government and the public have now grown accustomed to the existence on the statute books of these measures, indefensible except in the context of emergency.

At a conference of the study group on internal relations in June 1979, Professor J.D. Van der Vyver warned that arbitrary powers exercised according to the dictates and whims of authorities amounted to "lawlessness on the part of the government which, in my opinion, is the worst form of anarchy". In consequence, he said, the South African government had come dangerously close to losing its sense of justice and "a genuine feeling of what is right". The result can be a dangerous one, for when a government loses its sense of right and wrong the example spreads through to all sections of the community. "One must admit", said Professor Van der Vyver, "that South Africa has come dangerously close to the situation where government actions have lost track of the sense of justice generally entertained by a substantial portion of the South African population and where the need to honour the judicial and political institutions of the country seems no longer to be inspired by a genuine feeling of what is right".

The extent to which this can be manifested was brought out in the Steve Biko affair where the officials of government were able to act in a manner clearly indicating that torture and suffering had ceased to have upon them the effect which, in normal circumstances, they would produce. This applies not merely to the actual prison officials who inflicted this torture, but also to those higher in the scale, reaching all the way up to the ministerial officials involved. Their conscience did not seem in any way to be troubled by the fact that Biko, a rare flowering of intellect, courage and selflessness, had been tortured and killed for precisely these qualities. Indeed the suggestion has been made that the doctors who, despite obvious brain injuries, certified that Biko was fit to be put back into his cell, did not conform to the normal standards of integrity expected of medical practitioners. A complaint to this effect lodged with the South African Medical Association evoked only a belated response, thus bringing even this august body within the sphere of possible censure, as evidenced by numerous newspaper comments to this effect.[1]

Mr. Justice Brandeis of the American Supreme Court once observed in terms quoted by Professor Van der Vyver: "If the government becomes a law breaker, it breeds contempt for law; it invites every man to become a law unto himself: it invites anarchy".

City Life

The city white lives in the midst of petty apartheid. However conscientious he may be, he is placed by this fact in a situation of compromise with his conscience. He must live in the city. He must therefore live in a racially zoned area and use apartheid conveniences such as separate schools, transport, restaurants and toilet facilities. Each time he uses them he is subscribing to the system, but he has no alternative. He may desire to opt out of the system, but this is not always feasible. The other option is to stay within the system and fight its denigrations of the human personality. Yet each use of each privilege denigrates human dignity — not only the dignity of those who are victimised by the system, but also of those who derive benefits from it.

Unfortunately, it does not strike the vast majority of

these partakers of privilege that each use of a separate facility is a debasement of themselves. They consequently seek to perpetuate their enjoyment of these privileges, oblivious that by their conduct they are sowing the seeds of their own destruction.

A telling illustration of the effect of white city dwellers' attitudes was the recent re-introduction of segregation (prominently reported in the Cape Press in August 1979) by a restaurant in Cape Town. The explanation of the management as given to the press was that the enforcement of the segregation laws, was the result of complaints by white customers. The restaurant had earlier turned a blind eye to the segregation laws, but was now compelled to enforce them when white customers complained, and it was brought to the firm's notice that it was liable to prosecution.

Consequently the firm displayed a notice, "We have been granted a permit to serve both White and Coloured Customers in this restaurant. However, in order to comply with Government regulations, we have provided separate seating facilities for the customers of the two communities. We are grateful for your co-operation in using the section of the restaurant reserved for you". Note the wording "reserved for you" as though the obnoxious segregation system were in fact a privilege.

The case cited was not the only instance. Several restaurants which had chosen to ignore the legislation were compelled by the complaints of white customers to re-impose eating apartheid.

The Cape Times in an editorial on August 22, 1979 observed that it was high time the government stopped pandering to blatant race prejudice in the restaurants. "All over Cape Town restaurateurs have tried to 'normalize' eating — in the same way that sport is being 'normalized'. But their applications to provide non-segregated eating have all been refused". The editorial suggested that the complaints were only by a minority of whites. This may well be true, but it is not good enough for the majority to remain passive if it were indeed their wish that this abnormal state of affairs should not continue.

It is of interest to note that in the case cited the company's legal representative is stated to have flown from Johannesburg and held discussions with officials under section 21 of the Group Areas Act (36 of 1966) and was told that the officials were prepared to grant a permit to admit coloureds to the restaurant only on the following conditions:

1) The hours of business would be normal shopping hours.

2) A separate entrance and serving area for coloured people should be provided.

3) A dividing screen of at least 25 metres should be erected.

4) The permit would be withdrawn at any time at the discretion of the Minister of Community Development.[2]

It may well be that government policy is moving at Prime Ministerial level towards greater relaxation, but in South Africa there seems always to be a gap between the pronouncements of government policy and their implementation by government officials. The work of the Prime Minister in attempting to create a better climate is drastically negatived by such official action, and the white city dwellers — even the minority of them who are the active complainants — seem to be getting away with it all the time. A government truly committed to reform needs to be more than alive to the need to co-ordinate the policy in the field with the policy in the ministerial pronouncements. Failing this, such little hope and sympathy as the outside world can entertain. for South Africa must fast fade — and the white city dweller will have played an important part in this dire result.

Attitudes of Superciliousness

The traveller in South Africa seeking to probe the reasons for its topsy turvy legal system often hears many justifications in its defence. There is on the part of some few South Africans an articulated belief in racial superiority. Others may believe in this but may not articulate their views. In fact a discussion with some, who are more frank than others, has more than once resulted in the statement, "Of course, I don't believe in this but the vast bulk of whites in this country do believe in their racial superiority and will not tell you so".

Openly expressed attitudes are easy to meet, for they reveal a gross ignorance of world history. Some of these attitudes are the result of direct indoctrination in the classroom. It has not been unusual for white children to be taught in their early years that the brain of the African is inferior in capacity and size to that of the European. Some have been taught that Africans are lower in the scale of evolution and have not completely shaken off the animal qualities of the ape. It takes considerable unlearning to shake such beliefs once they are consciously implanted in young minds and the effort to do so is not always forthcoming.

The unarticulated belief in white superiority is however more difficult to counter. It manifests itself in a superciliousness when talking of the blacks and coloureds, which is difficult for an outsider to stomach and must be intolerable for the local non-whites. When such attitudes precipitate a confrontation with the visitor, the speaker tends to withdraw into his or her shell and skirt around the subject.

In fairness it must be observed that those who manifest these attitudes covertly or overtly are only a small minority of the persons one meets, but sufficient to indicate that there is here a greater problem than meets the eye.

It is a pity indeed that when such false attitudes generally prevail the Dutch Reformed Church, which ought to provide so much Christian leadership, in fact reinforces these beliefs by its active teaching and doctrine. More is said of this elsewhere. What surprises the outsider is that the basic Christian message of love to all men without differentiation of race or colour has become so distorted at the hands of theologians as to permit of a teaching of superiority, dominance and paternalism, which is obdurate enough to carry through even to the point where it can set South Africa and the world on fire.

As if to lend point to this observation, there appeared after this was first written, a news item in the international press on January 18, 1980[3] describing an incident in a Johannesburg church. Almost two hundred mourners — many of whom were blacks and Indians employed under the deceased — attended the church for a funeral service. The minister refused to conduct it because blacks were present. In the words of the widow, the clergyman "dashed into the church, silenced the organ player and announced that he could not deliver the service with non-whites present in his church. Some of these people had been working with my late husband for fourteen years and respected him very much. It came as a terrible shock. We did not know two lorries full of non-whites would take the trouble to come to pay their last respects".

The sequel was even more interesting, as showing how white worshippers are sometimes ahead of the church in their attitudes on these matters. The widow decided that all the mourners would leave the church and there was a walkout from the funeral service.

That the minister was reportedly criticised for his conduct by two other ministers is not in point. A clergyman, the source whence light and understanding should radiate to the community, was with all the authority of God's spokesman, telling a God-revering community that people of a certain colour were not fit to sit with whites in the house of God. If such attitudes still linger to this day, one can well imagine what attitudes held sway in the uninhibited past and what 'righteous' superciliousness they have produced over the generations.

If this superciliousness is to be attacked, it must be done educationally, and the Church needs to join in this process both as teacher and, more humbly, as learner. It is to be hoped that some at least of the younger members of the Church will participate in this process of spreading the spirit of humility which lies at the heart of the Christian message.

Verligte and Verkrampte

One does not stay more than a day in South Africa without hearing the terms *verligte* and *verkrampte*. The former means "enlightened", "progressive" or "liberal", the latter means "reactionary" or "conservative".

One must not however make the mistake of imagining that the *verligte* is enlightened, progressive or liberal in the common connotation of these terms. A *verligte* is one who is liberal by the standards of the Nationalist Party. He may well be a believer in discrimination or in apartheid. The two words thus express a division within the context of the Nationalist framework, and the South African *verligte* may well be described as an arch reactionary or conservative in another country.

The attitudes of the current Prime Minister, which are more fully discussed elsewhere, are commonly referred to as *verligte* in South Africa — so liberal as to cause consternation in *verkrampte* circles. The rest of the world would, however, scarcely agree with this classification, and he would probably stand to the right of some of the world's most rightiest leaders.

It is a pity that when many South Africans speak in terms of *verligte* and *verkrampte* they in fact think they are speaking of liberalism or conservatism in the commonly accepted sense.

The division between *verkrampte* and *verligte* in a sense splits the Nationalist Party but on the main issues there is still sufficient unity to keep the party together, except perhaps for some extreme right wing *verligtes* who may

choose to break away. It is to be remembered that the
verligte has not abandoned his Afrikanerdom. Rather he
attaches more importance to Afrikaner culture than to
Afrikaner race, more importance to building bridges than
building walls. He disagrees with *verkrampte* thinking which
holds that the process of change once begun cannot be
contained and will move inexorably towards a total surrender
of power. He believes that apartheid has at least in some
respects operated with harshness and cruelty and is anxious
to mitigate some of its asperities. Unlike the *verkrampte*,
who will hold on to power regardless of the unrest that must
ensue, he believes that reform is the only means of avoiding
unrest and revolt.

In *verligte* thinking lies any hope there is for South
Africa, and the *verligte* needs to be worked upon by the
outside world, so as to encourage him to enlarge his liberalism. This force for change, already operating within South
Africa, needs to be tapped.

British and Afrikaner [4]

Readers will have gathered from the comments made
thus far that South Africa presents not only a black/white
problem but a white/white problem as well. English and
Afrikaner, though not at daggers drawn, are two groups
which do not mix easily, each suspicious of the other, each
seeing in the other the embodiment of much that is antagonistic to its cultural ethos. English students at Stellenbosch have complained to the writer how difficult it is for
them to penetrate the social reserve that surrounds the
Afrikaner, and Afrikaners have complained at English inability to understand the Afrikaner viewpoint. They find it
difficult also to forget the period when they were at the receiving end of the sharp lash of British colonialism.

It must be remembered that the Afrikaner is a proud
race with a long history of suffering. Reference has been
made elsewhere to their checkered history. At the hands of
Dutch Company officials and of the British, they have indeed been one of the world's long suffering peoples fighting
for independence. A visitor to the castle at Cape Town is
taken to the dungeons where recalcitrant Dutch farmers
were imprisoned and tortured by the authorities. One
meets Afrikaners, anxious for change and liberal in their outlook, whose attitudes are deeply seared by the knowledge
that their mother was born on the *veld* in the face of advancing British columns, after the home in which she had

been born and bred had been razed to the ground. Others still remember through family tradition which is strong among them, how their grandmother and grandaunts and great grandparents perished in the British concentration camps where 20,000 Afrikaner women and children died.

The following quotation from Pakenham's recent book on the Boer war, highlighted in *Time* of November 26, 1979, graphically illustrates the sort of situation which lingers in Afrikaner memory and is vividly recounted to this day: "The charge of two hundred horsemen galloping across a plain is designed to be an irresistible force. It does not stop simply because the enemy would like to surrender. 'Draw sabres — lances!' In neat lines, the Dragoons and Lancers began to thunder across the plain . . . Half a mile away, the Boers, unaware of their danger, had saddled up their ponies and begun to jog back the way they had come. The charging line of horsemen caught them broadside, like the steel prow of a destroyer smashing into the side of a wooden boat. People heard the crunch of the impact — steel against leather and bone and muscle — and saw the flash of the officers' revolvers, and heard the screams of the Boers trying to give themselves up. The Lancers and Dragoons swept on, leaving dozens of Boers, and some of their African retainers, spiked and splashed on the ground. Back came the cavalry for a second charge. ('Most excellent pig-sticking...for about ten minutes, the bag being about sixty', said one of the officers later.)... The Boers fell off their horses and rolled among the rocks, calling for mercy — calling to be shot, anything to escape the stab of the lances. But a story had got round that the Boers had abused a flag of truce and, anyway, the order was no prisoners".

The Afrikaner likes to keep his traditions alive. The great trek is re-enacted annually with young people drawing the wagons up the hills. At a dozen camp fires the folklore of Afrikanerdom takes life before the flickering flames to engrave itself in the minds of Afrikaner children. There is much in common between Afrikaners and Jews in keeping ancient tradition alive. It is not without significance that in 1956 a Jewish group presented Prime Minister Malan with a silver plate, hailing him as the 'Moses of the Afrikaner people'.[5]

Linked also to this traditionalism is the love of independence, which set off the great trek, and the love of the Bible and of the family. These are values for which the Afrikaner will gladly lay down his life. He is an essentially God-fearing, family-loving, Bible-reading man who sees the world through very special spectacles liberally equipped with side blinkers. His vision of the world is narrow and intense, and he is a man with a mission. The narrowness is the result of his being tucked away in the farmlands, far from contact with other races or civilisations, and this lack of vision needs to be penetrated.

Afrikaner distrust of the English is formed also by the belief, not perhaps unjustly held, that the English are prepared to enjoy the benefit of apartheid while laying all blame for it at the door of the Afrikaner. English concepts of equality before the law are, in their view, proclaimed with little sincerity by English South Africans no less than by English people in their homeland. The former are happy to receive the social advantages and the latter the financial dividends that apartheid brings them. Afrikaners resent being the whipping boy for British vested interests.

This point made, it must be conceded that there is, as far as casual observation goes, a much greater readiness on the part of the English as opposed to Afrikaners to concede the iniquity of the system. A recent survey showed that while 20 per cent of Afrikaner voters support power sharing with blacks, a majority of English voters do so.[6] The English concede the need for change and power sharing and make fewer attempts to justify existing arrangements. The difference is noticeable when one compares the reformist activities of the student bodies of the University of Cape Town with those of the student bodies of the Afrikaner University of Stellenbosch. The difference is so significant as to make a strong impression upon the visitor. Billboards proclaiming the activities of a dozen reformist groups fearlessly announce in Cape Town that whatever the repression of the system, the student body is openly for change. Many students court police banning and surveillance, including loss of career prospects, for these open expressions of their views. Nothing comparable is to be seen at Stellenbosch, however liberal-minded the individual student may be.

Likewise in society there are probably more dedicated workers for change among the English rather than the Afrikaners. The visitor clearly receives this impression, though it is difficult to obtain the exact statistics. Another dividing factor is language. The revival of Afrikaner consciousness and the nationalist victory in 1940 meant the intensification of language divisions between English and Afrikaner, and the identification of the Afrikaans language with nationalism. Indeed one of the tests adopted by the Broederbond in screening its new membership was a secret surveillance of the extent to which the candidate showed devotion to the Afrikaans language by adopting it as the language of his home. The flowering of the Afrikaans language and the appearance in the 1920's of a significant body of Afrikaner poetry were also important contributory factors in raising the level of acceptability of Afrikaans.

The resurgence of Afrikaans carries with it the danger of a neglect of English and a corresponding increase of the insularity that plagues the Afrikaner. The rural Afrikaner speaks English with some difficulty, even at the University stage. Many students at Stellenbosch could express themselves competently in English but some of the rural students were not altogether at home in the language and would for this reason sometimes avoid expressing their views in the open classroom, preferring to indicate their views privately after the class was over. Out in the farmlands of the Transvaal, the real power base of the Afrikaner movements, the emphasis on Afrikaans to the exclusion of English is thus a tendency fraught with some political danger, in that it adds linguistic to geographical insularity and delays the day when the Afrikaner will see the evils of apartheid as the world sees them.

One other factor bearing on English-Afrikaner relations needs to be mentioned. The sharp edge of Afrikaner anti-colonialist feeling was blunted by the achievement of independence from the English, but the independence thus achieved was only political. The economic dependence of the Afrikaner on the English is still strong. The majority of Afrikaners are still farmers while the majority of English are associated with business and industry. English interests are still in control of the financial and business worlds[7] and this still breeds resentment.

Sufficient has been said to show the complexities of the intra-white situation in South Africa. These complexities do not end with the Afrikaner-English dichotomy. Within Afrikanerdom too, there are significant differences. The city-dweller, more exposed to foreign influences than his country cousin, is more likely to accept the need for concession and change. Nor is it entirely a matter of residence. Deep historical currents run through the division. Perhaps one-third of Afrikaners still think along the lines of the Botha-Smuts-Hertzog tradition, seeing true South African greatness to lie on the path of co-operation with the English.[8] On the other hand, the Nationalist cause is dependent on a sentimental concentration on all things Afrikaner and to that extent binds up its supporters in a self-centred cocoon. The resulting bitterness between the two sections has been thought by some observers to exceed the bitterness between English and Afrikaner.[9] If the Universities can bring these two strands of Afrikaner thought close enough to each other, for the 'Afrikaner-Afrikaner' to understand something of the 'English-Afrikaner's' thinking, an important bridge will have been built towards a solution of South Africa's racial problem. Perhaps there is, here, a challenge to the Afrikaner Universities, which has not, thus far, been adequately met. One of the missions of Universities is to shake people out of their insularities. This yet remains to be done by the white Universities of South Africa.

The Broederbond

Readers outside South Africa will perhaps not be aware of the seminal influence on South African government and life wielded by the secret organisation known as the Broederbond.

The Broederbond was formed in 1918 to redress the humiliation suffered by the Afrikaner community during the Boer War and in the years immediately thereafter. The war was one of intense humiliation for the Afrikaner. Not only did he suffer a crushing defeat. Amid the smouldering homesteads and the ravages of war it seemed as if the viability of a separate way of life for the Afrikaner was now for ever in doubt. His spirit, his culture, his language — all seemed destined to be crushed under the heel of the conqueror. The succeeding years showed divisions in the ranks of Afrikanerdom, for the Afrikaner knew not whether to submerge his culture in the all-enveloping British or to cling doggedly to such strands of it as remained.

In the despair of defeat and division there arose the Broederbond, the brotherhood of Afrikaners pledged to restore their race to its lost dignity and to regain the independence and cultural integrity they had once enjoyed.

The Broederbond was vowed to secrecy. It had for its objectives the advancement to power of the Afrikaner, the elevation of the Arikaner language, and the revival and fostering of Afrikaner culture. None could join the brotherhood except after the most careful screening. Several levels of inquiry preceded even the prospective Broederbonder's awareness that he was being considered for membership. When all preliminary inquiries had been concluded, and the prospective 'brother' informed of his acceptability, a solemn ceremony enacted in secret and by candlelight saw the new Broederbonder swearing to uphold and foster the ideals of the brotherhood. This oath was binding till death. It meant among other things that he would not indulge in Sunday sport or divorce his wife or marry an English speaking South African. It meant also that wherever he might be in South Africa the powerful helping hands of fellow Broederbonders would reach down to raise him into the higher echelons of power and responsibility.

By degrees the organisation grew in numbers and in power. It had its successes and its reverses as well, for it came into conflict with both Hertzog and Smuts. But there was no stopping the Broederbond and in course of time it had infiltrated into all the key positions in the South African government. It nominated candidates for Parliament. It nominated cabinet ministers. It nominated rectors of Universities, police and military commanders and heads of government departments. The nominees, as Broederbonders, owed first loyalty to their society and its ideals.

The intense secrecy of the organisation extended to such details as that members should not assemble for a meeting in such a manner as to give the public the impression they were gathering, that they should meet in farmhouses rather than public places, that they should not all arrive in individual cars, but should travel three or four to a car so as to avoid attracting attention, that they should not post large batches of mail in the same postbox and wherever possible should deliver mail by hand. The jealously guarded secrets of the organisation were however, given away in 1977, when from a secret source there was a surprising leak of information to the Sunday Times, Johannesburg. This resulted in the publication by Ivor Wilkins and Hans Strydom of *The Super Afrikaner.* the wealth of detail in the book, down to a complete list of members, makes it an invaluable document.

However the publication of this information has not weakened the Broederbond. It is still one of the lynchpins of South African politics and the South African state. All cabinet ministers bar two are Broederbonders. The brothers still meet in secret and there is no doubt that many of the decisions of the South African government originate in the Committees of the Broederbond.

This remarkable organisation is such a power in South Africa as to render it debatable whether Parliament or the Broederbond is the more powerful entity. On the brotherhood's fiftieth anniversary in 1968, H.J. Klopper, its first

Chairman, told his fellow members, with ringing confidence, "Do you realise what a powerful force is gathered here tonight between these four walls? Show me a greater power on the whole continent of Africa! Show me a greater power anywhere..." He was correct. The Broederbond is the most powerful secret society in the world.

The visitor to South Africa, when scheduled to meet a person of importance in the country, would do well to inquire ahead whether he is a Broederbonder. If he is, this is now sufficiently well known to be easily ascertainable. If one has this information, the entire conversation will fit easily into place.

Against this background it will be evident that there cannot be any major change in the South African situation unless that change has the approval of the Broederbond. This is a reality that all who hope to effect change in the South African situation must bear in mind. It is consequently of great importance to consider ways and means by which the message of those seeking reform can penetrate to the rank and file of the Broederbond. They are all, it must be stressed, extremely religious and committed Christians, and this is the best level at which they can be reached. If reached and persuaded with understanding at this level, there is hope. If they are not reached, the exercise of achieving peaceful reform in South Africa is likely to flounder.

Calvinism

Reference has been made more than once in these pages to the deeply religious nature of the Afrikaner. The circumstances of Afrikaner history were such that religion could not stand aside from matters of practical politics and government. At every stage in his history, from the days of the first settlers, through colonial rule, the great trek, the founding of the early republics, the formation of the Union, independence and eventual Afrikaner supremacy, the Afrikaner people felt themselves adrift in unknown waters. It was their deep faith that sustained them and their church which gave them a sheet anchor when the seas were rough.

It was natural that church leaders and laymen should select for their guidance a Protestant philosophy which specially suited their circumstances and their willingness to cast themselves adrift in sole reliance upon the guidance of God. They had not far to search.

John Calvin, Swiss divine and reformer, born of French parents in 1509, provided to a large extent the religious basis for Afrikaner attitudes. His religious doctrines were intended to furnish a statement of the faith for persecuted Protestants and in a very short space of time wielded immense influence and authority. Among the countries most deeply influenced by them was Holland, and the Dutch colonists took it with them to South Africa.

Calvin, immensely austere in life as in belief, sought to purify the individual, society and the state through deep penetration of Christian principles into every aspect of life. It was central to the achievement of this purity in private and public life that God's plan for mankind be strictly adhered to. This plan, as Calvin saw it, was that God had preordained a Chosen People for leadership and entrusted to them the great destiny of realising this providential plan.[10] The State is divinely ordained and created and in the fulfilment of its God-given responsibilities which permeate every department of life, has exclusive powers over its citizens. "The rulers of such a state are God's earthly agents, acting in His name".[11] A strong belief in predestination and in the assignment of each individual to a predestined station in life underpins the entire doctrine.

Translated into the context of South Africa this doctrine was seen by the Afrikaner as meaning that just as the chosen people of Israel were led through the wilderness to the promised land, so the Afrikaner was led to the promised land as he moved northwards on the Great Trek. He was escaping from the Egypt of British imperialism into the rich lands of Africa where he was to exercise his divinely given leadership over the heathen. Those who came under his dominion owed a complete duty of obedience to their rulers, for their station in life, like their State, was preordained and had the sanction of God. It was to their spiritual and material advantage to subscribe obediently to this divine plan. The very division of mankind into different nations and races was divinely ordained, a notion the Dutch Reformed Church was not slow to elaborate upon, with various scriptural passages invoked in support. Notions of equality and sovereignty of the people stand contrary to such doctrine. Calvinism was authoritarian where it was established — as in Geneva — and revolutionary elsewhere — as in England. It knew the strength of organised revolutionary movements. In South Africa when it established itself, it practised the authoritarianism which went naturally with its doctrine, and suppressed dissent, of whose mechanism as well it had first hand knowledge.

Afrikaner history supported this belief in predestiny. When, in unquestioning trust in God, the Afrikaner sold his farmstead in the Cape and moved away from Western civilisation into the wilds of Africa, he was taking far greater risks than the American pioneers who rolled back the frontiers of the West. He had only his faith to rely on. Attacked by the Zulu, he made a Covenant with God on the day of the Battle of Blood River and God answered him with victory. As he moved northwards in expectation of the promised land he found vast stretches of the world's richest territories unfolding before him as if prepared by an unseen hand. That land was God's gift to him, prepared for him from the beginning of time and by this title deed he would rule it till time and life ran out. Calvinism thus gave him both his land and his right to rule.

Calvinism resulted also in a symbiotic alliance between the rulers and the Church. Each supported the other, for the ruler swelled in authority when the church pronounced him divinely ordained to rule, and the church basked in the reflected authority of the ruler. Ruler and church were in constant communication with each other, often in such close relationship as to be practically indistinguishable. In South Africa this is reflected in the rather irreverent observation that the Dutch Reformed Church is the Nationalist Party at prayer.

The thread of Calvinistic influence runs through the history of South Africa, which cannot be understood either socially or politically without some knowledge of this background. Prime Minister Botha reflected this deep religious streak when he stated, on being appointed leader of the Nationalist Party, "We shall go forward in faith and we shall go forward in humble obedience to God who controls the destinies of men".[12]

The Church in South Africa

The number of Christian churches in South Africa is such as to cause the utmost surprise to those accustomed to the formal church organisations of the outside world. They vary from the august Dutch Reformed Church to the African "castor-oil" church, where baptism takes place in castor oil. From the cathedral to the tin shack in which many a church is housed, the church is vibrantly alive at all levels of society. Just as the early white settlers gave high priority to the construction of church buildings despite their privations, the poorest shanty towns throw up improvised sheds for divine worship in a manner which leaves a lasting impression upon the visitor. That shed soon becomes a focal point for community activity, being used as a school or meeting room when not in use for religious services. A cross made of two sticks and tied to the roof of a tin shack is symbolic of the faith of black South Africa.

Likewise, the priest or minister is a greatly respected figure in society, greeted in centres of affluence as well as in shanty towns with a friendly reverence that has a distinctly old-world flavour.

There was a time when the black churches took their guidance and direction from the white churches, especially the Dutch Reformed Church. That influence is now greatly reduced. A growing number of black pastors openly identify with the demand for social and political reform and will not be held back, as their predecessors were, by the fear of incurring the displeasure of their white counterparts.

Approximately seventy per cent of all South Africans identify themselves as Christians. The 1970 census figures, the most complete available, are listed below. The most powerful of the churches is the NGK (Nederduitse Gereformeerde Kerk) or the Dutch Reformed Church. It has three daughter churches — the NGKA (African), the NG Sending (Coloured) and the Indian DRC. Next in power are the Anglican, the Methodist and the Roman Catholic. While the adherents of the NGK and its three daughter churches are exclusively of particular racial groups, the other churches have a mixed following, though, especially after the Group Areas Act, this does not mean mixed congregations. Many parishes turn out to be exclusively white, coloured, or African as the case may be.

The Churches listed as African Independent are so various as to defy enumeration. Some three thousand of them, great and small, command the loyalties of hundreds of thousands on the one hand and of individual families on the other.

Church	White	Coloured	Asian	African	Total
NGK	1,487,080			924,820	1,487,080
NGKA					924,820
NG Sending		573,400			573,400
Indian DRC			830		830
Gereformeerde	113,620	3,940			117,560
Hervormde	224,400	1,620			226,020
Anglican	399,950	333,200	5,930	937,720	1,676,800
Presbyterian	117,250	7,570	320	329,320	454,460
Congregational	19,640	144,760	70	185,320	349,790
Methodist	357,410	115,810	2,540	1,676,080	2,151,840
Apostolic Faith Mission	110,960	52,380	590	138,360	302,290
Lutheran	40,620	83,510	250	759,740	884,120
Roman Catholic	304,840	195,630	13,820	1,329,980	1,844,270
African Independent				2,761,120	2,761,120
Other Christians	321,030	327,420	26,250	1,367,640	2,042,340
	3,496,800	1,839,240	50,600	10,410,100	15,796,740

South Africans take their religion seriously and one of the greatest factors favouring a peaceful resolution of their problems is that nearly all component elements of its population are responsive to the Christian message. To be sure, some of them have received it misguidedly, but it will be easier to convert the oppressor in South Africa through the Bible rather than through the sword; and the oppressed, when he triumphs, as surely he will, will be held back from vengeance by the Christianity lying deep within him more potently than by any other single factor.

The Church in South Africa has been sharply divided on the issue of apartheid. The South African Council of Churches (SACC), representing some fifteen million South Africans, rejects and on occasion defies the apartheid laws. The Dutch Reformed Church on the other hand defends apartheid, and cites scripture in its support.[13]

The churches of the SACC, though opposing the concept of apartheid, have not always acted consistently with their convictions and are open to much criticism on this account. There have, in their ranks as well, been conformists — too many of them — who have been prepared to toe the government line rather than get themselves into trouble.

Yet there is a great stirring of consciousness in the ranks of the SACC. At its annual conference in July it made a policy statement openly encouraging civil disobedience. It condemned the remaining restrictions on inter-racial contact as "morally so objectionable we cannot obey them with a clear conscience". Later in the year, Bishop Tutu urged Denmark to participate in anti-apartheid boycotts and not to buy coal from South Africa. In December Archbishop Bill Burnett announced that defiance of the state was legitimate even if it meant disintegration of the church.

This significant pronouncement was made when the provincial synod of the Anglican Church of the Province of South Africa issued a summons on the Rev. David Russell, a priest under a banning order, to attend the Synod at Grahamstown. The Rev. Russell advised the magistrate of his district of his intention to attend, but did not technically ask for permission. In terms of his banning order he was restricted to the Wynberg magisterial district and could not therefore leave it without permission. He was also restricted from any form of publication of his views or writings. Not only would the Rev. Russell be violating the Internal Security Act by his attendance, the church authorities too, could be charged with violating the Act by summoning him to the synod, as well as by publishing the notices of motion given by the Rev. Russell. It was reported in December 1979 that the security police had referred the matter to the Attorney-General and that further proceedings depended on the extent to which the Attorney-General desired to pursue the case.

Significantly for the history of the Church in South Africa, a resolution of the Synod authorised Church bodies to ignore the law applying to permits for church functions, if efforts to have these rules changed or abolished should fail. In other words, the Synod was prepared to defy the civil administration if change did not come. Archbishop Burnett's pronouncement went dramatically further.

The SACC churches are on the move in South Africa and are one of the great forces for change to be watched. How far they are prepared to go may well be the question on which much of South Africa's future depends.

The Dutch Reformed Church

The daughter churches of the NGK have hitherto taken their guidance on doctrinal matters from the main Dutch Reformed Church but the situation has now been reached wherein these daughter churches are no longer content to accept without question some of the guidelines laid down by the parent church. In particular the question whether there is scriptural justification for the doctrine of apartheid has run into rough weather at the hands of these daughter churches.

One of the great anomalies of church history in South Africa is that the parent Dutch Reformed Church has been able to find doctrinal justification for the doctrine of apartheid. It is of course not spoken of by the church in terms of apartheid but of "pluriformity of creation" and of "parallel development". This dogma has gained great acceptance with the hierarchy of the Dutch Reformed Church and through them has provided a moral justification for the doctrine of apartheid as practised in South Africa. · It is to be remembered that the most influential party, namely the Nationalist Party, consists almost entirely of adherents of the Dutch Reformed Church. When the Dutch Reformed Church takes up this position as part of its scriptural instruction, there is no doubt it must deeply influence the thinking of the government party. Indeed it is this identification between the activities of the government party and of the Dutch Reformed Church which has given such force to the jest already mentioned, that the Dutch Reformed Church consists of the Nationalist Party at prayer. Certain it is that there is very close connection between these two entities — a matter demonstrated recently in the context of the information scandal when it was revealed that funds of the government had secretly been made over to the Dutch Reformed Church. The Dutch Reformed Church has now admitted this and is taking the stand that the money has been properly received and properly expended, although not all Ministers even of the white Dutch Reformed Church are prepared to accept this position. In fact some members of the white Dutch Reformed Church have in protest, made personal contributions of R100 for the purpose of returning the money which the church obtained from government and which in their view the church is not entitled in conscience to retain.

In discussions with ministers of the Dutch Reformed Church I was able to probe into the doctrinal position of the church on apartheid — a matter which the Christian in any other country will find difficult to understand. I was able in these inquiries to gather some information regarding the origin of this unusual church stand, the documentation on which it is based and the resistance it is now encountering from within the church itself.

The Dutch Reformed Church's emphasis on the doctrine of pluriformity of creation is traceable in large measure to the very strong influence wielded by the philosopher Kuyper in Holland in the 1930's. He taught that the divine dispensation for mankind was a pluriformity of creation rather than a stereotyped uniformity. Each division of mankind was hence required to retain its own identity, which could only be done by keeping it separate and providing for its parallel development in relation to other groups rather than by attempts at integration.

This view has been developed with special reference to South Africa and has been propagated in a solemn document issued in October 1974 by the Dutch Reformed Church, titled "Human Relations and the South African Scene in the Light of Scripture". This document, approved and accepted by the general synod of the Dutch Reformed Church, still embodies its orthodox teaching and official doctrine. It is available in English translation from the offices of the Dutch Reformed Church in Cape Town and Pretoria.

Reading this document one sees that reliance is placed upon scriptural references to the existence of a diversity of people (Matthew 28:19; Acts 2:5; Romans 1:16). In fact emphasis is laid on the statement in Acts 17:26 that God appointed specific times for the various nations as well as boundaries for their homelands.   It is pointed out that the New Testament, while often referring to the diversity of nations, never characterises it as sinful and never calls upon Christians to renounce their nationality.   Article 13.6 of this document has already been cited in Chapter 1.[4]

It is interesting also to refer to the previous article which points out that the New Testament accepts the diversity of people as a fact but does not elevate it to the only or highest principle.   Although in Galatians 3:28 it is stated: "there can be neither Jew nor Greek, there can be neither bond nor free, there can be no male and female: for ye are all one in Christ Jesus", the article points out that:

> "To read in these passages a mandate for social integration between peoples would be to abuse them. It is obviously the purpose of these verses to emphasise the all prevailing importance of the new unity in Christ, but not to deny the existence of individual and diverse communities".

The same document has much to say on the question of mixed marriages in Article 64.   It points out that while marriage is in the first instance a personal and family matter it also has social, religious, political and juridical significance. Hence, such a marriage does not fall entirely outside the concern of society, church and state.   As far as the church is concerned it most certainly has a pastoral calling to warn against the contracting of such marriages especially where the social situation is one to which racially mixed marriages are foreign.   This is stated to be a pastoral obligation of the Church, not merely in view of the unfavourable complications of such a marriage for the partners themselves but also more particularly because of their unfavourable consequences for their progeny.

According to the Synod the equilibrium of a multi-racial and multi-national situation may be disturbed by the contracting of racially mixed marriages and in these circumstances the preservation of "peace" in the biblical sense would be of more importance to the authorities than the free choice of marriage partners by certain individuals. Strange though this may seem, all this is official doctrine bearing the solemn stamp of approval of church and ruling party in a very powerful state.   Unfortunately, it so happens that a Synodal document of this degree of solemnity requires a long process for its revision.   The leaders of the church at this moment are scarcely in a mood to recognise that the Synodal document of 1974 was a grave error. The process of change is complex and requires to be set in motion from the grass roots level of the church till eventually it filters through up to the General Synod. This process takes years, rendering it unlikely that there will be any rapid revision of this doctrinal statement. In any event it is not till 1982 that there will be another General Synod. However, the forces that need to be set in motion to achieve it are already conscious of the obligation that lies upon them, and both from within the white Dutch Reformed Church and from within the daughter churches, the movement is gathering strength which will eventually result in its revision.

Another alleged scriptural justification of the doctrine of apartheid — more prevalent outside the Church than within it — is the Noah Prophecy (Genesis 9:24-27). Canaan, the son of Ham and all his generations were cursed by Noah, and there are indeed many in the ranks of Afrikanerdom who believe that the black races are the descendants of Ham and thus condemned to a life of servility to the white races, descendants of the other children of Noah.

There is at least this much to be said for the stand of the Dutch Reformed Church, that in the scriptural document referred to (paragraph 9.2) there is a repudiation of the Noah prophecy as being an acceptable basis for the doctrine of apartheid.

Later on in this work there is an attempt to point out ways in which foreign churches can make their own influence felt on the thinking and practice of the Dutch Reformed Church in South Africa. The area of doctrinal justification of the practice of apartheid is pre-eminently one such. The pressures which the foreign church and the foreign branches of the Dutch Reformed Church can bring to bear upon the South African Dutch Reformed Church can be of vital importance in the immediate future.

It is significant that the 1978 Synod of the Dutch Reformed Mission Church (the Coloured Church) passed a resolution that the system of apartheid is diametrically opposed to biblical teaching and takes its point of departure from the untenable concept that reconciliation between peoples is impossible. It held that biblical teaching demands a unity of the Church and therefore that there is no justification for separate Churches and called on all members of the Dutch Reformed Church to form one unified Church. It is likely that the Black Church and the Indian Church will follow this lead, thus presenting the mother Church with a situation of open dissent it has never yet encountered. Also of significance is the report of the DRC's Commission on Racial Affairs in October 1979 flying in the face of the accepted stance of the church, and stating that "a church which silently tolerates...prejudice within its own ranks...is itself dominated by the power of that sin". The report condemned discrimination as "evil" and was instantly challenged by Dr. Koot Vorster, brother of former Prime Minister, John Vorster, resulting in stormy debates between the traditionalists of the church and the innovators. A compromise formula emerged, acknowledging that certain forms of discrimination "are in conflict with the word of God". The word "evil" was dropped.

There are signs therefore that there is movement even within the Dutch Reformed Church. That movement is slow, still hampered by traditionalists, and by General Synod pronouncements. It will need to be speeded up.

The Church and Western Culture

An important rider needs to be added to the general statement that Christianity commands the respect of all sections — black and white — of the community.

Especially among the more inquiring young black people of South Africa there is a smouldering resentment at the manner in which the early missionaries confused Christianity with Western culture. In introducing the first, they were in fact introducing the second, often unintentionally but sometimes by design. The missionary was frequently in the vanguard of imperialism without quite realising this, and 'missionary imperialism' was often destructive of ancient and time-honoured ways of life.[15]

Steve Biko instances the fact that when an African became a Christian he or she was expected to drop traditional garb and dress like a Westerner. Many other customs dear to the blacks they were expected to drop, although there was nothing in them which conflicted with Christianity. They conflicted only with Western ways of life.[16]

To add to this manner of dictation, there was dictation also through the social hierarchy of the church, which was rigidly white/black. Responsibility for church affairs was, till recently, exclusively white. Hence the church was hardly influenced in its contours by the black presence in the midst of which it moved.

These factors have prompted a certain measure of questioning of Christianity — not of Christian faith but in Biko's language of its "Western package". This has led also to the development of black theology in the context of black consciousness.[17]

There are some strong views that black consciousness is contributing to black theology. It points out for example that long before Christianity, Africans had a belief in the Supreme Being. Because of their ancestors' proximity to the Supreme Being their power was enhanced. They were not seen as gods, as is sometimes supposed, but as intercessors, because of their proximity to the Godhead — not very differently from the Roman Catholic's appeal to the saints as intercessors. The African does not approach his tribal chief direct, but through intercessors. The Catholic idea is no different from the African principle. Indeed the African takes a world view which gives him a sense of belonging to a community not confined to those who are alive. The Christian notion of community is thus expanded by the African to a sense of oneness with beings past, present and future. Those who have died and those who are yet to come are as much part of the African notion of community as those who are alive today — a view akin to that of Spinoza in European philosophy. What happened in the past and what will happen in the future are as much parts of one's world as what happens in the here and now.

All this richness of insight which African culture could have given to the church was lost sight of by the missionaries. In Bishop Tutu's words, "many of them came to think that things European were intrinsically Christian and everything else was pagan. So many African insights which might have been vehicles for the Christian faith were condemned, out of hand, not recognised... We were often made to feel guilty and ashamed of things African".[18] The traditional religiousness and spirituality of the African were denigrated rather than used for the enrichment of the universal Christian tradition.

Black consciousness also emphasises that whereas the Church has identified itself largely with power and wealth in South Africa, Christ himself was not merely on the side of the poor. Some black consciousness thinking sees Christ as having identified with the guerilla resistance by the oppressed element of the Jews against the might of the Roman Empire, whereas the high priests identified with the Romans. Black theology therefore sees one of its roles in Africa as being the duty to be active in throwing off the yoke of oppression.

There is another aspect as well concerning the Western church which is of the greatest political significance, and is often overlooked by the church in South Africa.

The way in which the church, of nearly every denomination in South Africa, fell docilely within the discriminatory guidelines of government policy, has affected the credibility of the church throughout black Africa. Africans of many countries wonder how churches calling themselves Christian could in any way compromise themselves in regard to the simple Christian message of love and humility and equality, when their clear duty was to court government displeasure and even persecution in the upholding of the basic tenets of their faith. Some individual churchmen have acted as black Africa would expect Christian religions to act, but the churches as a whole have failed. In particular the Dutch Reformed Church has by its stance reduced black Africa's regard not only for itself but for Christian churches in general. The damage resulting from this to Christianity — a continuing and increasing damage — is turning many away from the church and is likely to turn away many more unless there is a swift correction of attitudes. This aspect of the DRC's disservice to Christianity as a whole cannot pass unmentioned in any review, however brief, of the church in South Africa. It could in time become difficult for a black African to continue to be a Christian without incurring the stigma of identification with colonialism and privilege. Should this possibility ever become a reality, the Dutch Reformed Church in South Africa would have contributed largely to this unhappy result.

White Indoctrination

It is well within the ability of a government in supreme power, as the South African government is, to use its educational apparatus for the purpose of indoctrination of its school children. The South African government has not been loath to use this power. Afrikaner leaders, architects of the policy of apartheid, are magnified in school textbooks to the level of national heroes. Visits to Afrikaner shrines, re-enactments of the great trek, education in the doctrines of the Dutch Reformed Church, indoctrination in the belief that the Afrikaner is God's chosen race with a divine mission on the African continent — all add up to a grand total of belief in a God-given superiority and mandate to rule.

Nor is this accidental. In 1978 a motion on school education led to a heated debate in the assembly, and the Nationalist Party member who introduced the motion, said that in the face of the onslaught facing South Africa, children should be indoctrinated to become true patriots who will guard jealously their own culture and traditions. A member of the opposition P.F.P. attacked this suggestion that children be indoctrinated, and suggested that the government should stop looking to Russia for its methods.

Special importance attaches to the effort made through the Dutch Reformed Church to give moral and apparently scriptural support to the doctrine of apartheid in the formative minds of young school children. Where the dictates and pronouncements of religious authorities loom large, and where there is as yet no sense of discrimination with which to sift the chaff from the wheat, there is a very grave danger that such indoctrination may form life-long attitudes which cannot be shaken off even in the face of later experience.

A South African Teachers' Council of Rights has been constituted in terms of Section 4 of Act No. 16 of 1976. Although some teachers expressed concern that the Council was composed only of whites, the Minister of National Education said in the Senate that government policy on this matter was clear — the Council was for whites only. It is significant that the professional code of conduct for teachers drawn up by this body, and now gazetted, contains in its preamble a requirement that teachers pledge themselves as teachers, to honour and obey the laws of the country.

The attempted indoctrination of Afrikaner culture in the minds of black students was one of the immediate causes for the Soweto uprising, and that attempt has been defeated in so far as black children are concerned. There is nevertheless the fact that even they, and all other sections of the community, are exposed to thinking which does not portray the previous leaders of South Africa and the architects of apartheid in proper perspective.

There is no doubt also that the process of indoctrination takes place at home. The description by a Stellenbosch student of family reaction to his liberal ideas is the subject of one of the vignettes in Chapter 1. The family rallies round the parental view and persistence involves the danger of ostracism. In an intensely patriarchal society with close family bonds, this is too great a penalty for all but the stoutest spirits, and the student would capitulate.

It is in this mix of parental, school and church indoctrination that young Afrikaner minds are cast. The mould is so cleverly fashioned that the contours last for life.

Sport

In August, 1979, the Minister of Sport made an announcement that the Cabinet had given long and careful consideration to the whole question of sport. It had discussed three alternatives — the alternative of total segregation; the alternative of opening the floodgates; and a third alternative, which the National Party had chosen. It was stated that the Cabinet felt that if there was one way in which South Africa could be destroyed, it was by following the advice of people on the extreme right who argued for a continuation of total segregation. The middle position adopted by the Cabinet, was to authorize sports bodies and school authorities to decide for themselves what was best. As far as the schools were concerned, the principals in consultation with parent-teacher associations and school boards would be able to determine for themselves whether they wished to extend invitations to or accept invitations from other schools. Permits, with the long drawn-out procedure involved, would no longer be deemed necessary for mixed sport. There was, however, a note of warning from the Minister when he pointed out that anyone wishing to misuse the privilege for their own ends would have the privilege withdrawn. This was the right which the Government reserved to itself.

This so-called "advance" still leaves apartheid very much alive in the sphere of sport, for there is in the first place the power of the Government to withdraw the privilege and in the second no prohibition whatsoever against schools deciding to pursue a policy, however reactionary or exclusive it might be. It cannot be argued that on the basis of measures such as these the South African government has given its approval to mixed sport.

Outside areas where there is some compulsion towards integration, there is little effort in such a direction. For example, on a visit to a gold mine, the writer heard the manager speak at length about the attention they were paying to sport on the part of the black workers in the mine. When specifically questioned on integration, the manager was obliged to acknowledge that the company had not given any thought as yet to integration in sport.

Even where sport is mixed, there are many practical realities behind the facade of equality. For example, a baseball player who became the first black sectional member of the Wanderers in Johannesburg, was to be allowed, according to a club official, to play sport in the category for which he had applied, and would also be allowed to take part in any post-game activities in a private room which had been provided for by the Wanderers. However, he would not be allowed into the bar area of the main club unless signed in by a full member.

Wanderers' members wanted earlier in 1979 to open sectional membership of the club to all races, but in consequence of legislation, including the Liquor Act, the club could not grant full membership to blacks.

Black Eastern Transvaal cross-country athletes were forced recently to travel to South African Championships separated from white athletes. There were nine black runners from the Bracken mine complex, including the famous Springbok athlete, Matthews "Loop En Val" Mothswarateu and Vincent Rakabaele. Of this incident, Johnny Halbestadt, the South African marathon and half-marathon champion, announced that "it goes to show that the Springbok blazer is merely window-dressing to the rest of the world".

It was also announced by the chairman of the Eastern Transvaal Cross-Country Association that parents of juniors selected for the province threatened to withdraw their children if the black athletes travelled in the same bus.

Halbestadt drew attention to apartheid in sport by declining to accept a Springbok blazer "because I couldn't live with my conscience if I did". This action is said to have rocked South African athletics to its foundations, for the blazer is the highest award any South African can earn in the realm of sport.

Halbestadt drew attention to another of the realities of South African apartheid in sport when he pointed out that Loop En Val Mothswarateu could not get a South African passport to run in America. Loop En Val had a scholarship waiting for him at the University of Texas at El Paso, one of the greatest opportunities any athlete in the world could get, but Loop En Val was denied a passport for weeks until it was too late for him to accept the American offer. The reason for the refusal was the attempt by the South African authorities to compel him to accept Bophuthatswana citizenship if he wanted to go to America. "Loop En Val is not the only athlete who has had a raw deal. What about people like Humphrey Kohsi, Benoni

Malaka and Daniel Metsing, who ran for South Africa over-seas, but never got their Springbok blazers because those were the days when it was only for whites?   On Tuesday evening I told the Springbok team manager I was with-drawing. It was the hardest decision of my life".

Despite the announcements by the government, apartheid is a great reality in the realm of sport.

Since this was written, the international news media on January 8, 1980, announced that Springbok cricketer Eddie Barlow was to boycott all restaurants which ban blacks, in protest against a Cape Town restaurant which refused to serve his coloured team mate Omar Henry. "Dickie Jeeps will be here shortly with Basil D'Oliveira and his British commission to investigate any progress to-wards the normalisation of sport in South Africa.   I say don't even come, as there can be no finding other than 'nothing much has changed' ", he is reported to have said. The window-dressing of apartheid in sport for world con-sumption can never carry any conviction so long as the fundamentals of apartheid remain.

Overseas Business

The managements of overseas businesses have signed various codes of conduct in relation to the principles appli-cable to their South African establishments.   These codes concentrate on discriminatory practices in the workplace and are intended to prevent these businesses falling under the slur of being willing parties to the practice of apartheid.

A common criticism of these codes is that they do nothing more than create a moral atmosphere about investment in South Africa. For example, at the Human Rights Conference mentioned later, Dr. Alex Boraine, Progressive Federal Party M.P., accused managements of being 'derelict' in their responsibilities and of signing codes of conduct in order to avoid the disinvestment debate overseas.   The British Anti-Apartheid Movement, the Haselmere Group and End Loans to South Africa commented regarding the EEC Code that it would only lead to a 'sweetening of apartheid' and not its removal.

Still, subject to these limitations, codes of conduct deserve examination and offer much potential for amelior-ation of the South African worker's lot.

There are four main codes — the Sullivan Code,[19] the EEC Code, the Urban Foundation Code and the Canadian

Government Code. They were all framed with the South African situation in view, and cover Trade Unions, Desegregation, Employment Practices, Remuneration, Training, Development, Social Responsibility and Migratory Labour.

A principal difficulty in the implementation of the Codes lies in making provision for their monitoring. Employers are themselves slow to report on progress in implementing their Codes. The Inkatha movement announced in July that it would monitor the implementation of the Codes, as an alternative to a call for disinvestment. Such a step was not slow to arouse resentments from white trade union leaders as an attempt by a political movement to interfere in labour relations. The Consultative Committee of Black Trade Unions, however, expressed support for the proposal. If there is indeed any sincerity in the intention to implement these codes, one can see no objection to their being monitored by those most concerned — the representatives of the black population. If they are not permitted to do this the whole operation could be described as a sham. And a sham it is in many instances, for one of the reasons adduced by firms who did not introduce integrated facilities was that South African landlords and building managers did not allow American tenants to integrate leased facilities.[20] However, the Codes do in some cases produce results, and there has been some improvement in integrating canteens, washrooms, toilets and medical facilities. Still, such integration only touches the surface of the matter. In many workplaces where such integration has in theory been introduced, in practice the old discriminations continue, with the whites and non-whites using separate facilities.

The four main codes of conduct are summarised below, a summary appearing in the TUCSA Trade Union Directory 1978 and in the 1978 Survey of Race Relations.

It will be seen that the EEC Code specifically recognises African trade unions and encourages collective bargaining with African workers. This goes much further than the Sullivan Code which merely acknowledges generally the right of black workers to form their unions but is silent on the specific question of collective bargaining. The failure of American industry to recognise normal principles of trade union rights is a blot upon its record, which accords ill with its professions of interest in the South African blacks. Collective bargaining rights are crucial to any valid trade union recognition and it is surprising that U.S. trade unionism has not come out in strong insistence on this elementary right for black workers. The Secretary of the Commercial Catering and Allied Workers' Union of South Africa was well entitled to comment that the Code was "just good cosmetics for the outside world. To us, as trade unionists, we see no difference between American and South African companies".[21]

Apart from the incidence of petty apartheid in the workplace — integrating eating and washroom facilities — in which there has been some improvement, the more substantial aspects of apartheid in industry still flourish. In 81 per cent of the companies that have signed the Sullivan Code managerial positions are still held by whites, and only sixteen per cent of them recognise unions. Migrant labour, the great reservoir from which all industry draws its manpower, is still denied the most elementary human rights of family togetherness and association.

Signatories to the Codes, however well meaning they may be, have still a long way to go before they can exonerate themselves of the charge that they make use of the exploitative South African system for increasing their own profit. Perhaps the best proof of this was the report on the United States corporate interests in South Africa prepared by Senator Dick Clark, Chairman of the Africa sub-committee of the U.S. Foreign Relations Committee,[22] which revealed that the United States corporations had made no significant contribution to the relaxation of apartheid. On the contrary, they had assisted the South African government to strengthen its apartheid regime economically and militarily.[23]

There is no doubt that the more general adoption and enforcement of Codes of Conduct is one of the most powerful means at the world's disposal for making an impression upon the South African problem. A greater awareness among shareholders of the existence and potential of these Codes is much to be desired, and some suggestions towards increasing levels of awareness will be found in Chapter 8. It is indeed a matter of some surprise to students of apartheid that so powerful a means of reducing the iniquities of apartheid has been so little used. A perusal of the table that follows will show the vast scope that exists for the operation and extension of such Codes.

Apartheid — The Closing Phases?

Codes of Conduct   The table below summarises the four main codes of conduct:

	Sullivan Code (United States of America)	European Economic Community code of conduct	Urban Foundation/ Saccola	Canadian Government code of conduct
Trade Unions	Acknowledge generally the right of black workers to form their own union or to be represented by trade unions where unions already exist. Support the elimination of discrimination against the right of blacks to form or belong to a government registered union.	Encourage collective bargaining with African workers. Recognise African trade unions where they exist.	Recognition of basic rights of workers, freedom of association, collective negotiation, lawful strikes and protection against victimisation.	Companies to ensure employees free to organise collective bargaining units. Extend customary basic rights to such bargaining units.
Desegregation	Eliminate all vestiges of racial discrimination, remove all race discrimination signs, desegregate all eating, comfort and work facilities.	As far as possible employers should do everything possible to desegregate, notably at the workplace and in canteens, sports activities, education and training. Ensure equal working conditions for all staff.	Removal of discrimination in all aspects of employment practice.	Integrate working, eating, recreational, educational, and training facilities.
Employment Practices	Equal and fair terms and conditions of employment, provide non-discriminatory eligibility for benefit plans. Support elimination of all industrial racial discriminatory laws	Improvement of fringe benefits for African workers. No discrimination in any work sphere including promotion.	No discrimination based on race or colour in job advancement and fringe benefits.	Equal employment practices for all workers. Improve overall work situation of black employees. Equal fringe benefits for all employees.

Remuneration	Equal pay for all employees doing equal or comparable work for the same period of time. Ensure equitable system of job classification. Minimum wages to be well above the appropriate local minimum economic living level.	Companies to assume responsibility as regards African employees. Minimum wages to exceed initially minimum subsistence levels by at least 50% *Equal pay for equal work.*	Elimination of discrimination based on race or colour.	Equal pay for equal work. Employers should aim to pay above minimum datum lines for workers in lowest categories.
Training	Initiation and development of training programmes that will prepare substantial numbers of blacks for supervisory administrative, clerical and technical jobs.	Internal or external training schemes for blacks including to artisan status. Employers to reduce their dependence on immigrant White labour.	Training programmes or facilities to improve productivity and skills. Aim to achieve African advancement into technical administrative and managerial positions.	Provide training programmes.
Development	Increase the number of blacks in management and supervisory positions.	Encouragement of training to develop full potential and non-racial promotion policy.	No discrimination in selection, employment, advancement or promotion of all employees.	Provide job opportunities to facilitate movement of blacks into semi-skilled and skilled positions. Introduce blacks to supervisory positions on an accelerated basis rather than recruiting expatriate personnel.

The Border War

It is not commonly realised that South African forces are already constantly engaged in what is called 'The Border War'. South African radio and television broadcasts constantly speak of the 'boys on the border'.

South Africa, stable though it may seem from the outside, is thus constantly in a war situation and at various stages her forces have been in actual battle situations in Angola, Namibia and Zimbabwe. This is an important transformation that has shaken South African society more completely than can be appreciated from without. In January 1978 all white South African males were required to register for two years' compulsory military service, to be followed by eight annual camps of thirty days each. The young men at the Universities find their lives transformed by this requirement and sooner or later the immediacy of this war situation will cause increasing qualms of conscience among them. Even the military service and the camp service period may require active service at the border.

The northern border of South Africa is so vast and vulnerable that no amount of military strength can police it effectively. University students who have served on the border vividly describe this impossibility, pointing out how, despite every effort of the military, the movement of blacks from South Africa to the neighbouring countries proceeds under cover of night and of the terrain. The build-up of hostile forces across the border is strong — both escaped South Africans and the troops of neighbouring countries. Foreign troops such as the Cubans add considerably to the difficulties, and it is a bold South African soldier who would speak with any confidence regarding the army's ability to prevent infiltration from the borders.

It does not add to South Africa's peace of mind to realise that the local populations in the midst of which the soldiers operate are entirely hostile to their cause. The army are thrown largely upon their own resources, just as they would be in hostile territory. In addition, the fire power of the opposition is increasing daily. The Zimbabwe settlement is at best a temporary stop gap, and sooner or later realistic South Africans realise that the Zimbabwe border will be wide open to hostile action if apartheid continues.

When one places this in the setting of the constant possibility of a flare up at home and of a protracted guerilla style war with determined activists, one sees that the security problems of the government are many. From a security point of view the massive strength of the armed forces is not an invincible shield behind which South African politicians can foster their policies of apartheid. They realise the vulnerability of their position, and this is why the present, more than ever before, is a time in which they will be prepared to make concessions. The Prime Minister was defence minister for thirteen years and should appreciate these difficulties even more than most other politicians.

Conscientious Objection

Compulsory military service, an obligation lying upon all white males raises many questions of conscience, which, surprisingly have not as yet been sufficiently aired in South Africa. Compulsory military service for the national defence of any country is a cause which its nationals would not in general cavil at. However, when military service involves also the repression of one's own nationals who may, in defying the state, have reason and justice upon their side, the problem assumes an entirely different complexion. This is precisely the crisis of conscience which young white South Africans are called upon to face. Many go through their military service hoping they will never be called upon to support repression at home. Many shut their eyes to these possibilities and, if they choose to philosophise, sweep their qualms of conscience under the carpet of their duty to their state. Some migrate from South Africa in time to evade this crisis of conscience. The problem is there, however, and young South Africa must come to terms with it.

Jehovah's Witnesses have in general established a right to have their conscientious objection recognised but until 1979 there was a surprising absence of precedent in the case of non-Jehovah's Witnesses, only one of whom, Anton Eberhard, had served a sentence of two months in Pretoria for conscientious objection in 1977.

In 1979 Peter Moll set up a well documented case of conscientious objection to military service. He was a member of the Baptist Church and Chairman of the Students' Christian Association. He was studying for an honours degree in Religious Studies, part time, at the University of Cape Town. He was also studying actuarial science.

The case history is interesting as indicating the obstacles the conscientious objector faces.

Moll's thoughts in the direction of conscientious objection were first prompted when he was put on eight-hour standby by the Cape Flats Commando in 1976 and was required to keep a rifle in his room. He decided that if he was required to put down riots he would not answer the call. There was in fact no call-up. The following year he was called-up for border training. He requested non-military service instead, a request which was refused. He refused to attend camp, saying South African society was so unjust in terms of Christian morality that he could not be required to defend it. He quoted, on this aspect, Archbishop Bill Burnett — this would be the "defence of the morally indefensible". In court he argued that when the law of man and the Law of God are in conflict, the latter must take precedence. He received a sentence of three months, suspended for five years.

Again, in 1978 he requested a non-military alternative and was again turned down. He then requested Defence H.Q. to allow him to complete the balance of his training by teaching mathematics in Umtata, for which his knowledge of Xhosa would have suited him. The secretary of education of the Transkei backed his request. The request was refused.

When he was called up for training again, in 1979, he refused to attend, quoting Alan Paton: "the war is basically a civil war", and the *Cape Times:* "The guerillas are none other than our own deeply disaffected fellow citizens". He invoked Reformed, Lutheran and Catholic theology on the minimum requirements for a just war — that the war should be "for a just cause". How could the injustice of apartheid, which resulted inevitably in resistance among Blacks, be called a just cause?.

Information is not yet available regarding the final result of Moll's trial. He could face imprisonment, loss of employment and an order to repay the 6,000 dollars bursary money he was receiving. These are the pressures upon the young South African conscientious objector — apart, that is, from family displeasure and social ostracism. Nor is Moll's way of thinking permitted to spread. Possession of two of his writings — "Thinking No" in *National Student* (June 1979) and "To be a soldier or not to be" in *Contours of the Kingdom* (May 1979) has been banned by the authorities.

Civil Disobedience in the Light of Theology

The concept of civil disobedience attracted considerable theological discussion and clarification in July 1979 when the South African Council of Churches held its Eleventh National Conference. The theme of the Conference was "The Church and the Alternative Society". Major papers were delivered, among others, by Bishop Desmond Tutu, the General Secretary, Dr. H.W. Van der Merwe, the Director of the Centre for Inter-Group Studies and the Mennonite theologian Dr. John Yoder. The subject is of more than academic importance in view of the great influence wielded by Christianity over all component elements of the South African population.

The conference was unusual in that only 28 of the 115 participants were white (representing the approximate white/black ratio in the country), that issues of civil disobedience were openly discussed and that the delegates were housed together during the period of the conference.

Dr. Yoder's contribution was of special significance in that it drew attention to the need for churches to take an unambivalent attitude to violence. He argued for non-violence but drew attention to the fact that the Christian churches in the Western world had since the fourth century, accepted and worked out the notion of the 'just war'. The acceptance of the 'just war' idea and of conditional violence had been embodied in the Hammanskraal resolution of the SACC some years earlier and meant that in certain circumstances the taking up of arms was regarded by the Christian churches as justifiable i.e. for the purpose of fighting a just war. Dr. Yoder's sect, the Mennonites, had emigrated in the 19th century to the US and Brazil to avoid conscription as their religious beliefs did not permit military service. In accordance with these beliefs Dr. Yoder urged strongly that he was opposed to all violence.

Bishop Tutu challenged Dr. Yoder's stand, saying "I am not persuaded by your position in favour of non-violence". In taking this position he was not running counter to Christian theology, as already indicated, and was in fact advancing the traditional Christian position of conditional violence. This raised another theological debate, for some blacks argued that the South African regime was continuously guilty of institutional violence. Those who could resort to institutional violence could not reasonably denounce violence committed by liberation movements. If the institutions of the state could in a studied manner resort to planned violence, it did not lie in their mouths to say that others should not use violence in reply.

Dr. Alan Boesak of the Dutch Reformed Mission Church made an impassioned plea for massive civil disobedience and urged the black churches to take the lead.

From this discussion there emerged a further refinement of the civil disobedience idea — the notion of conscientious affirmation of inter-racial fellowship propounded by Dr. Van der Merwe. Dr. Van der Merwe drew a distinction between this notion and that of civil disobedience on the basis that the motivation for conscientious affirmation was positive while civil disobedience was negative. The former was concerned with the promotion of what is right in society, the latter was directed at what is wrong. Conscientious affirmation was concerned with laying the foundations for a healthy, stable, society, and had long term aims unlike the short term aims of civil disobedience.

As with many concepts and practices in South Africa we are probably here in the realm of semantics, for the two concepts often coincide. Yet the new formula has legal and other advantages, for the new notion is based on the conscientious duty to build up a Christian society and this is a dictate of the conscience that results in a personal commitment. It frees the debate of the concept of involvement or inter-meddling in affairs of state and avoids juristic discussions on the legality of laws. If a brush with the law results, that is incidental — it is not the purpose of the exercise.

The new notion attracted considerable public discussion and may give a more acceptable flavour to conduct which may otherwise be classed as civil disobedience.

The Yeast in the Dough

Although white South Africa has come in for heavy criticism in the foregoing pages, the general tenor of this book would have made it clear that there are many admirable elements in White South African society. There is not time enough to refer here to them all, but there are persons and institutions in white South Africa that would put to shame many a civil rights fighter or organisation in countries with a rule-of-law orientation. In South Africa, unlike in the United Kingdom, the United States or Australia for example, liberalism means taking on the establishment, sacrificing career prospects, being labelled a 'Commie', courting banning orders, imprisonment and torture. It means ostracism by the circle in which one has grown up and has one's roots. It requires deep courage and strong convictions.

The white community in South Africa has thrown up such heroes. Bram Fischer, whose grandfather was Judge President and whose father was Prime Minister of the Orange River Colony, threw away all the privileges of one of the most highly privileged Afrikaner families to take up the cause of the blacks in Johannesburg, and died serving a term of life imprisonment. Archbishop Clayton defied the government's racial legislation and made a declaration of open disobedience which could well have changed South Africa's recent history had he not, by a quirk of destiny, collapsed over his desk after signing this document. The Rev. David Russell placed himself under banning orders by defiantly pursuing his work for Black South Africans. The Rev. Bayers Naude, son of one of the founders of the Broederbond and minister of the Dutch Reformed Church, invoked all the wrath of the establishment to which he was born by facing sincerely the issues of conscience which his position and calling constantly thrust before him. Expelled from the church and banned by the State, he offers living witness of Christianity in action. Donald Woods, biographer of Steve Biko and formerly editor of the *Daily Despatch*, courted banning orders, possible imprisonment, loss of career, and exile from the land of his birth to fight for black liberation and inform the world of the plight of black South Africa.

Persons such' as these command respect from all ranks of the black community. They are not compromisers and do not seek merely to improve the status of the blacks within the framework, but to alter the framework itself. Only a few names have been cited, names which are generally known because they have attracted international attention. But there are many, many more, known only in their respective circles whether in Cape Town or Durban, Pretoria or Johannesburg, who are acting as yeast in the flatness of the white South African dough. Cumulatively they exercise an impact and that impact is increasing.

Not the least important are the academics. There are many Afrikaners among them. In their different disciplines — history, sociology, theology, economics, law, to mention a few — they are slowly but surely raising the white community's level of awareness of the injustices the system perpetrates. Steve Biko himself conceded that Afrikaner intellectuals were willing to consider change in their community.[24] In the law, for example, the writings of Van der Vyver, Barend van Niekerk, A.S. Mathews, John Dugard, presenting an unanswerable case for fundamental legal reform, have not produced answers of any depth from the ranks of establishment. In theology, the challenges are meeting with ever weakening responses. In the other disciplines likewise, the intellectuals are stimulating debate and putting the establishment on the defensive. This has not thus far occurred in South Africa on any comparable scale.

But over and above these individuals there are organisations as well which are selflessly working for the upliftment of the blacks. Some of them attract radical black criticism on the basis that they only tend to prolong apartheid by making it sweeter. Blacks do not want a lightening of their fetters. They demand their removal; and hence work which is directed at amelioration rather than fundamental change does not always command their approval. "We are accustomed to suffering and can take a little more for a purpose" runs their argument.

Still it cannot be gainsaid that a great social service task is being performed by a number of organisations of dedicated whites. Those who have attended some of their offices, as the author had the privilege of doing, can testify to the harrowing tales of human suffering where the only source of relief to which the sufferer can turn is an office like the Athlone legal aid office or the office of Dependants' Conference. It would be unfair to the people who dedicate their lives to this kind of service to decry their work. While fundamental change is imperative, the sort of relief these people dispense is of great humanitarian value. Nor would it be fair to these organisations to take the view that they contribute nothing to the reform of the system. They keep raising levels of community awareness and contribute their share to the massive cumulative effort that the circumstances demand.

The work of two of these organisations is briefly described in the ensuing sections.

The Black Sash Movement

The Black Sash Movement started as a movement of conscience and protest during the days when the Appeal Court was packed and the Senate enlarged in order to take coloured people off the common voters' roll. Since then it has worked consistently and devotedly in order to promote equity in South African society, and it has been uncompromising on the issue of civil rights.

It furnishes an opportunity for creative dissent and has many achievements to its credit, not the least of which is that it offers an avenue of service in a society where there is a blocking off of all such opportunities.

In the early days of the Black Sash Movement, thousands of women marched through the streets of Johannesburg. They trekked to the Union building and camped out there in the open for two nights in order to hand a petition to the Prime Minister. Hundreds of cars came in convoys from all corners of the country converging on Cape Town. On hundreds of occasions they have stood in silent protest at public places and outside Parliament, sometimes performing vigils of several days and nights around a flame of liberty.

The Black Sash Movement will shortly celebrate its twenty fifth year of operation. There are some who will decry its efforts claiming that it is not radical enough and that it still attempts to work within the establishment rather than to overthrow it. It is to be remembered however, that the movement has aimed consistently at removing or preventing unjust legislation and has not been prepared to compromise on any matter of principle.

Apart from protest, the Movement also has to its credit the establishment of advice offices where victims of unjust laws can turn for sympathy and perhaps legal assistance. It also maintains extremely valuable records built up over the years especially in the field of influx control.

One of the governing philosophies behind this sort of movement is that, while it protests against injustice, it provides also a mechanism for immediate help and assistance to many, many thousands who have cause to be grateful to it throughout their lives. It also adds to the fund of goodwill which may one day stand between South Africa and disaster or violent revolution.

Mr. R. de Villiers, Chairman of the Cape Western Region of the South African Institute of Race Relations, in an address to the 1979 Black Sash Conference spoke also of another dimension of the philosophy underlying this kind of movement. "Of course protest pays. But I would go further and say that even if it didn't seem to pay it would still be imperative to make it. Why? Because it gives fresh heart to those whose cause is being defended or espoused, it gives encouragement to those helped, and it helps to sustain the faith of those who do the work. All that is important, for without it the forces of reaction or of evil or of destruction would operate without any restraint at all".

Dependants' Conference

Dependants' Conference was formed in 1963 to help the families of the many hundreds of people arrested for political offences. This organisation, initially funded through the churches, became in 1970 a part of the South African Council of Churches.

Since 1963 it has given breadline subsistence to families while the breadwinner was serving his sentence. In many cases this assistance has been continued even after the release of the breadwinner, in consequence of the very real difficulties experienced by ex-political prisoners in finding employment. Appreciating these difficulties, the Conference has launched on schemes to rehabilitate such people by commencing farming ventures, transport businesses and small factories.

In the sphere of education as well, the Conference has been active and has helped not only with the education of ex-prisoners but also with the education of children whose fathers are in prison.

Perhaps the most striking part of the work of Dependants' Conference is the effort they make to enable members of families of political prisoners to visit detainees and thus keep up their spirits by showing them that their families still retain an interest in them. This is especially important in the case of long-term prisoners who may be serving sentences ranging to fifty years or even more. The families are often resident in distant homelands and even the effort of arranging one family member's visit involves considerable expense in transport, accommodation and incidental expenditure.

It is a memorable experience for a visitor to visit the office of Dependants' Conference and speak to family members who have been brought from distant homelands to see members of their family in detention. On one visit I met a young man, twenty years of age, who had come to see his brother, a boy of eighteen, who was in detention under a prison term of 140 years. Some of the various sentences imposed on him were concurrent, in consequence of which his total term of detention was to be 42 years. In any event this man would not come out until his late fifties, when every spark of independence in his being would perhaps have been extinguished. People in this predicament need moral support and the confidence that their families have not lost interest in them. It is to be remembered also that for detainees on Robben Island, remissions are never made in the term of their sentence.

Dependants' Conference also assists in legal defence and immediately after the Soweto uprisings assisted an estimated 600 people in this way.

The Conference assists also with funeral expenses,

with monthly grants to families who have lost their bread-winner, with assistance in payment of bail moneys and also in payment of a portion of the fines imposed.

The political importance of the work of Dependants' Conference can be gathered from the fact that the cream of South African leadership is on Robben Island. These detainees have a particularly high level of education, many being the holders of two degrees, if not doctorates. Nelson Mandela has been there fifteen years. They can constitute the future leadership of black South Africa and it is of vital importance that their morale should be kept high.

Only first degree relatives are permitted visits, that is, father, mother, brother, sister, wife, husband or child. No one under sixteen is permitted on Robben Island even as a visitor, and consequently many children now seventeen are seeing their father for the first time since their infancy. Many of the prisoners are life prisoners — and in South Africa a life sentence on a political prisoner really means life. Consequently there is no hope of their ever seeing their families except in circumstances such as Dependants' Conference have been able to organise.

Among the cases Dependants' Conference cites as illustrations of the potential leadership on Robben Island are those of a man who entertained a cousin charged with terrorism and paid his rail fare, in consequence of which he himself was later accused of terrorism. He was given a sentence of seven years and in the course of serving that sentence he has now collected two degrees. In another instance, eleven children between the ages of eleven and fifteen were walking from Cape Town intending to make their way to Swaziland where they felt they could get a better education. They were arrested near the border and detained. One of them was found not guilty and released after two and a half years' detention. The others found themselves on Robben Island.

A special significance of Dependants' Conference is its preoccupation with the victims of South Africa's iniquitous statute book. There is stark human misery in many countries but in most instances it is the direct result of poverty or natural catastrophe, which in some instances have led to dictatorships aggravating these miseries. South Africa suffers from neither poverty nor natural catastrophe but from the miseries created by its own statute book. It is appropriate therefore that some organisations at least should concentrate on alleviating the misery thus caused — not merely to the immediate victims but to their families, who are in most instances as hard hit as the immediate victims themselves.

Three cases cited in Dependants' Conference leaflets are here reproduced in order to show the sort of humanitarian work this Conference undertakes.

(a) Mr X was shot thrice in the arm by the police. He has had three operations so far, and has still not regained the use of his arm. He is married with four children to support, and at the time of his being shot his wife was expecting her fourth child. Charges against him were first withdrawn and then he was later charged with public violence and was found not guilty. During the time he was hospitalized the family had a small income of 20 rand per week from the wife's earnings, but as she was pregnant she had to leave her job and their income was nil. X approached Dependants' Conference for assistance, and his family have been assisted since October 1976.

(b) Y is 25 years of age and was shot in the back in November, 1976. He spent two months in hospital and was the sole supporter of the family as his father died in 1965. The Conference has assisted him with payments of hospital accounts and a monthly grant payable until Y resumes work.

(c) Z was detained in January, 1977, and was brought to court in June, 1977, charged with arson. He was found guilty and sentenced to three years in prison. While he was in detention the family was assisted with a monthly grant, and the Conference also paid a hire-purchase account which Z's wife could not pay due to lack of funds. The Conference felt that if the family lost the goods bought on hire-purchase this would be an irreparable loss, especially because the hire-purchase had been paid for more than a year. Employment has been found for Z's wife at a restaurant but her income is still not enough to maintain her six children. The Conference assists with rental and a monthly grant.

Should there ever be another riot or another Soweto, the work of the Conference will increase several-fold.

The Conference points out that 30 rand a month will assist a family to keep alive, and is the maximum grant that they are able to give. Many ladies are working very hard at keeping Dependants' Conference active and they do need appreciation and support.

The Erasmus Commission Report

All the world is aware of the scandal now commonly called "Muldergate" which in South Africa resulted in the fall of a President as Watergate did in America. The scandal erupted when Mr. Justice Mostert of the Supreme Court, conducting a one man inquiry into the operation of a secret multi-million dollar slush fund within the Department of Information, boldly laid bare a number of startling facts. Some of these had already been vaguely suspected, but the restrictive laws of the country had made disclosure difficult and dangerous. It was now no longer possible for officialdom to deny them.

The disclosures resulted in the public becoming aware
a) that the Information Department had illegally financed the start of a pro-government Johannesburg daily, *The Citizen;*
b) that funds had been misused to the extent of millions of dollars;
c) that a front company known as Thor Communications had been dishonestly started to cover up the operation;
d) that there had been irregular property purchases and irregular travel arrangements by members of the government.

For the first time a Cabinet member of South Africa's ruling National Party — Dr. Cornelius P. Mulder, Minister of Plural Relations — was forced to resign in disgrace. Mulder had been Minister of the Interior and Information under the previous Prime Minister, John Vorster, later the State President.

The government strained hard to prevent the ripples from spreading. Justice Mostert was publicly dismissed. The government was forced to appoint another commission of inquiry and this was headed by Mr. Justice Erasmus also of the Supreme Court.

The Erasmus Commission held that Vorster, now State President, was fully aware of the covert operation and of the illegal and secret spending of tens of millions of dollars to influence the media. The commission also concluded that Vorster had lied in sworn testimony concerning his role in the whole affair. The commission held that the South African government had not been able to account for 6.3 million dollars out of a sum of ten million dollars of government funds that went into an unsuccessful attempt to take over the Washington *Star* in 1974. Vorster, like Mulder, resigned in disgrace, his last act as President being to receive the report that compelled him to resign.

"Muldergate" has been hailed as a milestone of openness in South African government and as a demonstration of the power of truth and public opinion even against the government of South Africa.

While the episode undoubtedly bears resemblances to Watergate and demonstrates that considerations of propriety and fairplay do, in some ways, carry weight in South Africa, it is the contrast rather than the similarity to Watergate that stands out.

Watergate could have depended on investigative reporting and editorial courage. With all respect to the English language daily, the Rand Daily Mail, which led the way in pursuing the scandal, the legal restraints on its freedom of action were far too severe to permit it the openness of criticism that was possible in America. But for the findings of Mr. Justice Mostert, it is uncertain that the matter would ever have reached a point where the government was compelled to act.

Watergate was an inquiry conducted in the full blaze of world publicity. Muldergate was inquired into by government appointed commissioners often in secrecy or semi-secrecy. Watergate demonstrated that pure rule-of-law mechanisms such as subpoenas on the President were adequate to bring the President to book despite his claim of privilege. Muldergate, if at all, highlighted judicial inadequacies to deal with such claims. If the Muldergate issues had been taken to court, a claim by the executive that the matter involved official privilege would in all probability have ended the inquiry. Such a claim only strengthened the inquiry in the United States. Watergate resulted in the processes of government becoming yet more fair and open. Muldergate resulted in a tightening up, even to the extent of legislation drastically limiting the power of the press to investigate clandestine government operations. Watergate highlighted the right of the Amercian citizen to obtain information regarding governmental affairs. Muldergate highlighted the rightlessness of the South African citizen in the same field.[25]

Lastly, in regard to the Erasmus Commission itself, often hailed as another milestone on the road to freedom in South Africa. As Professor A.S. Mathews has observed in his paper on the Commission,[26] the real credit must go to the Mostert revelations, which made further denial impossible. Furthermore, the Erasmus Commission took the dec-

ision to hold its inquiries in camera. What is most important, however, is that the Commission glosses over some of
the most glaring deficiencies of the South African governmental system which it had every opportunity to criticise.
For example, it accepts uncritically the new legislation
which declares that every government department may have
secret funds.   It does not point out the vast network of
repressive legislation and secret laws which made Mulder-
gates possible in the past and will make them possible in the
future.   The Commission   did not point to the desirability
of a right to information in the public.

Granted all these defects, Muldergate is certainly
revealing in that it highlighted a deep-seated public expectation that honesty and integrity should prevail in high
places. If this aspect of the white South African conscience
can be touched and the lack of honesty and integrity in the
whole planning and structure of the legal system can be
brought home, there is yet hope for South Africa.

The Resilience of the Afrikaner

Those who advocate the need for exploring every
avenue of peaceful change are invariably met with the argument that the Afrikaner is intransigent. He will preserve
his privileges and fight for them even to the point of death
for himself and annihilation for white South Africa.

Two views are possible on this question, and opinion has differed sharply, some holding him to be a die-hard
and others believing him to be flexible. The view that the
South African situation is hopeless rests largely on the acceptance of the first assumption. This needs to be re-exam-
ined.

There is much to be said for the view that the Afrikaner is a pragmatist. His history has consistently been one
of reconciling himself to the inevitable and then seeking
other practical options. When British dominance of the
Cape became inevitable the Afrikaner reconciled himself to
this situation and commenced his great trek. This was an
option open to him which, however difficult, he chose as
the only means of preserving his way of life. When the
British sought to encroach on his new territory he resisted
the British, knowing that on his own ground his military
strength gave him a chance of survival. When the British
nearly defeated, brought in the full strength of their arms,
the Afrikaners capitulated in an effort to preserve by treaty
the options that were closed by war. When independence

came and in time they found themselves in power, they realised that if they were to preserve their privileges they needed to build a wall around themselves, and so devised and strengthened apartheid. But the inevitable is closing in on them again. The wall is cracking and even the most sanguine among them must see that it is not long before it will be massively breached. What then will the Afrikaner do? He will have no unexplored frontiers into which to trek, no defensive *laager*, physical or legal, into which to retreat. He will need to come to terms with his surroundings and devise a *modus vivendi* which will give him the maximum benefit. There can be no doubt that the pragmatist in him sees the writing on the wall and is already preparing himself internally for it. He will of course make public pronouncements of defending himself and his way of life to the death, but if past history means anything — and history is ingrained in the Afrikaner — he must know that, as in the Boer War, there is a point at which resistance becomes impossible and negotiation a necessity. As a perceptive writer has recently observed,[27] "the South African system of pragmatic racial domination is rather flexible in accommodating pressure and adjusting to new situations outside dogmatic racial ideologies".

It seems a mistake to assume that the Afrikaner is incapable of change. He could not have survived so long and so dangerously if he did not have the resilience for making adaptations necessary for survival. That is the author's view — which of course can be dissented from. But what cannot be dissented from is the proposition that one should avoid any attempts to convert the Afrikaner on the basis that the opposite proposition is unarguably true. At best the opposite proposition is open to argument and therefore uncertain. It cannot therefore be used as the justification for shutting the door to every avenue of peaceful conversion which can still at this late hour be attempted.

There is a mistake also in the assumption that the Parliamentary caucus of the governing Nationalist Party truly reflects the views of Nationalist Party supporters on the question of power sharing with the blacks. As a party elected on an apartheid platform it tends to stop up any crevices in orthodox apartheid doctrine, lest the structure itself should fall. Charged with a commission to support it, it can make fewer concessions than individual supporters can. It will therefore deny power sharing with blacks even though there may be a substantial number among its supporters who do not favour a denial of such power sharing. A recent survey by Professor H. Lever showed that although the government constitutional proposals left the blacks out of power-sharing altogether, 57 per cent of Nationalists felt the need for a new political dispensation for urban blacks. Although the government is firmly committed to the Homelands policy, only 17 per cent of Nationalist supporters saw this as a total solution of the problem of power sharing for urban blacks. Further, nearly 60 per cent of Nationalists oppose government policy and believe that blacks should be allowed to own land in white areas.[28] Official government policies must not hence be taken as true reflections of the actual thinking of the Afrikaner who may in fact be somewhat more ready for change than the government would be prepared to admit. This is perhaps one reason why the writer did not see, in conversations with a wide variety of Afrikaners, an attitude of blind unreason such as he had expected to encounter before he arrived in South Africa. Almost without exception, but with varying degrees of reservation, they conceded the inevitability of major change and the impossibility of a continuance of the present state of privilege.

A useful pointer to change in progress is that the percentage of whites who advocate power sharing with the blacks has risen from one fifth in 1974 to one third in 1977.[29] The change that has taken place between 1977 and 1980 perhaps brings this number to a position close to the halfway mark. A further change could well tilt the crucial balance and cause dramatic changes in South Africa. Such possibilities are well worth working towards.

It is submitted that it is a mistake to look upon the Nationalist government, entrenched though it be, as representing a solid phalanx of unchangeable opinion.

A Change of Heart — Is it possible?

Alan Paton at the 50th Anniversary Conference of the South African Institute of Race Relations declared rather emphatically that there was still ground for hope. "I cannot bring myself to believe that the Afrikaner Nationalist, or should I say the leaders of Afrikaner nationalism, cannot see that Afrikanerdom is at the crisis of its history" he said. "I cannot believe that the people who achieved nationhood after a long and bitter struggle, who faced each other with courage and intelligence, who picked themselves up from the dust after the defeat of their Republic, cannot face with courage and intelligence this greatest crisis in their history".

He condemned as the great obstructing factors, white fear, white pride, white greed. These three factors operating together produced an inertia that has been characteristic of South African rule in the last few years.

With a deep sense of history he pointed out that South Africa's history has been one of conquest, but although it was a history of conquest in the past it was by a political and not a military conquest, in which no gun was fired and no spear was thrown, that all South Africa was taken over by the National Party in 1948. However, the world has since then undergone a profound change. The relationship of conqueror and conquered no longer governs the attitudes of people one to another. If the white people of South Africa based their claim over the blacks upon conquest, that claim cannot be sustained. "The relationship of conqueror and conquered won't do anymore".

His speech was in effect a challenge to white South Africa to refute the contention that a white change of heart was a ridiculous expectation. Though the critics might point out that one could ransack the history books without finding an example of a change in heart of rulers, he thought that such a change was possible in South Africa. "Let me sound a sombre note; if there is another conqueror, then God help South Africa and all its peoples. That is why conquest must be undone, by us, not by anyone else".

It is true that no power holders in history have willingly given up their power except under pressure. What pressures can there be upon the present government to achieve such a result?

a) The pressure of the realisation that it is within the power of the blacks to paralyse and cripple South Africa. The blacks will cause themselves immeasurable harm in the process but the whites and their property will be destroyed. Moreover this threat has a sword-of-Damocles ring, for no one knows at what moment black South Africa will decide to rise. Its patience has been tried to breaking point and the government knows this.

b) The fear that foreign action can synchronise with internal unrest and produce a situation which will wear out South Africa's armed power.

c) The confused situation on the border, where apart from soldiers from other black African countries, thousands of escaped South Africans are reputed to be also training and under arms.

d) The example of Iran where, with one of the world's most massive military machines at his disposal, the Shah could not contain the anger of a population with whom he had fallen out of dialogue.

e) The fall of the White dominated South African buffer states—Zimbabwe, Angola, Mozambique and a confused Namibian situation.

f) The example of Angola and Zimbabwe where dialogue with the black leaders was so delayed as to make eventual settlement difficult. In Zimbabwe for example, even as Ian Smith delayed, Bishop Muzorewa's support weakened and Nkomo became more difficult to talk with. Delay in South Africa in establishing a dialogue only worsens the situation and South Africa realises this.

g) World pressure, which South Africa affects to be unconcerned with, but with which she is in fact deeply concerned. The boycott in the field of sport has had telling effects on South African pride, and South Africa earnestly desires to rejoin the company of the civilised world rather than remain an outcast. It is extremely sensitive, in a proud sort of way, to its universal condemnation.

h) The fear that foreign encouragement and propaganda can incite a black uprising.

i) The fear that further delay in mending the situation can lead to the spread of internal communism.

j) The inability to find any continued ideological justification for its stance.

k) The failure of the homelands policy which was the king pin of its earlier plan for a separation of the races. The presence of ten million urban blacks puts paid to this plan as an ultimate solution. With its failure the whole scheme falls apart and the urban African must also be recognised as a future power sharer.

For all these reasons and perhaps many more it seems a fair inference that the government is anxious to start dialogue with the blacks. Yet there is an obstacle, for the homelands policy and separate development of the races, the inspired brain child of its prophetic leaders, cannot in one fell swoop be jettisoned. The Afrikaner's pride, and his sense of mission and inspired leadership do not as yet permit this. He is looking around for a formula on the basis of which he can commence discussion without admitting that his prophets and high priests misled him. He will not make this admission immediately and is hence speaking now in terms of removal of some of the petty inconveniences of apartheid. Once the process gets under way and builds up momentum there is prospect of more substantial concessions in the next two or three years.

Whether black South Africa will wait for white South Africa to make up its face-saving formulae is problematic. Its patience has run out and it is surprising it has waited so long. It is to be hoped that Alan Paton is correct and that the pressures we have set out will combine with the hopes he has expressed, to help white South Africa rather than the outside world to undo its conquests.

FOOTNOTES

1. Since the time of writing it has been announced that the S.A. Mental and Dental Council is inquiring into the conduct of two of the state doctors who attended Biko and that a Pretoria judge has dismissed an application by the Chief District Surgeon and the Principal District Surgeon of Port Elizabeth who had tried to stop the Council from inquiring into their conduct — London Times, Dec. 17, 1979.
2. Cape Times, Aug.21, 1979.
3. *The Australian*, p.9, quoting *The Guardian*, London.
4. The population distribution among the whites is approximately 57 per cent Afrikaner, 37 per cent English speaking and others 6 per cent.
5. Munger, *Afrikaner and African Nationalism*, 63.
6. Survey by the German Arnold Berrgstraesser Institut, referred to in Mathew Midlane, "The Crisis Facing South Africa", *The Round Table*, Commonwealth Journal of International Affairs, April, 1979, p.107 at 116.
7. Munger, *Afrikaner and African Nationalism*, 64, assesses 'English' control at four-fifths in 1967.
8. Leo Marquard, *The Peoples and Policies of South Africa*, OUP, 1969, p.62.
9. Marquard, *ibid.*
10. See R.H. Tawney, *Religion and the Rise of Capitalism*, p.102.
11. W.H. Vatcher, *White Laager*, p.110.
12. The *Guardian*, Sept. 29, 1979.
13. See p.89.
14. See p.12.
15. See Bonn, *The Crumbling of Empire*, 1938, p.40, and the present author's *Equality and Freedom*, p.53.
16. See Bernard Zylstra's interview with Steve Biko, December-January 1977-78, *Canadian Forum*, 15.
17. See p.156 *infra*.

18.   Jill Johnson and Peter Magubane, *Soweto,* pp.118-122.
19.   Named after Rev. Leon Sullivan of the Zionist Baptist Church
       who was instrumental in persuading twelve of the biggest
       U.S. firms operating in South Africa to accept a set of prin-
       ciples ending segregation and job discrimination. The com-
       panies were Otis Elevator, Minnesota Mining, Union Carbide,
       IBM, Ford, International Harvester, American Cyanamid,
       Citibank, Burroughs, Caltex, General Motors, and Mobil Oil.
       Many more firms later subscribed to these principles.
20.   *1978 Survey of Race Relations,* 257.
21.   *1977 Survey of Race Relations,* 190.
22.   *U.S. Corporate Interests in Africa,* Report to the Committee
       on Foreign Relations, U.S. Senate, U.S. Government Printing
       Office, Washington, 1978.
23.   That the Codes are not satisfying the blacks of the absence of
       discrimination was shown recently when the international
       press on Jan.12, 1980 reported that 700 black workers had
       walked out in protest at racial discrimination from the Ford
       motor company's plant in Johannesburg, Thozamile Botha, a
       leader in this movement was later detained by security police,
       arrested as he was about to address a meeting to discuss in-
       dustrial action in Port Elizabeth.
24.   See his interview with Bernard Zylstra, 1977-78 *Canadian
       Forum* 15 at 20.
25.   I have drawn on Professor A.S. Mathews address on The Eras-
       mus Commission Report delivered at the Annual General
       Meeting of the Natal Region of the S.A. Institute of Race
       Relations on March 21, 1979, for many of the ideas in this
       discussion.
26.   See note 25 above.
27.   H. Adam, "Ideologies of Dedication versus Blueprints of Ex-
       perience" *Social Dynamics,* vol.2, no.2, 1976, p.84-5.
28.   These figures are quoted by Mathew Midlane, "The Crisis
       Facing South Africa", *The Round Table,* The Commonwealth
       Journal of International Affairs, April, 1979, 107 at 116. They
       come mainly from a statistical survey appearing in the Eastern
       Province *Herald* of June 12 and 19, 1978.
29.   Midlane, *ibid.*

CHAPTER   **5**

Black South Africa

Soweto

Soweto is a vital nerve-centre of the world political scene. What happens in Soweto today shapes the fate of South Africa tomorrow and on the fate of South Africa hang many major problems of the African continent and the world.

Soweto is a crucible of black aspirations. In its intense concentration of urban Africans and in the white heat of its sufferings, a new philosophy and a new determination are being forged which no physical weaponry can resist. It is a privilege to visit Soweto and catch even a glimpse of the beat of life in that sprawling expanse of black vitality.[1]

Soweto is unique. It is no mere replica of tribal African life re-enacted in an urban ghetto. Nor is it a replica of the Western oriented urban lifestyles one sees so often among the black population of American cities. It draws its institutions and traditions fresh from a dozen tribal cultures, mixes them with their Western counterparts, and welds the whole together amidst the urgencies and stresses of the black urban situation. The result is a phenomenon of throbbing power.

The Sowetan black, especially the younger Sowetan, is a confident breed. The togetherness of nearly two million people packed in one township under a common set of grievances justly felt, is a force which the planners of apartheid did not envisage or reckon with. Its collective will cannot, in its escalating intensity, be forever contained in a straitjacket of white regimentation. It is truly a matter of amazement, that a conclusion which strikes a foreigner as so patently obvious, has not seeped through to the majority white consciousness in South Africa.

The Sowetan has settled into a relaxed urban lifestyle shorn of the uneasiness that characterises colonial peoples in white dominated society. Three or four *shebeens* (pubs) flourish on every street in Soweto. They are all illegal and constantly raided by the Liquor Squad, but if one is closed down another opens down the street the next day. The Sowetan cherishes his *shebeen* which is warm and friendly, unlike the cold impersonal beerhalls, representative of alien culture and domination, which were burnt down during the riots. "They can bring the army here, but they won't close the *shebeens*" is a commonly heard comment, typical of the defiantly independent attitudes of Soweto.

Soweto is alive in literature, theatre, music, painting, sculpture. In each one of these are blended the old and the new, the tribal and the Western, suffering and aspiration, lamentation and hope. Nine hundred churches tend their flocks in Soweto as do five hundred *sangomas* or witch doctors. Young gangsters called *tsotsis* pickpocket and stab on streets and trains while young intellectuals plan selflessly for the day when the black man comes into his own in South Africa.

Soweto is not only the most important of the black townships. It has also passed into world consciousness as symbolising freedom movements both in South Africa and in the wider world.

Afrikaans, the language of the master race, was by decree of the Department of Bantu Education in 1974, to become the language of instruction in secondary schools. English, the lingua franca in which Africans of different tribes communicated with each other, was also the language of protest against apartheid. If English was to be displaced in favour of Afrikaans, this extension of authority of the master race was not to occur without resistance from the young people of Soweto. "We are fed the crumbs of ignorance with Afrikaans as a poisonous spoon" they proclaimed in banner headlines. Soweto erupted in protest. Several thousands of students demonstrated peacefully. Police replied with teargas and bullets. The dead children of Soweto now belong to world history and there is no purpose in recording here what has been recorded in thousands of writings across the world. All that need be added here, from a visitor's impressions, is that the memory of the hundreds (local recollection places it at thousands) of deaths is still fresh and that the community is alive with tales of mounds of dead bodies, mass graves, mass funerals and of wards full of dead and dying children. The spirit of defiance has not been suppressed by the shootings, and some of the defiance of the young has been absorbed by elders who till then had resisted it.

Soweto unleashed a chain of events whose full implications are yet to be seen. On the one hand it extracted from the government a number of concessions — for example on the language of instruction — which might not otherwise have been possible. On the other hand the government was able to tighten and perfect its plans for the repression of the Sowetos of the future. It served notice on the white community that the patience of the blacks was running out. It served notice on the black community that conciliation and compromise would not be the methodology of the future. It served notice on the world that black South Africa was stirring and that South Africa was a potential powder keg. It was a world event of startling importance.

Crossroads

Crossroads is both important in its own right and symbolic. It has been referred to, symbolically, as a crossroads in modern South African history. It typifies many of the problems of black South Africa. The Crossroads problem arose in this way.

Government policy, that blacks should not live in urban areas, meant that Cape Town's existing black townships, Langa, Nyanga and Guguletu saw no new construction of family houses since 1966. There was an official waiting list of 1,400 families. Existing houses — two bedroom, generally — were overcrowded with up to fourteen people per house. Migrant labourers were expected to live in mammoth unisex dormitories, eight, or more often, sixteen, to a room and seeing their families two weeks a year.

The desire of wives and families to be with their menfolk, legally or illegally, compounded the problem. The result was that, as had happened before in modern South African history, the people constructed dwellings in various locations hoping to build new townships where families could live together. Modderdam, Werkgenot, Unibell and Crossroads were among these.

This of course was contrary to government policy. Systematically the government set about demolishing Modderdam, Werkgenot and Unibell, depriving 25,000 persons resident there not only of shelter but of the comfort of being with their families.

The 20,000 inhabitants of Crossroads were told officially to dismantle their shacks and return to the homelands. By June 1978 the newspapers were reporting that despite all appeals not just from residents, but from responsible church, social, politcal and other substantial sources "it seems likely the juggernaut is about to roll again".[2] Early one morning police and inspectors in several vans surrounded the camp from about 5 a.m., stopped people on their way to work and arrested those without passes. The use of the communal taps which serve the entire community was denied to them.

A delegation met senior Administration Board officials. "Every day they come to Crossroads and arrest our people. We can't go to doctors or clinics, and we can't even use the taps," they complained.

Still the authorities appeared unswervingly determined to clear Crossroads by the end of the year. The Divisional Council which administered Crossroads as an emergency camp and the Administration Board served notices on all residents warning them the end was coming and asking them to make "timeous arrangements" to leave. In one hundred or so cases where husband and wife both qualified to live in the area, they were to be allowed to move their shacks to a vacant area between Nyanga and Guguletu.

Men lawfully working in the area but living illegally with their "permitless" wives were to report to the unisex dormitories and to send their wives back to Transkei, Ciskei or wherever they came from, despite the fact that some of them had lived in the area for twenty or more years. The government in its magnanimity was prepared to give such people rail warrants to travel to their appropriate areas.[3] To qualify for this concession one had to prove registration in Crossroads. If one was merely a squatter in another person's shack one would not qualify for a warrant.[4]

It is significant that in the course of the year, one of the methods resorted to by the police was to charge men whose permits were in order with "harbouring" their wives. There were fifty-eight such cases. The others arrested in droves in pre-dawn raids, were charged in the court at Langa.[5] There were 477 such cases and almost all the accused were sentenced to fines of R.50 and in default 50 days' imprisonment. "Attorneys battled against impossible odds to represent these unfortunates with pleas in mitigation. It was impossible to interview the accused before they appeared in the dock, and attempts at cross questioning at that stage failed dismally. Much distress was caused to all concerned".[6] On the morning of September 14, 1978 under a pall of tear gas, 400 fresh arrests were made. They were charged and dealt with in the Langa court. The penalties, heavy and remorseless as before, are thought in September alone to have earned for the government R.40,000 from this impoverished community.[7] Many are thought to have lost their jobs and much pay as well owing to their confinement in police and prison cells.

The matter had reached such a pass even by July 1978 that a day of prayer was called for the people of Crossroads. In preparation for this even some pastors of Crossroads issued a leaflet so poignant and so reminiscent of Hebrew lamentations of the days of bondage that it is quoted in full:

"We, Ministers and Priests responsible for the pastoral care of members of our congregations at Crossroads, feel bound by our calling to speak out once again about the situation at the Emergency Camp, where the family life of 20,000 people is under immediate threat.

Our people at Crossroads are being persecuted for trying to live a normal family life.

It is their Christian right and duty to seek to live together as families. We call upon those in authority to hear and obey the Word of God:

'What God has joined together let no one put asunder'. (Matt.19.6)

What does this say about the sickness of this land, that a man can be brought before the courts for harbouring his wife?

Such a law stands in direct contradiction to the The Word of Jesus and challenges those in authority:

'Why do you disobey God's command, and follow your own teaching?' (Matt. 15.3)

Our people at Crossroads are being persecuted because they are black.

Where else in the world are people denied the right to live as families because of the colour of their skin? Yet this is happening here in Cape Town — This is why the authorities refuse to allow wives and families to live with their husbands

Jesus wept for Jerusalem.

We believe he weeps over this city when he sees families being told to separate — when he sees people singled out for this cruel and unChristian treatment because they are black.

We appeal once again to those in authority not to discriminate against black families at Crossroads, but to allow them to live together here in Cape Town near their places of work.

A PRAYER FOR THE PEOPLE OF CROSSROADS

O God our Father, who made of one blood all people on earth, we pray at this time for the healing of South Africa.
We lift up to you the people of Crossroads Camp.
Send your Holy Spirit to be a power of hope and faith in them.
Protect and save these your people
That they may rejoice in you, Father, Lord of all.
Bless them and strengthen them as they seek to live in peace
Together as families, in obedience to your command:
Those whom you have joined together, let no one put asunder.
Father Almighty, stay the hand of those who seek to scatter your sheep.
Touch the hearts of all in authority, that they may hear your Word and find your Son, Jesus Christ, in their neighbour.
Lord hear our prayer, and let our cry come unto thee.
Lord, have mercy
We have failed in love of our neighbour,
Failed in our love of you, Lord.
Cleanse us, rid us of fear, indifference, selfrighteousness,
and a sense of hopelessness.
Fill us
With your Spirit of hope,
With faith in your power to save and transform,
And with your love which enables us to do all things —
offering our very selves that we, your people, may find and build your peace and justice —
free in fellowship one with another.

We praise you, O God.
We give thanks to you.
Your will be done
Your Kingdom come
AMEN."

The Crossroads problem, more than any other, focussed government attention on the impossibility of implementing apartheid's grand dream of transferring all the urban blacks to the homelands. The government realised it had to accept the presence of some at least of these teeming millions and that a start needed to be made somewhere. Crossroads was fortunate in that it occurred just when this realisation was dawning and at a time when tokens of a change of heart were required. In a grand gesture there came a dramatic reversal of official attitudes towards Crossroads. The Minister concerned visited Crossroads, appeared on the same platform as its leaders and announced that Crossroads would not be demolished. Temporary residence permits were to be issued in favour of all residents of Crossroads, entitling them to live there for six months. Employers of Crossroads residents who obtained these permits would be free of prosecution. The Minister promised a new township for the residents as the Board would decide which of the residents qualified for entry into the new township.

But this was only a temporary interlude. What was to happen after six months was still problematical. The officials patrolling the borders of Crossroads refused on many occasions to recognise the permits issued under this dispensation, saying that they were not recognised passes. Many a Crossroads resident was ordered off the roads by such officials, and they had nowhere to turn for relief. The survey of residents was said to be completed at a certain stage and by September 1979 it was being announced that unless Crossroads residents had a "very good excuse" for not already having applied for a temporary residence permit, they would no longer be able to obtain one.

The people of Crossroads have organised themselves well for the struggle ahead. They will need to ensure the acceptance into the new township of the maximum number of Crossroads residents. They will need to ensure that the rents in the new township will not be exorbitant. They will need to ensure that ministerial promises are honoured by ministerial underlings.

The community is united and has from its inception shown a marked capacity for the ordered administration of its affairs. An election held in August 1979 resulted in the election of Mr. Johnson Nxgobongwana, who polled 5837 votes as opposed to his two rivals' polls of less than a hundred each. The community thus had an unofficial mayor. It is remarkably crime-free. The people have built their own schools and churches, and run literacy classes, craft groups, sports clubs, women's centres. They have set up within the community, dress making establishments, furniture shops, car and shoe repair shops, small grocery stores. It is a viable, Christian, law-abiding community. If the South African government does not keep trust with this community it will have demonstrated its total inability to negotiate with the black community. It is the government of South Africa that is on test at Crossroads.

Robben Island

One of the grim realities behind the life of blacks in South Africa is this little island, lying off Cape Town. It is one of the most vital symbols of black South Africa's struggle.

On this island, South Africa's maximum security prison for black political activists, there have languished Mandela, Sisulu, Mbeki, Motsoaledi, Mlangeni, Toivo, Tuhadeleni and many others. Many of them intellectuals of high calibre, all of them collectively representing the flower of black leadership, they live out the remainder of their lives labouring in the quarries or collecting seaweed from the cold Atlantic. Shut off from their people, they are nevertheless an ever-present reality, for their spirit and their ideals permeate black South Africa.

On 29 January 1980, the Department of Prisons released figures showing that 489 political prisoners are currently serving sentences on Robben Island. Of them all are black except for eight coloureds and ten Asians. Their terms of imprisonment range from two years to life imprisonment. "Life imprisonment" in the context of Robben Island means "life imprisonment". No reprieves are expected and none are given.

Political prisoners are cut off from the outside world not merely physically. They are not permitted radio, television or newspapers and even non-political magazines are censored.

Nor are all the detainees on Robben Island convicted prisoners. Many are there otherwise than by judicial decree. Robert Sobukwe, for example, after an initial term of three years' imprisonment, was detained on Robben Island by an Act of Parliament for a further period of six years.

Black South Africans who have served a term on Robben Island come back to the community with a halo of martyrdom that keeps warmly glowing for years. The experience and its implications of courage and high principle are looked upon by many as an almost indispensable qualification for black leadership. Nelson Mandela is widely looked upon as a potential Prime Minister of South Africa, if there is a transition to black rule.

In 1977 the Government allowed five journalists to visit Robben Island in an effort to convince the world the prison was not as bad as generally believed. There are indeed reports of relaxations of some of its rigours, especially after the Biko episode. But Robben Island is still a foremost symbol of South African repression.

The Wife of the Political Prisoner

We have referred elsewhere to the manner in which the families of political prisoners are cut off from their menfolk, often for life. The authorities often do not stop at this. Where the wife or the family are known to be active sympathisers with the prisoner, they are often themselves the subject of persecution.

An outstanding instance is the fate of Mrs. Winnie Mandela, wife of the internationally known Nelson Mandela, a life term prisoner on Robben Island since 1964.[8] The way in which pressure can be progressively applied in an attempt to break even the most resolute spirit, is well worth recounting, item by item.

1) A banning order was served on her during the trial, in 1963, which confined her to Johannesburg.

2) After the life sentence on Mandela, the banning order was intensified, restricting her to a particular area of Soweto. This meant the abandonment of her job.

3) The order was then intensified further, preventing her from publication of anything at all.

4) The screws were tightened further when in 1967 she received a sentence of fourteen months' imprisonment for breaking the banning order on a visit to Robben Island to see her husband.

5) Two years later she was arrested and interrogated without pause for five consecutive days and nights, her questioners taking turns in this form of torture. After sixteen months in solitary confinement she was acquitted.

6) She was banned again, being confined this time to

an even smaller section of Soweto. Her banning order expired the next year (1975).

7) After the Soweto riots she was arrested, imprisoned for five months without trial and released.

8) Another banning order was issued, this time as stringent as was physically possible. It confined her to her house.

9) Her spirit being still unbroken she was banished to a remote Afrikaner village in a barren part of the Orange Free State. Here she was a stranger and was confined to her house every night and every weekend.

10) Two women drove 500 miles from Johannesburg to meet her. This meant she was breaking her banning order as she was meeting more than one person at a time. She was prosecuted for this violation.

11) The two women, who refused to give evidence against her, were charged and sentenced to terms of four and three months' imprisonment.

12) Mrs. Mandela's letters are regularly tampered with. Some are permitted to filter through the security net. Others are intercepted. Her calls, taken from a call box, (she has no telephone) are tampered with.

What has happened to Mrs. Mandela can happen to the family members of any political prisoners if they show concern with the political issues which led to their man's imprisonment. The state's surveillance and punishment do not end with the imprisonment of the actual 'offender' on Robben Island.

The Black Homelands

The viability of the Black Homelands Scheme was one of the underlying premises of Verwoerdian Apartheid. This underlying premise has collapsed completely.

There are many fantasies involved in this Verwoerdian dream. In the first place there was the fantasy that a place could be found in the Homelands for all the South African blacks, thereby freeing the entire white area for occupation by the whites. The reality is that there are at least ten million blacks who have no place in the Homelands and are a very real fact of life in the white areas.

A second fantasy is the manner in which the geographical areas have been carved out, some of them being little blocks of separate territory completely isolated in the midst of South African land and having no communication whatsoever with each other except by the grace of South Africa. Bophuthatswana for example is a patchwork quilt of ten different pieces of territory and a citizen of this 'state' would have to travel across South African territory to get from one part of it to another. Electricity, water and other services would likewise have to come from the mainland and can with the greatest ease be cut off.

A third fantasy was that housing could be found for all these people. Housing was wantonly destroyed in order to segregate communities by race. This piece of foolishness which in another society would be categorised as criminal and anti-social has proved itself to have been purposeless and in fact destructive of much that was of value both historically and materially. District Six in Capetown, has already been mentioned as an outstanding instance.

Another item of evidence that the Homelands Policy has collapsed is the subdued reaction of even the ruling Nationalist Party itself to the Declaration of Independence of Venda on September 13, 1979. Venda is the third of the Homelands to achieve independence and not even the Nationalists could have been serious in expecting this bit of land — described in the international news media as "A tiny cabbage patch tucked away in the north-eastern corner of South Africa" to be recognised internationally as a new independent nation.

Venda is a useful illustration of some of the most unsatisfactory features of the homelands scheme. Its 450,000 people are totally dependent on South Africa, and most of its men work in white South Africa. Of the territory's budget of forty million dollars a year, ninety per cent is provided by Pretoria. Venda has no rail links and no infrastructure to support any industrial growth. The Independence Stadium, the venue of its Independence celebrations, was sponsored by South African liquor and tobacco interests. The Chief Minister of Venda has quashed his opposition by packing his government with fellow chiefs and detaining most of his critics under security laws, the model for which no doubt comes from South Africa. Indeed rumour has it that the chief minister bought the support of his chiefs in the Venda Legislative Assembly by giving them forty suits hurriedly bought for the occasion. The Chiefs were also provided with a tour of the Manyeleti Game Reserve.   In fact Chief Patrick Mphephu was roundly defeated at the previous year's general election by Mr. Baldwin Mudau, but despite the greater popularity of Mr. Mudau, Pretoria's support went to Chief Mphephu who became the Chief Minister.   He now occupies a palace, paid for by South African taxpayers, and lives behind security forces and guard houses.

The effect of the Declaration of the Independence of Venda in terms of apartheid and the grand dream of Prime Minister Verwoerd is that 450,000 Venda people are automatically and arbitrarily stripped of their South African citizenship, thus joining about six million Transkeians and Tswanas — about a third of South Africa's black population — in being no longer considered citizens in the land of their birth.

Every black South African possesses in addition to his South African nationality, the citizenship of one of the various black Homelands.   This was in anticipation of the day when each of these persons could be transferred back to one of those Homelands as a citizen of that Homeland. Upon the attainment by that Homeland of independence he would then become a citizen of that Homeland to the exclusion of his South African citizenship.   Thus far three of the black states have achieved their independent status and consequently the citizens of those three states — Transkei, Bophuthatswana and now Venda — have lost their South African citizenship.   With the projected attainment of independence by all the other states, every black in South Africa would then eventually become a citizen of his own state and lose his South African citizenship.   That at least was the original scheme.

The effect of being a member of one of these states is well illustrated in the demand of some South Africans that once a black is a member of an independent state, the South African immigration authorities at the border should satisfy themselves that these persons, when they enter the South African Republic, have sufficient funds to look after themselves and also a fixed place of abode to stay in during their sojourn in South Africa.   The argument runs that all other countries in the world insist on these requirements for their visitors and consequently any of the blacks from the Homelands who enter South Africa should be treated as foreigners would be when they enter a host country.   A sufficiency of funds and a fixed place of abode are according to the argument some of the minimum requirements that a host country would require before permitting a visitor to enter their borders. A situation thus unrighteously created is used as the basis for an apparently righteous argument.

In the homelands there is considerable opposition to the government policy of granting independence, with resulting loss of South African citizenship. When the Prime Minister visited kwaZulu in August 1979 he was greeted with placards reading "pseudo independence" "equal expenditure on black and white education" and "an end to influx control".

Despite his talk of reform the Prime Minister still persists however with his emphasis on the establishment of a constellation of states in South Africa. The Chief Minister of the Ciskei, Chief Lennox Sebe, described black reaction to this eloquently, when he said at one of the formal receptions to the Prime Minister, that the dream of separate development was being "looked at and seen as a vacillating, penny-pinching, half-hearted effort" and that the promises of equal opportunity in separate areas, and equal facilities and equal pay were "today so much disillusionment".

There is now a demand for more land for the black territories and this has become a potentially explosive issue. On the one hand it has aroused black expectations, but on the other, the extreme right wing, the Herstigte Nasionale Party, and its right wing allies are using any readiness on the part of government to concede extra territory to the blacks as a weapon with which to take away white support from the government. One of the pieces of territory which is involved in a suggested handover to a black state is the historic town of Mafeking, which was fiercely fought for by Boers and British in the South African war. It would appear that some of the white business community of Mafeking are happy to have their town incorporated in Bophuthatswana, one of the reasons for this being that much of their trade is with the people in the black territory of Bophuthatswana. However, by parity of argument, if Mafeking should go to Bophuthatswana, East London should go to Transkei, or Ciskei and these concessions of territory are more than can ever be expected from the white rulership of South Africa.

Indeed, even areas which were once granted to some of the black homelands have since been excised, an outstanding current example being Batlokwa. In 1977 the Batlokwa area was excised by South Africa from Leboa much to the resentment of the tribesmen and the chiefs. Batlokwa is situated in the centre of a rich white farming belt and when it was excised from Leboa it automatically became a "black spot" in a white area. In the eyes of the master planners of the Homelands policy, "black spots" need to be removed, to preserve the integrity of white territory. In the case of the land of the Batlokwas, this meant that several thousands of hectares of good farming land would then become available to white farmers, and that 80,000 Batlokwa tribesmen would be removed from a land which had been their home for two hundred years into an arid waterless tract unable to support them and their livestock. The new settlement is nearly one hundred kilometers away from the network of tarred roads and comprises little more than a police station, a few houses, a provision store, a bottle store and a beer hall.

Batlokwa is just another example of what could be another great South African tragedy.

An indication of the government's real attitude to the Homelands is the location of factories built on the fringes of the Homelands. These factories tend to be within South African territory and workers from the Homelands thus form a convenient reservoir of cheap labour at the white employer's doorstep. As one travels, for example, into Bophuthatswana from Pretoria one sees large factories lying almost on the outskirts of Bophuthatswana. A closer examination reveals that these are situated within white South African territory. Indeed a large medical school that has been built for Bophuthatswana is also sited on the fringes of Bophuthatswana but on South African territory.

The homelands policy spells out misery in other ways as well. For example where people are moved from one location to another there are often squalid transit camps provided for them. One of these is called the "God forsaken home" — Katlehong near Germiston. According to a recent report the residents who are brought there often against their will have to scavenge for scraps of food from nearby rubbish dumps. The whole area is surrounded by rubbish dumps and the stench caused by blocked toilets is always present. Some of the rooms sleep several people and the larger families are given two rooms for use as bedroom, kitchen and dining room. These quarters are sometimes raided late at night by the police. There is no electricity and the residents need to buy candles to light their homes even by day in some of the hostels provided for workers.

The homelands policy needs to be seen against realities such as these if its full implications are to be appreciated.

Objections to the Homelands Policy

The homelands policy is based upon the supposition that once a black takes up homelands citizenship he has rights in that "state" comparable to the rights of the whites in South Africa. He can own his house, vote, practise a profession, develop an industry — all without the slightest restriction based on race.

The argument is hollow and the reasons are set out below.

a) the complete dependence of the homelands on South Africa has already been mentioned. This includes external direction from South Africa on all important matters of foreign affairs and defence and total economic dependence as well.

b) the reservation of eighty six per cent of the country's land area for the sixteen per cent minority whites violates all principles of equity.

c) the loss of South African citizenship rights,[9] implicit in the policy.

d) the passing over to the governments of the homelands of some of South Africa's more intractable problems — labour unrest, unemployment, education of the blacks, health services.

e) many of the Africans who will be relegated to the homelands have no roots there and will be in the midst of strangers.

f) they will have scarcely any opportunities for employment and will, in seeking employment in South Africa, become victims of the migrant labour system.

g) the Bantustans are the creation of a white government, not of the African people of those territories.

h) the Bantustans will perpetuate tribal divisions, which not all Africans desire and which certainly are not conducive to their viability or independence in the modern world.

i) being consigned to a homeland is equivalent to a sentence of bitter and grinding poverty.

j) the homelands are much too dependent on the authority of the Chiefs who, understandably, tend to take South African authoritarianism for a governmental model. The judicial system of these territories is not sufficiently developed to ensure the citizen any guarantees of his rights.

k) the fragmented nature of these territories, which makes it necessary for a citizen to pass through South

African territory on his way from one part of his homeland to another, and which renders their dependence on South Africa, total.

l) the reliance of some homeland areas on South Africa, for electricity and water, which can be cut off at any time.

The Future of the Urban Blacks

The failure of the Homelands policy is indicated by the fact that the Prime Minister is now speaking in terms of according a greater measure of recognition to urban blacks and foresees some place for them in his planned constellation of Southern African states. The details of the sort of recognition which he intends to give to the urban blacks are by no means clear. It is significant that the Afrikaans newspaper, *Die Burger*, emphasises that whatever status is given to these Homeland blacks, it should be done with due consideration to the links of these blacks with their black Fatherland.

The problem of recognition means nothing if it does not mean national political rights and nowhere in recent pronouncements has any importance or even mention been given to national political rights for the urban blacks. This seems however to be furthest from the intentions of the government, for Dr. Piet Koornhof, the Minister of Co-operation and Development (black affairs) at the Nationalist Party's 1979 congress in Bloemfontein reiterated that the bonds between the urban black and his 'National State' should be strengthened. "The black man's political rights must be exercised in his own national black state", said Dr. Koornhof. If this is indeed the government's plan for the advancement of the condition of the urban black, it will earn immediate disapproval from every rank of black leadership. All that the government envisages is that the blacks would be granted some sort of community councils regulating their affairs. These councils would not even be extensions of municipalities but would be supervised by deputies and would contact their Homeland at ambassadorial level through the Department of Foreign Affairs. This only exacerbates the problem by emphasising the blacks' inferior status in 'white' territory.

A useful indication of the government's attitude towards devolution of power is that the new constitutional proposals speak of three parliaments — one for each of the groups — whites, Asians and coloured. The blacks, the country's vast majority, do not come into the picture despite the professed concern with the rights of the urban blacks. In the face of these sorts of proposals, the government cannot expect to be taken seriously when it speaks of political rights for the urban blacks.

The Loss of South African Citizenship

An obnoxious feature of the Homelands legislation is the way in which the black citizen is deprived of his citizenship. A clarification of this matter is required in view of the false assertions one hears both inside and outside South Africa that membership of a homeland does not deprive a person of South African citizenship.

There is in this area a negation of earlier political and legal promises. The politicians, when they first formulated the homelands scheme, gave guarantees that all black citizens of South Africa who would be moved there would still retain their South African citizenship. This continued to be official policy even till the amendment of the Bantu Homelands Citizenship Act 1970, which provided by section 2(4) that "A citizen of a territorial authority area shall not be regarded as an alien in the Republic and shall, by virtue of his citizenship of a territory forming part of the Republic, remain for all purposes a citizen of the Republic and shall be accorded full protection, according to international law, by the Republic".

Any black citizen of South Africa could have rested on this legislative assurance that even if he were relegated to one of the homelands he would not lose his citizenship. When, therefore, the very same Act provided that "Every Bantu person in the Republic shall...be a citizen of one or other territorial area..." this provision did not hold the terrors it now holds for the blacks.

What happened in 1976 was a complete political and legislative *volte-face*. When the Transkei attained "independence" in that year the Act providing for it — The Status of Transkei Act — provided by section 6(1): "Every person falling in any of the categories of persons defined in Schedule B shall be a citizen of the Transkei and shall cease to be a South African citizen". The same position was repeated in the Status of Bophuthatswana Act in December 1977.

What does this mean for the blacks? No less than that every black citizen of South Africa, whether he wills it or not, is now, according to government policy, under the threat that some day he will lose his South African citizenship and become the citizen of an impoverished puppet state. He would not be able to recover his South African citizenship, though he would be able to apply to exchange the citizenship of one homeland state for another. If such application is granted — of which there is no guarantee for it depends on executive action — he would become a citizen of another homeland. If that homeland is not already independent he would then regain his South African citizenship, but when eventually they all become independent it would be finally lost. For practical purposes, therefore, these Acts completely deprive the whole of black South Africa of its right to South African citizenship — whatever the contrary official pronouncements may be when officialdom is questioned on this matter. Every black child born in South Africa is registered as the citizen of one or other of the homelands in terms of the earlier cited provisions of the Bantu Homelands Citizenship Act and must eventually expect to have to make his home there, even though it be hundreds of miles away and he is a complete stranger to it. They must await with apprehension the day when the homeland to which they have been assigned attains "independence". That·day they will lose South African citizenship even as three million South Africans lost their citizenship when the Transkei became independent in October 1976.

    Once thus deprived of South African Citizenship, these people will almost inevitably drift back to South Africa as migrant labour. As foreigners they cannot be legally heard to complain if all manner of restrictions are placed upon them such as are placed upon aliens. Already one hears official justifications in regard to Transkei and Bophuthatswana labour, likening it to the migrant labour that drifts from one European country to another. They have no citizenship rights and are under all manner of restrictions — justifiably, say the authorities, for they are foreigners.

Unemployment

    One of the great spectres hanging over South Africans, black and white, is unemployment. For the blacks it means starvation and an intensification of their suffering. For the whites it means something even worse — social unrest and a growing army of discontented citizens who could upset their regime. The blacks are perhaps prepared to go through this additional hardship. They can survive it as an entity. The whites cannot.

Consequently foreign investment is essential from the whites' point of view. A million blacks already unemployed in the latter part of 1979 were a grave potential danger. Several millions would be an irresistible force. Indeed this could well be the thinking behind Prime Minister Botha's promised concessions to the blacks. Every year the ranks of the unemployed can be swelled by upwards of a quarter of a million. In 1978, only 37,000 of the 274,000 new members of the workforce found jobs. The growth rate of around 2.5 per cent annually is insufficient to generate the jobs. Four times that growth rate is required. This cannot be achieved without strong infusions of foreign capital, which perhaps will not come in unless apartheid is substantially relaxed.

Furthermore, a relaxation of apartheid and an improvement of the black man's lot means the growth of a tremendous internal market for South African consumer goods, now almost completely bypassing them. To capture this market would be a shot in the arm for South African industry and could relieve unemployment. Indeed considerable pressure is currently being applied on the South African government by the South African business community to achieve just this.

Black leaders do not fear unemployment so much as do the whites. Their view is that a little extra suffering will not materially enhance the black man's burden. It is the white leaders who do.

The Pass Laws and Employment

In July 1979 the case of Mr. Dickson Kohlakala aroused a great deal of interest. Mr. Kohlakala was fined R.50 for allowing his wife to stay with him because their baby was ill.

This will look strange to anyone in the world outside South Africa. Yet this sort of judicial decision is probably being handed down several times each day in a dozen courts in South Africa. Mr. Kohlakala's case was fortunate enough to attract publicity. The many hundreds that do not, pass entirely unnoticed.

We must begin at the beginning. The Pass Laws make it illegal for a non-pass holder to live even one night in an urban area. An employee in an urban area, whose employment requires his or her residence at the place of employment, would have a pass entitling such person to residence in that area — but the pass would be personal to the employee. The spouse of such an employee would need to remain where the law has decreed he or she should be — in the African townships, or, in the case of migrant labour, in the homelands. In the case of Cape Town migrant labour, this means a location hundreds of miles away.

Now, Mr. Kohlakala was a stable hand in Constantia and was not, of course, entitled to have his wife stay with him.   It so happened that the Kohlakala's 11 month old baby was suffering from tuberculosis, pneumonia and malnutrition and needed expert attention.   Mrs. Kohlakala brought the child to Cape Town in a desperate bid to save its life and had the temerity to stay with her husband in order to look after the child. The magistrate said the baby would not need its mother's care as it would be well looked after in hospital. Mr. Kohlakala was fined R.50. Dr. Alex Boraine, PFP Member of Parliament for Pinelands was so disturbed that he telegraphed Dr. Piet Koornhof telling him that apartheid was not dead but "alive and kicking unfortunate people about". The reference was to Dr. Koornhof's statement in America earlier that month that he had declared war on "dompas" — the pass system.

The resulting public furore gave Mrs. Kohlakala a chance of staying in Cape Town — not with her husband but at an international four star hotel; not for the three month duration of the child's hospitalisation but for a period of two weeks. Mrs. Barbara Versfeld of the Athlone Advice Office stated that the Kohlakalas were fortunate in the publicity they received but that hundreds of other cases, with rulings as flagrantly harsh, would have slipped through unnoticed.[10]

Far from there being an amelioration of the Pass Laws there is in fact increasing severity. The Laws on Plural Relations and Development, Second Amendment Act, created a great deal of heartache in 1979 by increasing the fines on employers employing Africans who do not have passes.   The fine was increased from R.100 to the deterrent level of R.500.

Many 'live in' maids and other domestics had been employed in Cape households for so long that they had virtually become part of the employer's family.   They stayed with their employers and sent money back to their families in the homelands.

The huge fines caused hundreds of employers to serve notice of dismissal on employees who had served them faithfully for years. Families in the homelands almost exclusively dependant upon the remittances were condemned to penury. Stormy debates in Parliament attended the passage of the Act. A white Cape Town employer wrote a letter to a Cape Town newspaper[11] saying "I am a criminal. At any time my doorbell will ring, and, taken to court, I'll be given the option of paying R.55 — which I haven't got — or going to jail for three months. It is a severe sentence and the crime which merits it must, one would think, be correspondingly heinous — like mugging, arson or drug-pushing. My crime is less violent. It is a refusal to commit a crime against conscience". The writer pointed out that the employee, a widow, was the sole support for her old mother and three children in Transkei. "Without her monthly remittance they just don't eat. In spite of this financial stress with its consequent temptations this hard-working, conscientious woman has proved her complete honesty on innumerable occasions. When illness or other causes take me from home I know that the domestic routine will continue, the house cleaned, locked and guarded. How can I face this unfortunate woman and say 'You have done nothing wrong but you must go. You don't want to and I don't want you to, but somewhere some public servant neither you nor I have seen or heard of — but whose salary I help to pay — has taken it upon himself to decide who may and who may not work in my kitchen. That would be a crime. Now that I am coming closer to the end of a long and interesting life I must ask myself: How can I, on meeting my Maker, plead for mercy having myself shown none?"

What has been described is one aspect only of the viciousness of the Pass Laws. To pursue their many ramifications into the deep wells of human misery would need an army of full time researchers.

The Labour Bureaux

The establishment and operation of the labour bureaux provides one of the best examples of the elaborate nature of the legislative scheme by which apartheid is established and maintained.

At the heart of this legislation is the Bantu Labour Act of 1964 and a series of government proclamations promulgated in 1965 and 1968. Under these laws and regulations the structure of labour bureaux has been established at all levels, local, district and regional, and these operate both in white South Africa and in the homelands. They number several hundred.

Every employer of black labour in South Africa is required by law to register at a local or tribal labour bureau as a potential employer. The same applies to employers of black labour in the homelands. Should a vacancy occur in any sort of employment, this vacancy must immediately be notified to the bureau within fourteen days. Likewise every contract of employment must also be registered by the employer.

Viewed from the angle of the employee, the regulations require that the work-seeker should upon registration be placed in a category of employment, of which the 1968 regulations list seventeen. Once categorised in this way the work-seeker is virtually tied to this category for the rest of his life, for the process of change is extremely difficult. It is true that the regulations require the labour officer to have regard to the work-seeker's preference at the time of registration, but in the event of failure to do so there is little, if any, remedy that the work-seeker would enjoy. He is to a large extent at the disposal of the registering officer in regard to the kind of employment for which he will be registered. By the whim of a petty official, nearly every black South African thus becomes condemned to be a mason or factory hand or what you will for the rest of his life. The mobility of labour, which humanity achieved when it emerged from serfdom, does not exist for the bulk of South Africa even in these closing years of the twentieth century.

The impossibility of registering one's preferences effectively may be realised from the fact that there is such a scramble for employment in these employment bureaux that there is great risk in offending the labour officer who may indicate some area of preference where labour is needed.

Now to the recruiting process itself. Prospective employees form long queues at the labour bureaux in anticipation of the visits of recruiting officers. The exceedingly high rate of unemployment in the homelands makes these people only too anxious to procure a contract on whatever terms. Contrary to all basic principles relating to contracts of employment, the department of Bantu administration has generally considered it unnecessary for a black worker to receive a copy of his contract. In fact, his signature is often placed upon the contract of employment before even hours of work or rates of pay are specified. Indeed there is scarcely any individual explanation of the terms of a contract, the general practice being that a brief explanation of the conditions of service is given to all the assembled contracting workers and they are asked to raise their hands in case they approve. This is invariably done out of the desperate need in which they find themselves. There is scarcely a possibility against this background for a negotiation of contractual terms and conditions.

Should it be the position of a black recruited labourer that he did not fully understand the terms and conditions of the employment which he has undertaken, there seems no effective way in which he can obtain any form of redress. The records of the Black Sash Advice Office contain numerous complaints of lack of explanation of any of the implications of the contract before signature or thumbprint was affixed.

Should there be a vacancy in a job category, other than the category in which the work-seeker has been registered, he would have very little chance of obtaining it.

The Labour Bureau has tended to become entrenched in the South African system for the reason that many of the homelands rely for much of their revenue on fees, derived from contracts of employment. Not only do the homelands levy a fee on each contract of employment. There is also a monthly payment to be made for each worker employed. Although the system is inimical to the interests of the black population it thus has an inbuilt ability to draw support from the homelands governments, which is another instance of the manner in which the South African instruments of oppression are so constructed as to be difficult to dislodge.

It will be seen overall that these labour bureaux are not merely an apparatus for obtaining cheap labour for the economy. They are also a skilful means of maintaining vigilance over the workforce, for every labourer is documented and it is extremely simple for the authorities to trace him through all his meanderings between the homeland and the industrial centres. He is also extremely easy to locate by reason of his job categorization and this also helps the administration by preventing the mobility of labour.

Reference has been made elsewhere to the way in which a person once recruited needs to leave wife and family behind in order to assume the position to which he has been appointed.

The labour bureaux are only one of the external manifestations of a labour system which is vicious in its conception. They are tied to the Homelands policy. We see here again how black misery in South Africa cannot be alleviated so long as the Homelands policy continues.

Black Education

Governmental attitudes towards the education of blacks were best summarized by Dr. Verwoerd in 1954 when he said: "The Bantu must be guided to serve his own community in all respects. There is no place for him in the European country above the level of certain forms of labour ... it is of no avail for him to receive a training which has as its aim the absorption in the European community, where he cannot be absorbed".[12] Government education policy has closely followed the guidelines there set out.

To begin with, the cost of building a white primary school is currently more than 600,000 rand while African schools cost between 40,000 and 50,000 rand. These figures appeared in a paper on current trends in racial discrimination in South Africa prepared by the Centre for Inter-Group Studies in Cape Town.

Until very recently, there was no provision for free textbooks or stationery for black children, whereas for many years white children have had these provided to them. There has been an announcement of a change of policy in this regard but it still remains to be seen to what extent this policy will be effectively implemented. As regards teacher/pupil ratio there is a discrepancy again. In regard to white pupils the ratio is 20 white pupils per class compared with 30.8 coloured, 27 Indian and 58.5 African. In addition to the African teacher thus coping with almost twice as many pupils as a coloured teacher and three times as many as a white teacher, the African teacher may also be required to do double session teaching, thus being required to teach up to 100 children a day.

There is also a shortage of black teachers, itself a result of prior education policy. There is a need of 7,000 to 8,000 new teachers per year to keep pace with the yearly increase of 200,000 pupils. Hence a large number of unqualified teachers are employed: 15% of African and 5% of coloured teachers have neither matriculation nor any other teaching qualification. There has also been a heavily discriminatory rate of pay between the different racial groups in the teaching profession. An Indian teacher receives 80 per cent and an African teacher 65-75 per cent only of a similarly qualified white teacher's salary.

The drop out rate is also alarmingly different. For a white child the drop out rate before standard ten is considerably less than half, whereas for the African children the rate is as much as 98 per cent. Only one African child in 500 reaches the final year at school and one in 1100 succeeds in his matriculation. It is largely from the ranks of these one-in-a-thousand blacks that their potential leaders come, but when they show signs of political leadership they are most often arrested or banned as were Mandela and Sobukwe and Biko and countless others. The high drop-out rate in the educational system thus makes political control all the easier, for rather than cut down the whole tree it is far easier to clip the few flowers that keep appearing.

Syllabus content again reveals a heavier strain upon the African child, who must from his or her first year at school learn three languages, a burden that is especially difficult when there is a shortage of school time caused by the double session system. There is no requirement for white, coloured or Indian pupils to learn an African language. Absence of light and warmth and a congenial place for study are other drawbacks for the blacks.

It is to be noted also that it is an offence for a person to establish, conduct or maintain a school other than a government Bantu school unless the school is registered.

The prerogative to register rests with the Minister. There have indeed been prosecutions of persons who have allowed young children to gather together, as, for example, a prosecution of a 76 year-old African some years ago for allowing young children to use his stable as a club, where the children learned to sew, knit and make dolls. He was arrested and indicted under the Act, but was acquitted after thirteen appearances in Court because there was no evidence that actual school instruction was taking place.[13]

This system also quite evidently deprives parents of the essential right to choose freely the kind of education they wish their children to have.

A provision recently introduced in regard to political detainees is that they will not be permitted to self-educate themselves beyond matriculation stage. Till recently it was possible for a political detainee to pursue his higher education, which he invariably did through a correspondence course from the University of South Africa. There have been notable instances of political detainees obtaining more than one degree in this way, if not doctorates, but from now on this seems no longer possible. The educational structure is thus linked with the leadership question. It does a great deal to prevent the emergence of black leadership and gives white governments the argument that there is a dearth of education and leadership among the blacks.

The Black Parents Association

The Black Parents Association is one of the many phenomena resulting from the Soweto episode.

Some days after the disturbances started a number of black organisations realised the need to give assistance to the numerous families that had funeral arrangements on their hands. There were several hundreds of these, many of them quite unable to provide for the sudden eventuality which had descended on so many of the families of the community at such short notice. A funeral would usually be an occasion on which various connected families and neighbours might give assistance but in this instance it was not possible for individual families to expect this in consequence of the fact that so many hundreds of families were simultaneously affected.

In order to render assistance, parents formed themselves into a Black Parents Association, and the sympathy of the entire community was enlisted in order to assist with coffins, taxi fare and all that was necessary for a mass funeral which was contemplated. Indeed 700 taxis had been arranged for this massive funeral which the community planned. The application for the mass funeral was however turned down, with the result that each of the families had then to make its own separate funeral arrangements.

These were the circumstances in which the Black Parents Association was formed, but once formed it was found that there were numerous other purposes which this association could serve. In particular,there was the question of the resumption of the childrens' education and the circumstances in which they were to resume schooling. The question of examinations and the need for a postponement also received attention. There was also a necessity to make special arrangements regarding the evaluation of students' performance in the course of that year, having regard to the exceptional privations and the unsettled conditions which they experienced.

In order to negotiate all these matters with the Department of Education, the Black Parents Association was found to be a valuable organisation able collectively to represent the black community and to obtain thereby greater concessions than individual parents would have been able to extract had they acted by themselves.

From its activities has resulted a more concerned attitude towards the problem of black education and the built-in impediments which make it so inferior to education in the other three categories, Asian, coloured and white.

Many black persons will tell you that it is out of such privation that any real organisation or worthwhile result emerges. In the stress of the days immediately following Soweto, when it was necessary to act urgently in order to identify corpses and the families to which the deceased belonged against a background of an absence of a public list of victims, one can become easily convinced that the more privation and suffering there is the greater will be the resolve and the organisation of black people to fight for a more equitable order for themselves and for South Africa.

Black Universities

There are three black universities in South Africa — sometimes referred to disparagingly as "bush colleges", or "tribal colleges".

Of these, Fort Hare, once an independent university which trained many black intellectuals of many African countries, was deprived of its earlier independence when the curiously named Extension of University Education Act restricted universities to different racial groups. Together, Fort Hare and the two other black universities have under 10,000 students. Coloureds are served by another university — the University of the Western Cape — and Indians by the University of Durban-Westville.

All these institutions lack the autonomy enjoyed by the white universities. They are strictly administered by government departments although enjoying the appearance and form of universities. For example, Durban-Westville comes under the Department of Indian Affairs and such academic freedom as exists is what the administering government agency is prepared to allow. Academics feel free to explore and research their areas of expertise until the moment when such research begins to acquire political relevance. At that point academic freedom stops, for the consciousness that the agencies of government are peering over one's shoulder acts as an immediate source of inhibition.

The white universities have a considerable measure of academic freedom, as evidenced by the work of many academics whose research runs counter to established government thinking. The work of white academics such as Barend van Niekerk, John Dugard, A.S. Mathews and Van der Vyver has already been referred to. Their work in the field of law cannot please the establishment, but is permitted and can be indulged in without fear. The lectures given by the author at the University of Stellenbosch, as for example the farewell lecture reproduced in Appendix A, attest to a wide measure of academic freedom in the white universities.

Whether this is so in the other universities is greatly open to question. Even if academics should desire to be as outspoken and liberal there will always be the consciousness that the same freedom will not necessarily be available to them, in the same manner that the freedom enjoyed by the white press is not enjoyed by the black. The lack of autonomy, the accountability to a governmental agency and the very fact of their being black, coloured or Indian, all combine to produce this result.

Some of these campuses, especially in the early days, were presided over by Afrikaner academics — quite often Broederbonders — who were constantly in touch with security police and did not hesitate to call them into the campuses in the event of unrest. Moreover, the existence of internal university regulations acts as a constant source of inhibition to academics minded to express their views on politically controversial questions.

It is not as though these universities have been thankfully accepted by the different racial groups for whom they are meant. Indians for example looked upon the creation of a separate university for them as an altogether unwelcome idea, and protested strongly against a segregated university. Still the government, intent on the scheme, forged ahead with its plans and constructed a magnificent campus at Durban-Westville to drive home the point that there was no intention to deprive this group of university education. Having no alternative, the community receives its higher education at this institution.

The theoretical possibility that a person may enter a university which is not of his racial group makes no difference to this pattern of racial segregation. Permits for this purpose depend, as we have seen, on the absence of a corresponding course in his appropriate university. These students are generally at a postgraduate level, and too few in number to make any real impact on the existing polarisation of the communities.

There is also power in the minister to control the admission of students to universities. He may refuse admission to a person if he considers it to be in the interests of the university concerned that such person should not be admitted, and he may limit the entry of students to particular courses.

The university scene, in short, presents one of the

best illustrations of the discriminatory pattern of South African life.

The black campuses are rich in leadership material and support comes to them also from the coloured and Indian campuses.

Those who have had the privilege of addressing student bodies on different racial campuses will know the contrast between their attitudes. The well-meaning liberalism of the white Afrikaner campus seems pale when compared with the more activist liberalism of the English speaking campuses. This seems pale again in the context of the other campuses. The burning anger and the sense of militancy of the non-white campuses is unimaginable from the sheltered groves of white academe. Black consciousness[14] has a great deal to do with this and the longer the government delays, the sharper will these attitudes become.

The Black Professional Man

We have noted in the preceding section the many difficulties with which the path of black education is strewn. With all these difficulties there are still the gifted few who make the grade. The writer was privileged to meet some of them - lawyers, doctors and academics - ornaments to any community but underprivileged citizens in the land of their birth.

In the major South African cities it is an interesting experience to meet a non-white lawyer functioning in chambers no different from barristers' chambers in any part of the English speaking world. Respected by his colleagues, handling matters of the gravest importance with acceptance to both bench and bar, moving freely in the company of his peers — these ordinary incidents in the life of a lawyer become strange phenomena when one considers that this same person is politically rightless, and socially discriminated against. He must help administer laws in whose fashioning he is incompetent to play the slightest part, he must live in a separate area from his colleagues, send his children to separate schools, and watch as a bystander when his country's general election takes place. Yet he must swear to obey and uphold the laws of his country in the same way as any member of the privileged race. Should he, for the sake of argument, become some day a Supreme Court Judge, he will still be a political outcast while being judicially supreme.

Take again the case of a Johannesburg lawyer or doctor who lives in Soweto. He will probably live in one of the more affluent sectors and not in the midst of the squatters' corrugated metal shacks. His house will probably be wired for electricity and he would not have to use the coal fires which cause the perpetual smog that hangs over Soweto. He will travel to and from the city by car and not be exposed to the pickpocketing and knifing that are daily features of the Soweto train and of the unlighted roads. Since he is probably not illegally in Soweto he will perhaps have less fear of the midnight knock and the search for illegal residents on his premises. But there end any privileges he may have.

He may add a room or two to his house, but 'his' house is not his property. He will never have pride of ownership in it, for it belongs to the West Rand Administration Board. It is contrary to government policy that a black should own land in such an area, for his proper place is in the Homelands. He — or his parents for that matter — may never have seen their particular homeland which is hundreds of miles away, but that is the place to which he will legally belong. If his home language is Tswana, for example his proper homeland would be Bophuthatswana. By the Bantu Homelands Citizenship Act every black child born in South Africa must be registered on birth as a citizen of one or other of the homelands and his children would therefore be registered as citizens of Bophuthatswana. Some day they will be liable to be relegated there even though they will be total strangers to that environment. This sword of Damocles hangs perpetually over his head, threatening the disintegration of his family.

He may wish to change residence because he dislikes the perpetual smog, the unlighted streets, the slush, the overloaded sewers, the pickpocketing and knifing. He cannot do this without permission from the bureaucracy and in no case will he be permitted to live outside Soweto.

If invited to a fellow lawyer's or doctor's house in the white areas, he will be able to accept the invitation, but he cannot invite his white friend home to repay this hospitality, for he must obtain a permit for this purpose. His social life is thus subject to official control and his non-black guests will be 'vetted'. Should a non-black guest pay him a social call without a permit, the friend is liable to be arrested and to spend the night in a police cell. This is more humiliation than the host can legitimately take the chance of imposing, and so all equal social intercourse must end,

151

even at a professional level. The black lawyer or doctor is the permanent inferior, condemned for life to live in a black ghetto.

These constant sources of humiliation are rarely seen by his white friends and are little understood. Nor is this surprising, for till a few years ago black places of residence such as Soweto were fenced off with barbed wire. To this day a prominent notice at the entrances to these settlements warns the visitor that he has no right to enter without a permit. If only the average white citizen of South Africa should see places like Soweto and understand their frustrations, there is no doubt he will squirm. The well lit, well paved, architecturally attractive, privileged, white city contrasts so strongly with the sordid squalor and under-privilege of the black, that the iniquity of it all cannot but be on his conscience. One of the tragedies of South Africa is that this natural human sympathy is prevented from being generated by a physical separation imposed by law. Few white citizens will go to the trouble of obtaining permits to see the squalor of their fellow citizens. Even less so is it with the professional man.

To be a professional, for a South African black, is not to enjoy privilege but to be exposed to even more humiliation than is the lot of the average black.

African Nationalism[15]

It is useful to remember that although the nationalist movements in other African countries have in recent years commanded greater worldwide attention than black African nationalism in South Africa, the latter was for long the deepest and most developed black nationalist movement on the whole continent. Since the 1950's the South African movement has continued to lose strength and been systematically suppressed whereas in the other African countries it was from about that period that the nationalist movements prospered and came into their own.

One often hears the comment that it is inconceivable that so vast a majority as the blacks in South Africa are not asserting themselves and showing more independent nationalism. An answer cannot be given to this comment without a historical perspective, or a knowledge of the apparatus of repression. The first is dealt with in this section and the second is the subject of Chapter 6 of this book.

The African National Congress was formed in 1912, but even before the grant of independence to South Africa

in 1909 the blacks already enjoyed far-seeing leadership.
In 1907 a delegation of African leaders went over to London
to argue against contemplated provisions in the South Africa
Act, which, far from extending to the other provinces the
non racial franchise already enjoyed in the Cape, in fact
prohibited blacks from sitting in Parliament. The delegation
met the Colonial Secretary but the British government
showed no response to these representations and proceeded
with the Act, which as observed elsewhere[16] was the rock on
which apartheid was built.

The African National Congress was inaugurated to
struggle for the political rights of the blacks on a scale
transcending tribal or local endeavours.   If this organisation can be criticised for its activities in its early days,
that criticism must be for its trustfulness and its restraint.
Its leadership was in the hands of western educated lawyers, doctors, ministers and teachers.   These leaders had
been accustomed to more intermingling with the whites than
is now possible. Separateness had not hardened into a legal
institution. As with the first leaders of independence movements in other colonial territories, these persons saw themselves as bridge builders between the races and the cultures,
rather than as demolishers of the existing order and architects of a new. This background probably accounted for the
pattern of their activities and they cannot now be blamed for
not foreseeing to the full the grotesque distortions which, in
Southern Africa alone of all British colonial territories,
characterised the process of emancipation from British rule.

When the Land Act of 1913 limited African ownership of land to 7.3 per cent of the total area and imposed a
feudal requirement of service on blacks who remained on
white property or when the 1917 Native Administration Bill
threatened separate governmental institutions for the black
population, the ANC response was one entirely within the
constitutional framework — deputations to London which
came away with nothing. In 1923, when the Areas Act
forbade black freehold tenure in urban areas, or when in
1936 the 1913 land legislation was consolidated and the
black Cape franchise abolished, their response was still within
the system. They called for a convention of leaders of all
shades of political thought, organised a 'day of prayer' and
despatched a deputation to interview Hertzog.

During these early years there were, however, some
mild protests. In 1918 African sanitary workers in Johannesburg went on strike demanding a pay rise for the menial
work entrusted to them and the ANC gave them encourage-

ment.   The strike was broken by imprisoning the leaders under the Masters and Servants Act, using African police to do the work, forcing the workers back to work under armed guard and ordering the flogging of those who refused to work.   There were also various protests on inadequate wages, but these were largely ineffective.[17] The technique of passive resistance encouraged by Gandhi sparked off some measure of activism on the part of the ANC but its record was scarcely one of activism until 1945.

In that year, encouraged by the Atlantic Charter, the ANC published a Bill of Rights demanding universal suffrage and by 1949 had grown sufficiently disillusioned with its gentler compaigns of earlier years to reject the method of petition and deputation.

From that point on the ANC record was one of increasing activism.   In 1952 it adopted the methodology of the Indian Congress' satyagraha in campaigning against the Pass Laws, the Group Areas Act and other unjust legislation. Large numbers of volunteers staged 'sit-ins' in white sections of post offices and waiting rooms, and courted arrest and prison sentences.   The scale of the protests was such that despite all appeals for non violence, violence did surface in East London and Port Elizabeth.   Leaders like Chief Albert Luthuli gave a new dynamism to the movement, proclaiming a Freedom Charter for Africans, advocating the burning of passes and courting banning orders and prosecutions for High Treason.

In 1958, ANC members defecting from it because they felt it was still not sufficiently activist, formed the Pan African Congress (PAC) and together these two organisations pushed for political rights.   Prime Minister Macmillan's "winds of change" speech in 1960 gave them a further impetus and the year 1960 saw many disturbances.[18] We have seen how these two organisations were banned in the wake of the Sharpeville disturbances.

Another black movement of note was the Industrial and Commercial Workers' Union (ICU) founded in 1917 by clements Kadalie a mineworker.   After an unsuccessful dock strike organised by it, the movement spread to achieve a membership of 200,000 by 1928.

From this promising beginning the ICU failed to progress into a major force in the country for reasons which have been the subject of much discussion.   Some reasons suggested are that it grew too swiftly to be adequately organised, and that Kadalie, knowing his support was largely revolutionary, desisted from mobilising it fully to avoid a confrontation with the state.

The Communist Party had the potential to provide the country with an inter-racial organisation and there were white radicals working to this end. These activities were prevented from succeeding and giving South Africa a united, race-free labour movement by internal dissension within the party and by the international repercussions of Hitler's rise to power. A directive went out from the Comintern to all its branches to align with groupings opposed to fascism, and the party, thus called upon to ally itself with authority needed to be all white. This is probably a forgotten turning point in South African history, for one tends to forget the existence of the poor white South Africans. Especially in the 1930's there were many demonstrations of working class solidarity across the colour line, black Africans and White Afrikaners both tramping together in the ranks of the unemployed, both scouring the streets together in search of food. That phenomenon passed from the South African scene, never to be seen again.

It is of interest to note that when Mr. Bram Fischer, Q.C. was charged and convicted in 1966 under the Suppression of Communism Act, he outlined to the court his reasons for joining the Communist Party. One of these was that the Communist Party had always refused to accept any colour bar, taking its stand on the brotherhood of all men. The other was that the white members of the Communist Party were, save for a handful of courageous individuals, the only whites prepared to forgo their privileges and give of their time and energy for the ending of discrimination. Mr. Fischer observed also that they were the only whites who threw themselves into the work of national movements.

The Influence of Mahatma Gandhi

Gandhi's influence on South Africa is an important strand in its history. His influence extended beyond the Indian community of Durban, where he lived and worked, and gave to black African movements their earliest methods of challenging unjust legislation.

A barrister of the Inner Temple, Gandhi left India for Durban in 1893 to represent an Indian firm which had an important case pending in South Africa. Racial arrogance was not new to him, for he had experienced this in India, but what he found in South Africa was very much worse. The Indian community in Natal, who had come there originally in 1860 as indentured labourers, prevailed upon him to stay on and assist them in improving their status. The original migrants had been followed later by merchants from Mauritius and Bombay. All alike had been denied citizenship and were contemptuously called "coolies", Gandhi himself coming to be known as the "coolie lawyer".

Gandhi plunged himself into the struggle, relinquishing his work as a lawyer to devote himself fully to the cause. He was more than once arrested and imprisoned and suffered frequent indignities. He protested against anti-Asian legislation and racial segregation of the Indians. He settled later in Johannesburg and also helped to set up the Transvaal British Indian Association.

In 1902 the Transvaal government, going back upon an earlier undertaking, imposed a humiliating requirement on all Asiatic settlers, men and women alike, that they should make application for a certificate of registration with a full set of finger impressions — a requirement previously demanded only of convicted prisoners. At a mass protest meeting in Johannesburg addressed by Gandhi the crowd took an oath to adopt passive resistance and court imprisonment rather than accept an unjust and insulting law.

The occasion was important for the entire world. It was the birth of organised passive resistance — the technique that led in India to independence and in America to the success of the Civil Rights movement of the 1960's.

In South Africa unfortunately it did not yield such dramatic results. Gandhi initially succeeded in persuading the British government to withhold the royal assent to the bill, but later the royal assent was given and the passive resistance movement was launched. Gandhi and other leaders were arrested but later the government compromised and agreed to voluntary registration. The government later reneged on their undertaking to repeal the Act and civil disobedience was renewed. After many hundreds of Indians suffered imprisonment the Act was finally repealed.

The Indian resistance movement organised by Gandhi was the first serious resistance a South African government was called upon to face. It was known as satyagraha,[19] the basis for which is the age old jurisprudential concept that an unjust law is not worthy of obedience. It elevates to a moral duty the need to refuse obedience. It calls upon resisters to court willingly the punishment the law imposes and to use that punishment as the motive force for change, on the basis that the sufferings of the oppressed will stimulate a change of heart on the part of the oppressor. The process was to be kept free of violence at all stages, and free of bitterness as well.

The African protest movements until the 1950's relied heavily on this philosophy, and even in the somewhat more militant movements thereafter there has been an element of satyagraha thinking.

An instance of African adoption of the satyagraha philosophy was the fight by the Transvaal Africans against the pass laws in 1919. When enormous crowds gathered outside the pass office the organisers over and over again took away from the assembled people any weapons they had in their possession. Police later used force on the crowds, fired upon them, arrested 700 and broke up the movement.

Chief Buthelezi

Chief Gatsha Buthelezi, the most powerful black personality in South Africa, is an unusually gifted person. He combines ease of social intercourse with clarity of intellect, a commanding public presence, impressive platform performance and drive, determination and organising ability. He is a Chief (but not King) of the Zulus, who form the largest ethnic group of the black population.

Buthelezi, extremely articulate both at home and abroad, has steered what may be described as a middle course in black South African politics. He is prepared to speak to and do business with the whites, but not prepared to fall in line with their master plan of "independence" for the homelands. He looks upon all South Africa as the territory of the black people and does not see that they can be confined, as the whites would have them, into the little pocket territories of the homelands.

He commands, according to a 1978 survey, 43.8 per cent of black support, of which the more radical leaders of the banned African National Congress command only 21.7 per cent. By contrast the chiefs of the homelands, such as Chief Matanzima of Transkei and Chief Mangope of Bophuthatswana command only 3.6 per cent and 2.7 per cent respectively.[20]

Buthelezi's Inkatha movement well organised and with 150,000 paid up subscribers is a political force to be reckoned with and so is its almost military youth arm. It even has the support of a quarter of the supporters of the ANC.

Still, with all this acceptance and power, Buthelezi faces some real opposition.

Steve Biko (in an interview with Bernard Zylstra, possibly his last major interview)[21] expressed this opposition pointedly from the angle of African youth when he said that Buthelezi "dilutes the cause by operating on a government platform...Gatsha is supported by 'oldies' for good reason, since Gatsha protects the stability that the older persons need. But we are young. We do not look upon the solution to injustice as an expectation but as a duty. Here lies the dilemma of the old: between duty and bread".

But Buthelezi has built up over the years a support which is not confined to a tribal following or the elderly group or the compromisers. According to a German survey conducted by the Arnold-Bergstrasse Institut 40.3 per cent of his supporters among urban blacks are not Zulus. The survey states that "The outstanding phenomenon in black urban politics is without a doubt Gatsha Buthelezi...not only is he alone of all homeland leaders a national political figure, but over and above this he is the political figure of black South Africa".

There is an increasing ring of defiance in his recent utterances. In a new year message for 1980, he warned the whites of "uncontrollable bloodshed" if there was any reversion to the Verwoerd or Vorster policies, adding that "the black political tiger" would go on the rampage destroying everything in its path".

Buthelezi is a very real figure on the power scene of South Africa, and, if South Africa should in the near future come under black rule, there is every prospect that Buthelezi will be one of the chief incumbents of the seats of power.

Black Consciousness

Till the late 1960's the students of South Africa divided into two organisations — the *Afrikaanse Studentebond* and the NUSAS (National Union of South African Students). The former supported apartheid and drew its strength from the Afrikaans universities; the latter opposed apartheid, and drew its strength from the English speaking campuses and was multi-racial. It included black students, who found in it a convenient and sympathetic forum for the expression of their views.

But the late 1960's were, throughout the world, years of student radicalism. Black students, like students everywhere else, were growing impatient with traditional liberal slogans and the inaction which accomapnied them. The NUSAS Congress held at Rhodes University in 1967 brought matters to a head, for the inability of even sympathetic white students to identify with the problems of the blacks was underlined by the separate accommodation given to the two groups of delegates. The white students were accommodated at the University, while the blacks had to live separately in an African township. Black students were convinced that, try as they may, the different groups were prevented by the system from identifying with each other.

The black students realised the need for an independent organisation, despite the overtones of racism involved, and in this realisation was born the South African Students' Organisation (SASO) and the black consciousness movement. It is to be remembered that in 1961 both the ANC(African National Congress) and the PAC (Pan-Africanist Congress) had been banned, that Nelson Mandela had been sent to Robben Island in 1964, that Robert Sobukwe had been sent there in 1960. Black aspirations were languishing, leaderless and inarticulate, and needed both leadership and an ideology.

Black consciousness was to provide these. No longer was the black intent on proving that the white was not superior or that he was equal to the white. The black man was a God created being of intrinsic worth in his own right, proud of his blackness, conscious of his dignity. He looked inwards towards himself, provided his own leadership, was his own model. Black consciousness aimed at inducing the black man to rediscover himself. He would no longer be led blindly by the norms of white society. He would generate his own "soul force".

It followed that the political, social and economic changes so urgently needed by the blacks could not come from within the system — neither from existing political parties nor from existing student organisations nor from existing patterns of dependence on whites.

The first dramatisation of this new consciousness occurred at a University Convocation. Abraham Tiro, chosen by his fellow graduates to speak on their behalf on graduation day at Turfloop, astonished the white chancellor, the white rector, the white guests and the few black parents who were admitted to the hall, by protesting against discrimination. "Right now" he said, "our parents have come all the way from their homes only to be locked outside. Front seats are given to people who cannot even cheer us. My father is seated there at the back. My dear people, shall we ever get a fair deal in this land? The land of our fathers?...Let the

Lord be praised, for the day shall come when all shall be free to breathe the air of freedom which is theirs to breathe and when that shall have come, no man, no matter how many tanks he has, will reverse the course of events".[22]

Tiro was expelled and when he was escorted off the campus and a petition for his reinstatement was rejected, the students began a sit-in protest. Food and water supplies were cut off and the use of the toilets denied them. The campus was sealed off. Across the country black students launched a campaign of protest. Across the country the police began a persecution of SASO. Yet SASO's influence was spreading. Even as its leaders were banned new leaders started appearing.

Black consciousness had come to stay. Black theatre, black journalism, black poetry, black theology, all came into their own. Each had its message for black society and there was little that authority could do to stem the flow of ideas.

In the midst of this resurgence of African consciousness was Steve Biko, one of the moving spirits and intellects of the Black Consciousness movement. Biko was largely responsible for the formation of SASO and it is not difficult to appreciate how concerned the authorities felt at his growing stature and charisma. His death under interrogation sent shock waves through South Africa and the world. No single event since Soweto convinced the world of the iniquities of the South African system or aroused its interest more than the manner of the killing of Biko, and the initial attempt at a cover up. It is an event still so fresh and raw that no conversation in South Africa concerning equality or freedom for the blacks can proceed far without a reference to Steve Biko's life and work and death. Apartheid needs no indictment framed by the outside world. It framed its own indictment when it killed Biko.

Black Attitudes and Strategy

Black consciousness will have no truck with the establishment, it believes that it is a birthright of the blacks to have power in their own country and is determined to achieve this by attitudes of militancy. It condemns all blacks who would be prepared to have truck with the establishment, whether for their own advantage or even for the sake of extracting from the establishment some concessions which might otherwise not have been available. It will hence have no truck with the Homelands leaders or with any who are prepared to parley with the establishment on the basis of the values of white society.

Although it is said by many that boycotts of South Africa will lead to privation in the ranks of the African blacks, black consciousness does not believe this to be an argument at all. It sees in this an argument of white industrialism to avoid a deep hole being cut in its own pockets. Black South Africa on the other hand is prepared according to black consciousness thinkers to undergo some further privation for the attainment of some definite objective. The traumatic suffering of thirty years has been endured with great patience to no purpose. The blacks are accustomed to suffering, and further suffering directed towards the attainment of a worthwhile objective will therefore be gladly undertaken. In the words of some activists the blacks do not want their shackles to be made more comfortable. They want them removed.

An interesting observation of black consciousness philosophy, made to the author by a black leader, was that, as in chemistry, so also in society, it is not the stable element but the unstable element that changes. Sanctions, boycotts, disinvestments, will all shake South African society by creating massive unemployment and industrial and social unrest. It is then only that change will occur.

Another important aspect of black attitudes is complete fearlessness. Black people are prepared to accept detention, torture, and death in the cause. Many of the leaders of the Soweto uprising were youths so imbued with courage as to be prepared to sacrifice their lives by the hundred in the attainment of their objectives. The author has had the privilege of meeting a person who had been through detention and torture. His description of his reactions was that after a few days of solitary confinement during which he agonised over his fate, he found that he had "passed the threshold of fear", after which it did not seem to matter to him what tortures were in store. After his release he continues to work for his ideals, fearless of the consequences. Whether this is true of all black consciousness one does not know, but the attitude is spreading that suffering is not to be feared. Terrance Makwabe, a slenderly built, bespectacled gentleman in his forties, when questioned by the prosecutor as to why, when serving a sentence on Robben Island, he was prepared to incur a further sentence by giving defence evidence in another case, briefly replied, "Andi soyiki" — "I am no longer afraid".

There are many whites in South Africa who believe that there is nothing an unarmed populace can achieve against the ordered might of a well-armed government.

They say that the Soweto uprising enabled the government to regroup its resources for the suppression of such an uprising in the future. Soweto taught the government the lesson that it should not be caught unprepared in the future. The government has now the most sophisticated plans to circle the black settlements with a ring of steel in the eventuality of such an uprising.

While this may indeed be true, black militants contend that the government cannot throw a ring of steel around the black settlements for any considerable period of time. The government needs the black labour of those settlements in order to keep the South African industrial machine moving. It will be compelled to permit members of the work force by the hundred thousand to leave these black settlements and move into the industrial areas by day. However strict its vigilance may be, it will not be possible by government action and by force to restrain these hundreds of thousands of workers from guerilla-type action should they be so minded. Herein lies the strength of black activism, for it knows that its united effort in the industrial sphere can produce telling results even on a government armed to the teeth with the weaponry of repression. On January 28, 1980 this aspect of black power flexed its muscles at Port Elizabeth, scene of violent confrontations between police and protesting blacks in 1976. An executive member of the Port Elizabeth Black Civic Organisation said: "Things will not be the same this time. We know better now and we have a better weapon than sticks and rocks". The weapon he referred to was worker power. The workers were confident that the real strength of the 350,000 residents of the black townships lay in their ability to cripple white industry.

This new weapon of black protest has been used effectively to hit multinational firms like Ford. The strikes, according to news reports, appeared to be orderly and highly organised. The official already quoted is reported to have commented on the impatience of young blacks and to have said, "We think we have learned that to burn our homes and schools is useless. Our power does not lie in the torch, but with labour".[23] In the words of the news report which is the source of this information, "They seem to be opening a new chapter in the black protest against apartheid".

There have been very careful studies of the type of guerilla action that would be useful to black militants in the South Africa situation, and it is generally recognised that established patterns of guerilla action will not necessarily be suitable for South Africa. Much guerilla style activity in other countries has been worked out on the basis of a peasant resistance in the countryside. Any guerilla activity in South Africa is likely to be an industrialised guerilla warfare, for it is in industrial areas that this kind of activity will be conducted. The possibility of sabotage in a thousand different factories and workplaces is a spectre which the government will find difficult to grapple with. Such industrial guerilla tactics have not thus far been conducted in any country on an appreciable scale and South Africa may well be the prototype. It is possibly through them that the crunch situation in South Africa will really emerge.

Advance warning of this new dimension to the struggle has come at the beginning of the nineteen eighties. On January 25 the world media caried the news that three black gunmen had held the staff and customers of a Pretoria bank as hostages for seven hours. Aged between thirty and thirty-five, they were members of the outlawed African National Congress. They demanded one million rand and the release of political prisoners including Nelson Mandela. They sent out two bank employees with a list of their demands. A special police task force prepared for just such an eventuality stormed the building and killed the gunmen. Two hostages died, and seventeen hostages and four policemen were wounded in the gunfight. "Let this action of the police be a warning and an example to all terrorists who have thoughts of aggression against innocent people and the state", warned the Police Minister. An ANC spokesman in Lusaka, on the other hand, said that the next time something like this happened, its men would kill all the hostages if police started shooting and that the ANC saluted the guerilla trio for dying for such a noble cause.

It is symptomatic of the mood of black South Africa that the funeral of one of the guerillas on February 10, 1980 attracted a crowd of 20,000 mourners in Soweto, turning it into the biggest display of public mourning in South Africa since the funeral of Steve Biko, three years earlier. The mourners, chanting freedom songs and giving black power salutes, carried the coffin thirteen kilometers to the cemetery. Five hundred armed police wearing camouflage uniforms fired tear gas at the crowd, set up roadblocks and cut off Soweto highway as hundreds joined in a procession stretching for two kilometers. There can be no better illustration than this that black South Africa is on the boil and that the minutes left for peaceful settlement are fast ticking away.

The incident is significant as urban guerillas had never before mounted such a direct and open challenge to white authority in South Africa. In the past three years there had been over one hundred attacks on police stations and government buildings, but nothing of this degree of defiance.

It seems a fair guess that when South Africa is harried on its borders, as the buffer states fall away and the borders become more exposed, at that time dissident elements within South Africa will begin to rear their heads. It may well be beyond the competence of even the efficient South African security forces to handle these two problems simultaneously. Both sides are aware of this fact and both sides are waiting for the moment of truth much in the style of Sumo wrestlers taking the measure of their opponents for interminable moments before committing themselves to action.

A factor militating against the blacks is the ability of government to incarcerate black leadership on suspicion and thereby nip in the bud even incipient signs of black leadership . Any type of organisation is likely to be detected soon not merely by the security police but also through the activities of informers. Yet the massive scale of the resentments felt by the blacks, like the rumblings of a volcano, may be containable for a while but will build additional pressure through every moment of containment.

Another factor to be considered is the crushing of black leadership which occurred after the Soweto uprising. The first flowering of idealistic youth was gathered and crushed after Soweto, and it will take time again for a fresh flowering to appear. However, it perhaps requires not more than a period of five or six years between such cycles of leadership and it may well be that in another two or three years another flowering of Soweto-type leadership in Soweto will emerge. This period could synchronise with the period of trouble on the borders and by this reckoning it is at most about three years' discussion time that still remains.

It is to be noted also that while the older folk among the black population may be prepared to accept with resignation the dominance of white leadership, the younger generation is impatient and intolerant of such attitudes. It will probably be prepared to make enormous sacrifices in order to throw off what it not unjustifiably regards as an intolerable yoke.

Black South Africa is the crucial factor in the future of South Africa. Millions of young blacks cherish the ideal of a democratic and free society in which all persons live together in harmony and with equal opportunities. It is an ideal which they hope to live for and to achieve. But if need be it is an ideal for which they are prepared to die.

The external world has an obligation as far as lies within its power, to ensure that this sacrifice of life is not called for. This responsibility rests not merely upon governments but upon ordinary individuals, for there are many steps that they can take.[24] Should they fail to do so, they - the average man and woman — cannot avert a share of the moral blame for the tens of thousands of deaths that will result.

FOOTNOTES

1. On various aspects of life in Soweto, see Jill Johnson and Peter Magubane, *Soweto Speaks,* Donker, 1979.
2. *Argus,* June 5, 1978.
3. For these facts see Annual Report, Athlone Advice Office, Oct. 77 — Sept. 78 pp.7-8.
4. *Ibid.*
5. See Ch.1. p.
6. Athlone report, p.7.
7. Athlone report, p.9.
8. See Bernard Levin's article in The Times, 13 December 1979. See also the account regarding Mrs. Mandela in Amnesty International's Political Imprisonment in South Africa, 1978, p.45.
9. See pp.138-9.
10. See on the details of Kohlakala Case, *The Star,* July 7, 1979, p.9.
11. See *The Star,* July 7, 1979, p.9.
12. *Segregation Rules the Schools,* The Times, London, Supplement on South Africa, May 31, 1960, page XVI.
13. *Bulletin of the Committee on Science and Freedom,* August 1957, No.9, p.5.
14. See pp.158-60.
15. In compiling this section, I have relied heavily on Tom Lodge's articles on Black Opposition appearing in The Sash issues of February and August 1979.   Major writings on the South African black political movements are Edward Roux, *Time Longer than Rope,* Madison, University of Wisconsin Press, 1964; Peter Walshe, *The Rise of African Nationalism in South Africa,* London, Hurst, 1970; Leo Kuper, *Passive Resistance in South Africa.* The last named book is banned.
16. See p.58.
17. See pp.155-7.
18. See p.62.
19. Literally, *satya* — truth, and *graha* — fight; the fight of truth or righteousness.
20. See the statistics in the *Eastern Province Herald,* June 12 and 19, 1978.
21. Reported in December-January 1977-78 *Canadian Forum* 15.
22. Denis Herbstein, *White Man, We Want to Talk to You,* Penguin Books, 1978 pp.72-3.
23. See *The Australian,* Jan. 29, 1980.
24. See Chapter 8 below.

CHAPTER 6

Blots Upon the Statute Book

a) *The Pass Laws*

"*Kaffir, waar's jou pas?*" — "Kaffir, where is your pass?". Thus runs one of the most hated expressions in black South Africa — a symbol of inferiority, segregation, broken families, regimented employment, arrest, prosecution, imprisonment, white dominance. The law under which this question is asked has caused more heartache than any other upon the statute book.

The African must carry a pass at all times — not the coloured or the Asian or the white. Failure to do so is a criminal offence. Even a black professional man, be he lawyer or doctor or engineer, must on venturing out of his home, check his pockets not only for keys and driving licence and purse, but also for his pass, for he spends the night in prison if he is caught without it. The author was once in the company of a black professional man who, on leaving his home, said with a curse that he must check his pockets for his "badge of slavery". The law requires every African over the age of sixteen to be fingerprinted and furnished with a reference book containing his identity card, employment particulars and other information required by law. It empowers a policeman at any time to call upon an African to produce it on demand under pain of a fine of R.20 or imprisonment not exceeding a month. If a black should fail to transfer his passbook when changing from one suit of clothes to another and should thereafter walk down the street he can find himself handcuffed and taken to prison no matter whether he is a lawyer, doctor, business executive or member of the Council of Ten, Soweto's supreme representative body.

Pass laws are not new in South Africa. They were not invented by Dr. Verwoerd and the Nationalists. Prior even to the Union each province had laws applicable to non-whites which were meant to control vagrancy and the flow of labour into urban areas. In fact, historically, they go back to British rule, for as early as 1809, Earl Caledon, Governor of the Cape, issued a proclamation prohibiting Hottentots from moving from one district to another without a pass issued by a Magistrate.[2] A time was reached, however, when Africans had to carry as many as twenty-seven identifying documents in connection with work, travel and residence.[3]

There was continuous protest over the inconvenience and humiliations involved. What the Nationalist Government did against this background was not to abolish these requirements but to enact in 1952 the Abolition of Passes and Co-ordination of Documents Act — a far more drastic piece of legislation. The numerous passes of the past were replaced by a single "reference book" containing the African's employment contract and many of the particulars contained in the documents he was formerly required to carry. Women, not previously covered by the pass laws, were now brought within them. African leaders complained that without a pass, an African man was worse than emasculated. He had no right to travel or to walk up a street, or even to be alone at home. Indeed the reference book was the precondition even to getting a house in an urban area like Soweto, or obtaining a marriage licence.[4]

In Chapter 1, one of the vignettes describes proceedings observed by the author in the Langa court. The case described was one involving a pass offence. This happens to the extent of a quarter of a million cases a year. The sentence regularly imposed is R.5 for not being in possession of a pass and R.50 for being in an urban area without a right to be there. This total of R.55 is generally beyond the means of the poor person who has been picked up on the pass offence and the sentence of imprisonment in lieu of payment of fine seems to average one day per rand. Consequently such a person would have an imprisonment order of fifty-five days imposed on him.

The tendency of many African families if they can scrape together a few dollars is to pass the hat around and collect sufficient funds to relieve a person who has been thus imprisoned. Consequently, these fines tend to be paid at least in part after a short term of imprisonment and the offender is "released".

In some courts the cases are disposed of almost at the rate of one every three minutes, thus attracting the name among some liberal workers of "sausage machine" courts. The accused is generally asked whether he is guilty or not. As he is quite often undefended the plea of guilty comes back within a few seconds of the question, whereupon the magistrate passes sentence.

But prison sentences were not all. The system of Farm Gaols was a convenient method by which the white farmers joined with the police in a mutually beneficial scheme of keeping the prison population down. Persons convicted of the purely statutory pass offence would be sent to the farms as free labourers. There they would dig potatoes with their bare fingers, with overseers standing over them with whips which they did not hesitate to use. The "convicts", many of them boys, lived in barracks under guard on a diet worse than prison fare. The State President, C.R. Swart, praised these "farm gaols" on the ground that "They relieved the country of the expense of accommodating offenders, they helped farmers — and they rehabilitated criminals".[5]

There are offices such as the Athlone Advice Office which make it their business to give legal backing and support to persons who have been picked up on the pass laws. Attorneys from a number of firms are briefed by the Advice Office and act free of charge. In this way hundreds of people charged under influx control or illegal squatting legislation have been defended but this is still only a drop in the ocean. These organisations also tend as far as possible to station a representative in court whether the accused is legally defended or not, in the belief that the presence of an outsider in court keeps the proceedings a little more orderly and reasonable than they otherwise might be. A visit to any of these courts is a must for a foreigner in South Africa. If he has not seen one of them and its queues of helpless accused persons, he has missed a good part of the South African problem.

A great deal of trouble and harassment attends the first issue of a reference book to a young person. Numerous complaints have been received of arrogance, authoritarianism and obstruction on the part of the West Rand Administration Board Officials and the Department of Plural Relations in the issue of this first book. Young people are told to come to the office in order to swear affidavits and are driven from pillar to post in order to furnish such other evidence as the bureaucrat may in his unfettered discretion demand. Once an applicant has been fortunate enough to receive his identity document, he has to run through the entire procedure afresh, with the Labour Bureau demanding affidavits on all manner of irksome details.

People visiting the Athlone Office with pass law grievances would, but for the services of this office, have no opportunity whatsoever of obtaining relief. A lawyer would be beyond their reach; and approaching any government office would be courting an unsympathetic reception and an intolerably long exchange of letters.

Any visitor to the Athlone Office would see at first hand the sad plight of persons who are at the receiving end of the pass laws. A man would come in for example with a statement that he had misplaced his pass book. This may or may not be true. If indeed it is, as may well be the case, it means that he must establish by an affidavit to the satisfaction of an unsympathetic bureaucrat that his pass book has in fact been lost. His particulars must be capable of reconstruction sufficiently for the purpose of creating a duplicate of the pass book. Until these almost impossible conditions are satisfied, he would be a person adrift in his own country and in very real danger of being apprehended and deported to one of the homelands. A woman may come in with the statement that her husband had been picked up three nights ago, that she had lost contact with him and she did not know where he was or whether he was in need of any kind of assistance or whether he was undergoing torture or harassment by the police. By herself she would be completely unable to establish contact. With the aid of the Athlone Office, very often the prisoner is located and not infrequently legal representation arranged.

In addition to the misery of loss of earnings caused to the millions of people who have been prosecuted under the pass laws, they also serve — as Professor John Dugard observes[6]— to terrorise many other citizens whose documents may not be in order.

b) *The Bantu (Urban Areas) Consolidation Act*

For an African to be entitled to remain more than seventy two hours in an urban area, he must be able to prove, 1) birth and continuous residence within that area since birth, or 2) continuous employment with one employer for ten years, or 3) employment in the area for fifteen years, or 4) that he or she is the wife, unmarried daughter or son under the age of eighteen, of one of those qualified as stated before, or 5) that he or she has a special permit. This right of residence is the much prized Section 10 right.[7]

It will be seen that the specified conditions impose a most onerous set of requirements which severely curtail liberty of movement. Continuity of residence is theoretically broken even by an absence of three months. If for example a person resident in Soweto should go to school in Swaziland or to the University of Cape Town or to Durban for a job and is away for more than three months, he can lose his right to residence in Soweto. It matters little that he has lived there since birth. A person can lose his status by obeying the time honoured African custom by which a grandson spends a year or two in his grandmother's village helping her with the chores and the tending of cattle. Such persons are in grave danger of being parted from their families for ever. However the courts' interpretations of 'absence' for the purposes of this provision have been liberal, but it is only a minute proportion of those affected who can reach a court with its formalities and expense. The majority must be content with a bureaucratic decision, which in most cases is excessively severe.

The specified conditions mean also that the right to found a family is delayed till almost beyond the normal age at which a person may expect to found a family, for a person needs to wait fifteen years serving several employers if he desires to obtain permission to live in a city environment. Assuming he starts work at twenty, he would be thirty-five by the time he can think of establishing a family.

The conditions also have the effect of delivering up employees bound hand and foot to their employers. As an employee piles up years of service and approaches the magical ten year period, he can on no account suffer his continuity of service to be broken. He must therefore cringe to every demand and humiliation the employer may load upon him. The employer holds over him a whip not merely of dismissal from his job but of exile to distant homelands and of break-up of home and family.

The system means cringing also to the official who issues the pass. He is the bossman — 'baas' in South African parlance. When one reports at the pass office one puts aside one's personal pride and dignity. "Yes, baas, no baas, oh yes, yes, baas",[8] is the order of the day at the pass office. The white official swells with satisfaction and self-importance. The black pass seeker seethes with an internal resentment which will shortly be uncontainable.

Another section of the Act (Section 29) empowers a police officer to arrest any African without warrant in an urban area if he "has reason to believe" that he is "an idle or undesirable person". The unhappy citizen is then brought before a Bantu Affairs Commissioner and asked to "give a good and satisfactory account of himself". If the Commissioner is not so satisfied he may order such person to be sent to his homeland or a rehabilitation centre or a farm colony or to an approved employer on contract for a specified period.

A recent amendment now lays down a specific period of unemployment after which a person may be declared "idle or undesirable". In practice, one understands, a work seeker does not usually become a victim of these laws. The fact is, however, that the laws are there and can be implemented in a given case.

New powers given to a Bantu Affairs Board under an amendment of this Act in 1956 enable the Board to order the removal of an African from an urban area where "his presence is detrimental to the maintenance of peace and order in any such area". This power exists even where the African was born and domiciled in the area.

c) *The Bantu (Prohibition of Interdicts) Act*

It is an accepted principle of all civilised systems of law that access to a court of law ought not to be denied to groups within the community merely on grounds of race. It is one thing to say that a particular species of order is not justiciable by the courts. It is another thing altogether to admit that such a matter is ordinarily justiciable by the courts but will not be so because of the petitioner's racial group.

This is precisely what South African law ordains through the above Act. It specifically prohibits an African from obtaining a court interdict to suspend the operation of any banishment order pending an attack upon the validity of such order. An African, even if he be ordered to leave an urban area without any authority for such an order, must first leave — maybe to a homeland six hundred miles away — and then contest the order. One of the most repressive measures in South Africa, the wholesale movement of Africans away from urban areas and away from 'black spots' thus becomes for practical purposes free of judicial supervision. The Act applies only to Africans and deprives them, by reason of their race, of a right to invoke the protection of the courts, while that right is still enjoyed by members of other races.[9]

d) *The Group Areas Act*

Reference has been made at many points in this study, to the strange phenomena produced by the Group Areas Act, including the demolition of large mixed residential areas such as District 6 in Cape Town. The statutory basis on which this is done in the Group Areas Act, No. 41 of 1950 and its successive amendments leading to consolidating statutes in 1957 and 1966.

In pursuance of these Acts several thousands of persons have been served with notices to leave areas in which their families have resided or traded for generations. In some instances the housing occupied by them has been demolished. In others it has been taken over for the needs of another racial group. In some instances tidy profits have been made by white entrepreneurs who have taken over the houses of affluent Indians who have been asked to leave, and converted them into luxury housing for whites. In District 6, occupied by coloureds since 1834, 61,000 coloureds were moved out.

The Act is implemented in discriminatory fashion. Some whites have necessarily to be moved in order to achieve segregation, but the number of whites moved is far less than that of the other groups. By the end of 1975, for example, when 58,834 coloured families, 30,646 Indian families and 142 Chinese families had been moved, only 1,594 white families were moved.[10]

Nor are the courts upholders of the right of the individual to live where he pleases. In a recent case, mentioned to the author by a member of the Johannesburg bar, an Indian who had been evicted from his house and could find no alternative accommodation within an Indian area, had prevailed upon the owner of unoccupied flats in a white area to permit him to live in one of them. Upon a prosecution under the Act the defence of necessity was taken — the accused had no other accommodation to which he could go. The court made a great advance on prevailing practice and entertained the plea of necessity as a possible defence, but ruled that the accused had failed to prove necessity in that he had failed to eliminate the possibility that he and his family could have stayed in a hotel within the Indian area. At the time of the author's leaving South Africa this matter was under appeal before the Appellate Division, and the result is not yet known.

In fact the highest court, the Appellate Division, seems almost to have given its blessing to the Act, when it was attacked on the ground of inequality. It said, "The

Group Areas Act represents a colossal social experiment and a long term policy. It necessarily involves the movement out of Group Areas of numbers of people throughout the country. Parliament must have envisaged that compulsory population shifts of persons occupying certain areas would inevitably cause disruption and, within the foreseeable future, substantial inequalities".[1]

In travelling through the cities of South Africa one sometimes sees houses, evidently quite fit for human habitation, but marked for demolition. On some of them notices have been affixed; "Spare this house, people need it". This seems ironical in a community of acute housing shortage.

e) *The Population Registration Act. No.30 of 1950*

A number of legislative provisions dating back to 1911 defined the various racial groups in South Africa, but the boundaries were not absolutely rigid and there was a certain ease of movement from one group to the other. All this flexibility ended with the Population Registration Act which aimed at rigid race classification and its documentation through registers and identity cards.

The Act caused much humiliation, heartache and family disruption. Persons within the same family were sometimes classified in different racial groups on the basis of physical appearance. This happened most often in the case of coloured persons, some of whom had light skins while others in the same family were so dark-skinned as to be clearly non-white in appearance. The Group Areas Act, already referred to, made it necessary for these family members, thus separately classified, to take up residence in their separate areas. This meant not only the parting of brother from brother but often of parent from child. Moreover, one of the tests formulated for determining a person's racial group was the company he habitually kept. This requirement introduced an element of great reluctance on the part of the person enjoying the more privileged classification to associate with his less privileged family members.

Prior to the Group Areas Act there had been many instances of coloured and white persons living in the same neighbourhood. Likewise coloured persons married to African spouses might live in a coloured neighbourhood, without objection.

In the first case coloured persons who had grown up and been accepted as white might be subsequently classified as coloured and would have to leave the neighbourhood. In the second case the spouses would be separated, each being assigned to his or her own racial area.

In the case of such mixed marriages the lighter hued children might go to one school and the darker children of the same family to another. The siblings would now be territorially separated for life.

Indeed inspectors went round the schools to pick out children whose skin colour did not permit them to continue in the schools they attended. The inspector would initiate the necessary proceedings for the child's removal to his or her appropriate school and residential area.

On February 15, 1980, Susan Green, a widow arrived at a local magistrate's office to marry Aubrey Joose, a white man, with whom she had lived for three years. The magistrate examined her identity papers and found that she had been reclassified from white to coloured the previous year. The couple were turned away. Mrs. Green, as well as her children by her earlier marriage, had been reclassified by bureaucratic action without explanation and had tried in vain to have the classification altered.

The fate of most non-whites in South Africa is dependent on this type of arbitrary bureaucratic decision. An ultimate appeal lies to the Supreme Court from population registration decisions but only the minutest fraction of persons prejudically affected by such decisions have the resources to pursue the matter thus far. In any event there must be little satisfaction in having to obtain a declaration regarding one's legal status through the evidence of expert physiologists and anthropologists, much in the way biological specimens are classified but without even a pretence of scientific exactitude. Nor is there much joy in attempting to satisfy the court that one is a person who —

> "a) in appearance obviously is a white person and who is generally not accepted as a coloured person; or
> b) is generally accepted as a white person and is not in appearance obviously not a white person . . . "

This is the definition of a white person under the Act. Serious-minded judges, serious-minded lawyers and a sophisticated legal apparatus are all studiously engaged in operating this provision, which according to the thinking in every other part of the world could only belong to the pages of very imaginative fiction.

f) *The Marriage Laws*

The marriage and immorality laws have poisoned South African life at every level. One meets obviously coloured people desperately trying to convince one that they are white; people who married across the colour line before the Mixed Marriages Act, whose marriages were broken up by the Act; people whose domestic peace has been disturbed at midnight by vice squad detectives with dogs and searchlights. One hears of children removed from schools owing to the stigma of having a coloured ancestor in their bloodline; of distinguished South Africans forced to leave the country because they desired to contract a marriage across the barrier; of suicides by those who have been found violating the Act; of social ostracism in cases where a person is pronounced white by law but is apparently somewhat darker than a white is expected to be.

How strange this is to the outside world the average South African citizen does not apparently see. It is ironical too that the Afrikaner, on whom so much responsibility rests for these laws, is often dark-skinned enough to pass for Asiatic. Indeed there are many Asians and Middle Easterners much fairer than many an Afrikaner. One meets dark hued Afrikaners, many of them darker than the Burghers of Sri Lanka (descendants of the Portuguese and Dutch settlers), who claim most insistently that they are white. The author recalls a dark hued assistant at a Dutch Reformed Church book fair explaining to customers that some of the books on display were prepared for use in the coloured and black churches. " 'They' found it convenient to attend services in separate churches while 'we' also felt the same way about ours. Why shouldn't each group worship separately and be more at ease instead of their coming to our churches and our going to theirs?"

Nor is the administration of the laws any the less strange to the eyes of a foreigner. The relevant provisions of the Act are set out in Appendix C. Appendix D sets out a judgment picked at random from the Law Reports, showing how the courts set about determining the question whether a person is "white" or not. One has to keep reassuring oneself that this is indeed a real judgment concerning real persons in the twentieth century world, and not a flight of fancy by some imaginative writer.

The detection and arrest procedures are of the utmost interest. World news was made by one such prosecution in May 1979, when five policemen were charged with criminal injury to a 22 year-old white woman whom the police suspected of sleeping with an Indian South African in her Pretoria flat.[12] The man produced identity documents proving he was white. Counsel for the policemen, explaining the conduct of the police, said that the man appeared to be an Indian. "He acts, talks and looks like one".

Police Captain van Niekerk gave interesting evidence. He said that South African policemen were trained to listen for ten minutes before pouncing on lovers infringing the ban on sex across the colour line. He said the procedure was laid down in the police training manual.

At least two, preferably three, policemen should make the raid so that there would be plenty of corroborative evidence. Ideally a police photographer should accompany the raiding party. Binoculars for long-range surveillance, two-way radios and a tape recorder for snatches of conversation or sighs of passion were recommended equipment. Duplicate keys should be cut to avoid the noise of breaking down the door. The object was to catch the suspects in the sexual act. The bedding and clothing must be taken to a laboratory for analysis and the suspects taken to a district surgeon without delay for medical examination.

Though prosecutions are few under these laws, and have not been instituted as frequently as before, the laws are deep-rooted and perhaps no pronouncement of Prime Minister Botha has been bolder than his declaration in 1979 that he was willing to consider their amendment or abolition. This announcement caused dissension in the Cabinet and the Minister of Police and Prisons, Louis Le Grange, was reported to have said,[13] that "anyone suggesting that the government will do away with these Acts is telling a blatant lie. The Acts will merely be reviewed".

g) *Preventive Detention*

One of the greatest blots upon the South African statute book is the provision for preventive detention under the Terrorism Act, to which reference has already been made in Chapter 3. We have already seen how, contrary to every canon of civilised jurisprudence, it places on an accused person the burden of proving his innocence beyond reasonable doubt. It also refutes accepted legal principles in that although it was passed in June 1967, its date of commencement was June 1962! — five years retrospectivity, bringing within its net many things done long before the Act was even conceived.

This Act, providing for the detention of suspected

terrorists, was modelled on former provisions which had been of a temporary nature. However, not only were the provisions more tightly drawn, there was no limit of ninety days or any other period during which detention should terminate or be renewed by authority of a magistrate. The legislation was meant to be permanent, for the Minister said, "I believe this legislation to be of a virtually temporary/permanent nature, because the onslaught by the terrorists has only just begun".[14] The Minister rejected an amendment which proposed annual reconsideration and made no secret of the police pressures which lay behind the enactment.

The author met a civil rights worker who had been detained on suspicion under this provision. He claimed he was detained in solitary confinement for months, and subjected to constant interrogation for days on end except for periods when sheer exhaustion or demands of nature interrupted the questioning. The detainees are not informed of the charges against them but are aggressively and continuously questioned in the hope that some information would in a moment of weakness be inadvertently divulged. The worker in question said also that in the process of questioning, fake information is given to the person questioned in order to befuddle him and warp his judgment, for instance that a close friend of his has claimed the suspect was a terrorist or that a close friend, himself in detention, has confessed. After the Biko episode the police are apparently more circumspect, but are still not above causing physical harm. Deaths in detention have occurred even after the Biko case.

The South African Institute of Race Relations in a detailed report on the Administration of Security Legislation from January 1976 to March 1977, reveals that during this period alone, twelve persons died while in security detention. As at 25 March 1977, 471 persons were believed to be held in detention, of whom eighty-four were school pupils, forty-nine were university students and five were churchmen. During the same period, 366 persons were released from detention without charges framed against them — ninety-seven after detention for periods up to fourteen days, thirty for periods up to fifteen and thirty days, thirty-five for periods between one and three months, one hundred and forty-one for periods between three and six months, twenty-five for periods between six and nine months, eight for periods between nine and twelve months, and five for periods over a year. All these citizens are without redress for the loss of their liberty, not to speak of the solitary confinement and torture they probably underwent.

This "temporary/permanent" provision continued on the statute book from the date of its introduction and still remains the law. In 1979, a very influential South African, Dr. D.P. de Villiers in an important address delivered at the Rand Afrikaans University[15] drew the attention of the legal profession to its duties in regard to this provision.

He pointed out that it had now been twelve years upon the statute book when in fact the only justification for introducing such provisions was the hope that they would be speedily withdrawn when the immediate pressures ceased. He drew attention to the manner in which Israel has learned to live with constant danger and yet preserve the basic freedoms. He pointed out that detention could now occur for an unspecified time without even a prima facie case and questioned whether the distinction between legal dissent and criminal conduct was being faithfully applied.

Dr. de Villiers concluded that urgent action was required. I quote *in extenso:* "It must be positive: to devise a system which will contain the necessary checks and balances to serve, as far as possible, the fundamental rights and the sense of justice of the community on the one hand, together with the need for effectively combating terrorism and sabotage on the other. The endeavour should be to achieve this in a non-political way as far as possible. As in the Roman state at its peak, use should be made on a creative and advisory basis, of the best talents in the legal profession... An extended form of commission inquiry seems to be indicated". He concluded: "If the State does not itself take the initiative in this direction, I would contend that the legal profession should close its ranks and strongly and irresistibly insist upon it. Only then could the profession be truly worthy of the high standards of our great legal heritage".

This lecture was significant as an important expression of guilt feeling by a leader of the profession. Such a call to duty has been long overdue and the failure of the profession to concern itself with these blots upon its statute book is forfeiting for the South African legal profession the respect of the world. The call has come just in time and the government, in a mood to get moving with dismantling some of the apparatus of apartheid, has now responded with the appointment of a committee with far-ranging terms of inquiry.

h) *Banning Orders*

The extent to which a banning order can affect a man's personality is perhaps not fully appreciated except by those who have been under such orders or have been close to them. Steve Biko was once banned to the Magistrate's district of King William's Town and to his home which is in Kingsburg, and many accounts of the hardships involved have appeared in numerous books and journals. The ban meant that for five years he could not travel at all. He could not receive guests or relatives at home, he could not attend any gatherings or visit friends with his wife. If a banned person should enter a room in which there is already more than one person, all but one of the occupants must leave, for the banned person cannot speak to more than one at a time. If he does so, he courts up to three years in prison. A banning order gives the banned person a feeling of being a social outcast, as friends tend to avoid him for fear of incriminating him. Informers are everywhere, and there are few places the eyes of the police do not reach. The exchange of ideas with others, on which the vitality of thought is so dependent, is impossible. The banned person cannot publish or be published. He becomes a recluse. The banning order can be kept in force indefinitely without legal trial of the banned person. In fact banning orders are indicative of a lack of legal evidence against the person concerned, for if there were legal evidence of subversive activity, the state would in all probability launch a court prosecution. Reasons are not given for the order, nor is the person entitled to know why he has been banned. The terms of the banning order depend on the Minister and they vary from case to case. Few know how to interpret the regulations under which they are issued. Neighbours and friends and even relatives are often under the impression that it is somehow illegal to enter the home of a banned person or to invite him into one's own house.

Under the internal security legislation a person may have a number of different shackles clamped on him by the Minister of Justice. The Minister has power to prohibit a person from attending gatherings, to confine him to an area, to exclude him from an area, to subject him to house detention, to prevent him from being active in group activities, to prohibit him from performing specified acts, or from communicating with any person, and to require him to report at stated intervals at the police station.[16] Grant of power in almost every instance is preceded by the phrase, "if the Minister is satisfied". This means that recourse to the courts is little more than a theoretical possibility.[17] In the case of *R.* v. *Ngwevela*[18] the courts held that the notice was invalid for want of compliance with the rule that the accused should be heard before being shackled. This was in reliance on a basic common law rule that a person should not be condemned unheard. The legislature promptly intervened to neutralise this liberalism and by statute validated the notices in defiance of the common law principle. In 1964 the courts enhanced the citizen's helplessness by holding[19] that the Minister may refuse to furnish any reason other than the statement that he was satisfied that the applicant was "engaged in activities which are furthering or are calculated to further, the achievement of some of the objects of Communism".

Where a person is prohibited from attending gatherings there is an automatic prohibition upon the recording, reproduction, publication or dissemination, without the consent of the Minister of any speech, writing, utterance or statement of the person, no matter when or where they were made. By this token even the scientific writings of a brilliant researcher become subject to ministerial approval as a precondition to publication.[20] In fact, the ban upon the publications of a person who has once been banned from attending gatherings appears to be permanent and to be operative even after his death — a statutory severity which Attorneys-General have advised against enforcing after the order has been withdrawn.[21]

Reporting to police stations, sometimes as often as four times in the course of a single day, is another of the punishments the Minister can impose. Failure to comply almost inevitably involves prosecution and a term in prison which is mandatory, even if the failure to report was through forgetfulness.[22]

Being damned in the days of the Spanish Inquisition was not much different from being banned in South Africa today. The former happened centuries ago and is a shock to the sensitivities of the modern world. The latter is happening in the here and now, and is condoned by many who condemn the Inquisition.

i) *Capital Offences*

Two statutory provisions of 1963 greatly increased the circle of offences punishable with death under South African law. These provisions were contained in the General Law Amendment Act 37 of 1963.

These provisions are drafted in such sweeping terms that, theoretically, the most extreme results could ensue, though of course the courts would temper their extremism, and no government would seek to enforce them. These include:

a) a person who defended a scheme for United Nations intervention for non-white grievances would be liable to be hanged for his proposal or condemned to a minimum penalty of five years.

b) a person who proposed passive resistance to apartheid laws could be hanged. Gandhi if alive today could be hanged for his programme of passive resistance.

c) A South African who went to an English university at any time after 17 July 1950 to study communism for two years could, according to the strict wording of the Act, be hanged for furthering the aims of communism unless he could prove beyond reasonable doubt that such was not his purpose.[23]

Such provisions must be considered against the background of reversals of the burden of proof. The accused is under the burden of proving his innocence beyond reasonable doubt, and this does indeed place the shadow of death by judicial decree over many of South Africa's most freedom loving citizens.

That prosecutions may not occur in many instances covered by these provisions is not in point. The harsh reality is that the statute book does contain these provisions and neither parliamentarian nor judge nor lawyer has been able to persuade the government that these provisions are barbarous by all accepted legal standards.

j) *The Unlawful Organisations Act*

Act 35 of 1960 was introduced mainly in order to outlaw the African National Congress (ANC) and the Pan African Congress (PAC). Reference to the work of these organisations has been made earlier in the text.[24] The State President is given power to declare an organisation unlawful if he is satisfied that its activities seriously threaten the safety of the public or the maintenance of public order. The President's declaration is virtually unchallengeable.[25]

Once an organisation is declared unlawful, the provisions of the Suppression of Communism Act apply to it — (s.2).

The Act does not end with these suppressions of the right to associate. It goes on to effect what Professor Mathews describes as a "flash of executive magic", the like of which is perhaps unique in the legal systems of all time.

Section 1(3) gives the State President power to declare by proclamation that any organisation specified in the proclamation is and was at all times another organisation already declared unlawful. The former organisation will then be deemed to be the latter organisation for purposes of criminal proceedings.

Thus a person who is a member of an organisation which he believes is a black cultural organisation may suddenly find that by proclamation this organisation is deemed to be the Pan African Congress. He is then liable to criminal prosecution for carrying on the activities of an unlawful organisation. The law makes the government situation doubly watertight by providing that no court shall have jurisdiction to pronounce on the validity of the State President's proclamation.[26]

k) *Censorship*

The State President has the power by proclamation in the Gazette to prohibit the printing, publication or dissemination of any periodical or other publication. He needs only to be satisfied that the publication professes to be a publication for the spread of Communism, or that it was published by, or under the direction of an organisation declared unlawful under the Act.[27] Indeed it is an offence punishable with imprisonment for up to three years to be in possession, without the permission of the Minister, of a publication banned by the State President.[28] Even lawyers' offices must regularly toss out material which comes within the scope of a banning order. Other statutes under which censorship is imposed are the Publications Act, 42 of 1974, under which published works may be banned on grounds of undesirability and the Defence Act 44 of 1957, under which postal, telegraphic, telephonic and radio communications within, into or from the Republic can be censored — not merely during a state of war but for the prevention or suppression of terrorism, or for the preservation or suppression of internal disorder.

There are also restrictions on the registration of newspapers and bans on the publications of restricted persons. The registration of a newspaper is prohibited unless the proprietor has deposited with the Minister of the Interior an amount not exceeding R.20,000 determined by the Minister of Justice, and few proprietors are willing to risk such a forfeiture. The establishment of anti-government newspapers is thus a highly dangerous operation. Speeches, writings or statements of listed persons, cannot, without the consent of the Minister, be recorded, reproduced, printed, published or disseminated, and the power to impose this restriction on individuals may be exercised by the Minister in his discretion.

Recent legislation has made it incumbent upon newspapers to be in a position to prove the correctness of any proceedings they may print regarding occurrences in prisons or at the hands of the police. Consequently newspapers tend to leave these out of their coverage for the reason that they can scarcely afford to take the risk.

Even university professors have fallen within the ban, and the writings of Professor Simons, formerly Associate Professor of Comparative African Government and Law at the University of Cape Town, and the late Professor Roux, Professor of Botany in the University of the Witwatersrand, were banned at an early stage. Dr. Raymond Hoffenberg, Senior Lecturer and Research Worker, Cape Town Medical School, was banned in 1967, thus bringing his academic and research work to an end, despite his international reputation in his field.[29]

In consequence of all these various measures, dialogue is breaking down or, indeed, has broken down, and any means by which peaceful change can be effected becomes correspondingly more difficult.

It was observed at an earlier point in this narrative that the visitor to South Africa is pleasantly surprised by the degree of freedom allowed to the English speaking press to criticise the government. While this is indeed true, note must also be taken of the fact that the South African censor does strike hard in many areas, not commonly visible to readers of the English speaking press.

The Publications Act of 1974 instituted a vigorous system of censorship, which is applied to ban a number of publications emanating from academic and student circles. Indeed even some church writings have been banned under these powers.

A large number of student publications banned in 1979 included: *Bulletin Three* — a University of Cape Town publication, *DOME* — a publication of the University of Natal, *Wit Student* — publication of the University students of Witwatersrand, *NUX* — of the University of Natal, *Bona fide* — the University of Cape Town's Law Student Council's publication, and *SPOEG* — issued by the University of Cape Town's Fine Arts Student Council. So also *Varsity*, the University of Cape Town Campus newspaper, and *National Student* — the paper of the National Union of South African students.

Hardest hit appears to be the University of Cape Town whose publications criticising the administration in Namibia were banned, as well as a publication called *Statement Four*, dealing with a particular labour dispute that attracted a great deal of national attention — the Fattis and Monis labour dispute. So also a pamphlet commemorating the 1976 Soweto student revolt was banned.

In June and July this year *Varsity* and *National Student* were banned for ever.

Among church writings that have been banned are the Anglican newspaper *SEEK*, the April edition of which came under government disapproval, and *SA Outlook*, edited by Dr. Francis Wilson, and a British Council of Churches publication, entitled *Political Change in South Africa — Britain's Responsibility*.

Literary works that have come under banning orders are *Staff Rider* Vol.11 No.1., *Donderdag of Woensdag* by John Miles; *Africa, My Beginning* by Madingoane; *Burgher's Daughter* by Nadine Gordimer, and *Just the Two of Us* and *Muriel at Metropolitan* by Miriam Tlali.

Nadine Gordimer's novel has been described by the *New York Times* as "going to the heart of the racial conflict in South Africa...reminiscent of the great Russian prerevolutionary novels", while the London *Daily Telegraph* has observed of it that it is the most compelling novel of the year. *The Observer* says that it is a beautifully manipulated work of art moving towards a tragic and triumphant conclusion. The publication control board's reasons for its ban are, among others, that parts of the book bring a section of the inhabitants of the Republic into ridicule and contempt, that the publication is a political novel and the treatment of the theme is undesirable, that the book seen as a whole is harmful to the relations between sections of the inhabitants of the Republic, and that the book is prejudicial to the safety of the state and to general welfare and to peace and good order.

It is to be seen whether the relaxed attitudes which the present government speaks of will be implemented in the sphere of censorship as well. There is as yet no real evidence of such a relaxation.

1) *Separate Facilities*

In 1934 the Appellate Division was called upon to consider the validity of regulations setting up separate post office counters for blacks and whites. This kind of discrimination was not new in the world. The United States had practised it and the practice had received the stamp of judicial approval in that country in the 1896 decision of *Plessy* v *Ferguson*. In that case "separate but equal" facilities were held to be not unconstitutional. The Appellate

Division had little difficulty in arriving at the same conclusion and upheld the regulations on the ground that their
separation was not unreasonable, provided there was equality
in the facilities offered.[30]

Attitudes in the United States turned full circle by
1954 when in *Brown* v *Board of Education*[31] the Supreme
Court held that separation of black children from others of
similar age and qualifications was permanently detrimental
to them. In South Africa, however, discrimination was
heightened. The Reservation of Separate Amenities Act of
1953 encouraged the provision of separate facilities for
the different racial groups and expressly provided that no
reservation should be declared invalid on the ground that no
similar, or substantially similar amenity had been provided
for any other race or class. Legislation in 1977 (The Reservation of Public Amenities Amendment Act) went even
further. Whereas the earlier legislation encouraged the
provision of separate facilities, the 1977 Act enabled the
government to direct that separate facilities be established.
The same reservation applied — that the absence of similar
amenities was not to be a cause of invalidity.

The haphazard relaxation of petty apartheid that is
evident in many parts of South Africa has nothing to do with
revision of the laws. The laws relating to apartheid remain
very much alive. The law-makers of South Africa, if sincere
in their professions, should amend laws such as the above
rather than make attractive public pronouncements which
stand contradicted by their statute books.

m) *Migrant Labour*

One of the prime sources of black misery is the
legislation regarding migrant labour. At the age of fifteen
a person in the homelands is required to register as a work
seeker. This registration continues until the age of sixty-
five. Reference to the various hardships it causes has been
adequately made elsewhere in this book[32]— and there is no
need here to reiterate them. Job categorisation, employment
bureaux, contracts on terms not explained to the employee,
separation from home and family for fifty weeks a year,
unisex dormitories packed sixteen to a room, the whip hand
given by the legislation to the employer — all these add up
to a picture of total deprivation of industrial rights which
gives the migrant worker a status very nearly akin to slavery.

n) *Trade Unions*

Trade union consciousness among African workers has long been a feature of the South African scene. We have already, in discussing black nationalism, referred to some of the earlier labour movements in South African industry.[33]

In 1942 a war measure — War Measure No.145 of 1942 — totally prohibited strikes by African workers and provided a system for compulsory arbitration. In 1953 the principles of this Act were extended by prohibiting lockouts, sympathy strikes and the instigation of strikes.

The Industrial Conciliation Act of 1956 provided a system of collective bargaining in industry, but expressly excluded all Africans from these processes. The way in which the legislature set about this was by the simple device of refusing to recognise black employees as "employees". The Act ostensibly recognised trade unions, which are "any number of employees in any particular undertaking, industry, trade or occupation". It went on, however, to define "employee" for the purpose of the Act as "any person (other than a Bantu) employed etc". The word "Bantu" as we have seen is defined in South Africa as a person "who is, or is generally accepted as, a member of any aboriginal race or tribe of Africa".[34] By very simple legislative provisions, therefore, the very Act that recognised trade union rights for some was the Act which denied trade union rights to others. Recent legislation has rectified this gross anomaly by amending the definition of employee and giving registration to black trade unions.

Despite this amendment, black unions are still the victims of discriminatory treatment. Strikes organised by them are often broken by the police with police dogs being let loose on the strikers and the security laws being invoked against their leaders. When the author was in Durban, there was much talk that police dogs had been unleashed on strikers who had assembled outside a food processing factory. The incident was described as remarkable not for the use of the police dogs, but because one of the dogs had by accident attacked and injured a white foreman. In February 1980 the treatment of black union leaders in Port Elizabeth was the subject of angry comment by black unions.

Trade unionism must be viewed against the background of legislation so heavily penalising black labour that until 1974 it was an offence criminally punishable for a labourer to break his contract of employment — a position remedied, as we shall see in Chapter 8, not by any internal change of heart but by pressure applied by American unions.

For example, the Bantu Labour Act No.67 of 1964, not only made it a criminal offence to break a contract of employment, but even to harbour an African contract worker who had unlawfully left his employer.

Mixed trade unions, *i.e.* of whites and coloureds or Asians were denied registration by the Industrial Conciliation Act No.28 of 1956, and an amending Act No.41 of 1959 placed further restrictions on the operation of mixed unions. Another amending Act No.61 of 1966, prohibited strikes and lockouts for any purpose connected with the relationship between employers and employees.

Despite all these repressive measures industrial action by black employees is growing and especially in Port Elizabeth there has been mounting tension. On January 28, 1980, the government rushed riot police to this scene of earlier conflagrations, fearing that black industrial action may turn violent. Police stations were fortified with sandbags, turning them into military command posts. The methods employed on this occasion were a series of walkouts demanding better pay and working conditions.

The statute book needs urgently to open out safety valves for black industrial action. Else it will not be possible to keep down the lid that has at present been clamped on black discontent.

o) *Foreign Assistance*

The Fund Raising Act of 1978 prevents any South African organisation from receiving any aid from abroad without government authorisation.

In the past Black Sash, Dependants' Conference and many other social upliftment movements derived some part of their support from well wishers abroad. This most recent move of the government will necessarily have a crippling effect upon all liberal organisations and considerably lessens the scope for action by South African well wishers abroad. This strikes the outside observer as a retrograde step, especially disappointing in the context of prevailing hopes of increasing liberalism in government thinking.

The Uniqueness of South Africa's Statute Book

This brief and incomplete survey of some of the actual provisions of the South African statute book prompts an interesting reflection. It is common knowledge that some of the most authoritarian and wicked regimes in history have sought always to justify their conduct by reference to high moral principles and that their statute book reflects this tone of high morality. The statute books of despotic regimes often appear to harmonise perfectly with basic principles of fairness, justice and equality. One has only to look at the constitutions or the statute books of any of the admitted dictatorships of modern times (bar Nazi Germany) to see the procession of high sounding principles of morality and social upliftment which pass through their pages. Scarcely any ruler is so impervious to public opinion or so regardless of his image as to defy the principle that he must appear to be just. Even in war the principle of the just war, which rulers have down the centuries invoked when they commit their countries to battle, is based upon this regard for their image and public opinion. Nobody reading even the statute book of Idi Amin's Uganda would detect in it any major flaws in its apparent dedication to the highest principles of justice. It was not in the statute book but in the field that the iniquities of that regime were perpetrated. People might have been battered to death, judges might have been liquidated, bribery and corruption might have been rampant — but all these left the statute book as such, virginal and blameless. The dictator at the centre would disclaim knowledge of these iniquities, for he did not want to proclaim himself as publicly endorsing the manifestly unjust.

South Africa must be one of those rare instances in human history where an otherwise advanced state openly places upon its statute book legal provisions which no morality can justify.

The Concept of the Rule of Law in South Africa

The British constitutional lawyer, A.V. Dicey, writing at the end of the last century, gave the doctrine of the rule of law a specific content: 1) absolute supremacy of regular law as opposed to arbitrary power, 2) equality before the law, and 3) the constitution is the consequence and not the source of the rights of individuals. For nearly a hundred years Dicey's formulation has been cited as the starting point for any discussion of the concept of the Rule of Law.

Dicey's formulation applied primarily to unwritten constitutions like the British, but its underlying principles are cited in the context of written constitutions as well. The world of Anglo-American jurisprudence holds the rule of law in high regard and the expression is looked on by some as being almost co-extensive with the human rights concept. The jurisprudence of international human rights has indeed sought to extend the Diceyan rule-of-law concept into a universal one.

South African lawyers do not as a body take kindly to the rule-of-law concept. There are many reasons for this and perhaps the operation of some of the injustices of the South African legal system can be better understood in the light of some of them.

We have in the section on the judiciary referred to the anti-British sentiments dating back to Boer war days, which South African judges have carried as scars of that conflict. Members of the bar exposed to the same experience, no doubt reacted similarly. The Diceyan formulation, a British formulation in the context of the British constitution and the British historical experience, was therefore not likely to arouse great enthusiasm among them. Furthermore, they were trained in a different legal system, the Roman-Dutch which had a deep liberal tradition, and they did not feel the need for reliance upon English law for the humanistic aspects which were already sufficiently contained in their own system. What was lost sight of was that there was, in the Diceyan formulation, an important element of resistance to arbitrary power which was not so clearly formulated by the Roman-Dutch lawyers. In the general designation of the British rule-of-law concept this aspect tended to be neglected.

But this was not all. The South African constitution acknowledges the sovereignty of God, and the Afrikaner tradition elevates this sovereignty to a cardinal principle governing law and society. Hence the central theme of law lay not in the protection of the subject against the state but in the observance by all, including the government, of the principles of Christian rulership, such as they were believed to be. One of these principles, in the Dutch Reformed tradition, was that of obedience to the duly constituted rulers (who had a God given mission as God's chosen people). There was no room in such a philosophy for inherent citizen rights against the state. The ruler who betrayed his trust would be accountable in other forums than the workaday courts. The subject's duty was not to seek to enforce human rights against him but to comply with the divinely ordained duty of obedience.

To this thinking must be added also the strain of positivism which South African lawyers have displayed, perhaps an inheritance from Germanic jurisprudence to which they have been more exposed than their English counterparts. The law is to be obeyed because it is the duly ordained law of the State. It emanates from the ruler and is to be honoured irrespective of its compliance with or departure from accepted principles of justice. If the law is unjust it must be set aside by proper procedures but until such time it must be obeyed and enforced.

All these philosophies suited the proponents of apartheid well. The Afrikaner lawyer, himself a beneficiary of the system, had no great difficulty in formulating ideological grounds for the rejection of the rule of law if it stood in the way of his privileges.

The Universal Declaration of Human Rights

We have already pointed out that nearly every section of the Universal Declaration stands completely negated by the Statute Book of South Africa.

For convenience of reference, brief mention may be made of Article 1 which states that all human beings are born free and equal in dignity and rights; Article 13 which provides that everyone has the right to freedom of movement and residence within the borders of each state and that everyone has the right to leave any country including his own and to return to his country; Article 23 which provides that everyone has the right to work, to free choice of employment, to just and favourable conditions of work and to protection against unemployment and that everyone without any discrimination has the right to equal pay for equal work; Article 2 which provides that everyone is entitled to all the rights and freedoms supporting the declaration without distinction of any kind such as race, colour, sex, language, religion, political or other opinions, national or social origin, property, birth or other status; Article 16 which states that men and women of full age without any limitation due to race, nationality or religion have the right to marry and found a family; Article 7 which states that all men and women are equal before the law and are entitled without any discrimination to equal protection of the law; Article 9 which states that no one shall be subjected to arbitrary arrest, detention or exile; Article 10 which states that everyone is entitled to a fair and public hearing by an independent and impartial tribunal in the determination of his rights and obligations and of any criminal charge against him; Article 11 which states that everyone charged with a penal offence has the right to be presumed innocent and proved guilty according to law in a public trial at which he has had all the guarantees necessary for his defence; Article 19 which provides that everyone has the right to freedom of opinion and expression; Article 20 which provides that everyone has the right to freedom of peaceful assembly and association and Article 26 which speaks of everyone's right to education which shall be free at least in the elementary and fundamental stages.

Every one of these fundamental rights has not merely not received adequate recognition from South Africa. The Statute book indeed contains a total denial of each one of these rights.

Consequently we have in South Africa the situation not of a need to expand human rights but a need to introduce them and in this regard the legal profession has an important role to play. It has traditionally been content merely to function within the framework of the existing legal system but it needs more positive action on the part of the legal profession if this denial of fundamental rights is, in any way, to be altered or reversed.

It is of interest that although the Universal Declaration of Human Rights was passed without a dissentient vote, South Africa abstained from voting on the Declaration in the General Assembly.

It is of interest also that when the question of apartheid in South Africa was taken up in the United Nations in 1952, South Africa strenuously opposed the move on the ground that it constituted an intervention in matters which are essentially within the domestic jurisdiction of South Africa, and as such prohibited by Article 2(7) of the Charter of the United Nations.

It is ironical that the argument that has so often commended itself to Soviet Russia when repression within that system is sought to be investigated, has commended itself equally strongly to South Africa, which sees itself as ideologically the opposite of Soviet Russia in all things.

The denials of human rights implicit in apartheid need no further elaboration. Some general comments will not, however, be out of place.

Human rights can be viewed as both nominate and innominate. There are the specific human rights which are enumerated in the Universal Declaration and the many more which are emerging as a result of a growing international human rights jurisprudence — as for example in the Covenant on Economic, Social and Cultural Rights. On the other hand there is the innominate aspect. Specific rights do not need to be articulated. There is a basic concept of human rights apart from its specific formulations and this is based on the oneness and the humanness of all mankind. Human rights by their very nature are possessed by all humans and are possessed by them equally. If they are not possessed equally, the persons not possessing them equally are by implication read out of the human race. For South Africa this means four-fifths of its population.

One final observation, ironical for both South Africa and the world. It is not generally known that the Preamble to the United Nations Charter, in which the nations of the world "reaffirm faith in fundamental human rights and in the dignity and worth of the human person" was proposed by Field Marshal Smuts![35]

The Role of the Judiciary

There is room for criticism of the South African judiciary for not having taken a firm judicial stand on apartheid legislation. A clear indication from them that this legislation flew in the face of the basic assumptions of the Judaeo-Christian legal tradition would not have been without practical impact. All European legal systems, stemming from this tradition, as elaborated by the thinking of the seventeenth and eighteenth century philosophers, accept as axiomatic the equality of man. The South African legal system alone stands out like a sore thumb in denial of this fundamental concept. This is all the more ironic when we see it against the humanistic liberalism of the Roman-Dutch legal system, on which the South African legal system is based.

It is not here suggested that judges can override laws passed by the legislature. There is nothing however to prevent their constant voicing of an attitude of disapproval which in its cumulative effect must register an impression upon the mind of the legislator.

The South African judiciary is a respected judiciary. Its integrity and honour stand as high as in any country one may name. The pity is all the greater that a judiciary enjoying so much prestige should have chosen not to register its disapproval. Indeed the judiciary, through its attitude of leaving matters to the political authority even though they did raise fundamental issues relating to freedom and liberty, has often encouraged the legislature in the course which it was set on pursuing since 1948.

In seeking to understand this paradox of a judiciary trained in a humanistic legal system becoming the willing implementers of a dehumanised code of laws, we gain some insights from history.

Here, as elsewhere, the Boer war comes in, for it sharply devided the judiciary of South Africa. Judges left their judicial work to ride to battle — sometimes to death, sometimes to imprisonment, sometimes to become guerilla leaders. Hertzog resigned his judicial office a week before war was declared and became a skilled General. Smuts, a State Attorney, is reported to have been seen frequently with a gun in one hand and a book on international law in the other.[36] Three future Chief Justices of South Africa were Boer War personalities — J. de Villiers who was sent as a prisoner of war to Bermuda, N.J. de Wet who fought in the Transvaal, and J.S. Curlewis who was military censor. Senior lawyers, from whose ranks later judges were to come, suffered bitterly in the war and those who survived carried these memories to the end. Some senior prosecutors were killed in action, some executed by the British, some exiled, some confined in prisoner of war camps, where they died.

It is little wonder against this background that some of the judiciary should permit the liberalism of their Roman-Dutch tradition to yield to the exigencies of the hard-won and, at times, perilous, Afrikaner situation. This is no excuse for some of the judicial attitudes that one sees at work in South Africa, but is at least some aid to understanding them. How else could one understand for example such an unjudicial utterance as the following, by a judge trained in a system emphasising equality — "The statement that all are equal before the law cannot be accepted unreservedly. It is undoubtedly subject to important qualifications and as far as the Transvaal is concerned it is manifest that Europeans and non-Europeans have in important respects, never been equal. Separation runs through our complete social structure in the Union".[37]

It is to be noted also that despite some aberrations, South African judges maintained at one stage a fairly benevolent attitude towards the black people. "The judges likened themselves to the guardians of the black people, and delivered strong lectures to white farmers, policemen and others found guilty of violence to black persons".[38] But by the 1960's this benevolent attitude was no longer so apparent, the judges in many instances giving active support to the machinery of discrimination. Examples are numerous and indeed superfluous, but a simple one will suffice.

In *S.* v. *Joseph*[39] a woman was required by Ministerial order to report at a police station between 12 noon and 2 p.m. on a specified day. Through forgetfulness she delayed in reporting until 5 p.m., when she did actually report. The Criminal Procedure Act prevented the magistrate from suspending the entire sentence of one year's imprisonment that the statute demanded for this offence, but the magistrate, being merciful, suspended all but four days of the sentence. On appeal the Supreme Court frowned on the suspension of the major part of the sentence and expressed the view that such leniency was contrary to the spirit of the Criminal Procedure Act.

There have indeed been some outstanding examples of judicial resistance to the will of the administration, of which an example is the Appellate Division's declaration in March and August 1952 that the Separate Representation of Voters Act and the High Court of Parliament Act were unconstitutional. The judiciary's resistance was however submerged by the force of the apartheid wave and the judges not merely lost their spirit but came round to a stance of co-operation with authority. The attitude of resistance, shown by some, was not pursued either with sufficient consistency or with sufficient self-assertion. Time and again the South African judges have wiped their hands of responsibility for acts of the executive which are blatantly opposed to the fundamental principles on which the South African judges' legal training was based. Time and again they have in fact approved of the executive's increasing intrusions upon the liberty of the subject. Time and again they have refrained from clear pronouncements on the question where the judiciary stood in the conflict between human rights and state power.

There have been some occasions, all too few, when judges have, while upholding the position of the government and refusing relief to the petitioner, expressed themselves quite strongly against the legislation which has permitted injustice to occur in that particular case.

When the author was in South Africa, some judgments were reported, in which the judges quite clearly indicated their disapproval of legislation which in terms of the law they felt compelled to uphold. Justice Didcott of Natal in a judgment concerning the pass laws in August 1979, expressed his aversion for them while upholding the position of the prosecution. More recently, Justice Mervyn King in Pretoria held in connection with a charge that involved living in a white area without a permit, that the lack of accommodation for the Indian population was chronic and of alarming proportions, and went on to say that if he were sitting as a court of equity he would have come to the assistance of the person violating the Group Areas Act. He hesitated, however, to go further and say that in common justice he could not have upheld the contention of the prosecution. Such judicial reluctance to permit equity to override the law attracts occasional journalistic criticism. For example, in the lead article on the centre page of the *Sunday Times*, September 2nd 1979, South African judges were exhorted to follow the bolder approach of Lord Denning as displayed in many cases where he sought to do equity even in the face of contrary provisions of the law. The Roman-Dutch system, even more than the English, has a built-in component of equity. It is a matter worthy of study by South African lawyers and judges whether it is not possible in the name of a fundamental violation of equitable principles to override even a statute. If the judges cannot go quite so far, there certainly seems no reason preventing them from expressing their strong aversion for legislation which runs so contrary to the basic tenets of law and justice, which the judges are sworn to enforce.

Indeed, any legal practitioner or judge exposed for the first time to the South African legal system, necessarily suffers an initial shock at seeing judges trained in a liberal tradition prepared to uphold and enforce legislation of this sort. Most judges, no doubt desensitised to this legislation by having lived with it for thirty years, do not see it that way. It is essential, and this is said without any intention of disrespect, that they realise more strongly the great gulf that exists between their training and legal inheritance on the one hand, and the result of their judicial work on the other.

Chief Justice Lord de Villiers stated judicially in 1904, "It is the primary function of the court to protect the rights of individuals which may be infringed and it makes no difference whether the individual occupies a palace or a hut".[40] Is it too much to ask the modern South African judiciary, despite later contradictory judicial pronouncements, to regard this principle as axiomatic?

The Legal Profession

The South African legal profession has a high reputation for scholarship. The author, a lawyer trained in Sri Lanka, the only territory other than South Africa where the Roman-Dutch law prevails, knows well the depth of legal scholarship of the South African bench and bar. In order to practise the Roman-Dutch law in today's context one needs knowledge enough to move fluently between Roman law, Roman-Dutch law and English law and this gives a breadth of knowledge of legal systems which lawyers in few jurisdictions enjoy. It is to be noted also that in the original constitutions of the Boer Republics, heavy reliance was placed upon American Constitutional principles as well — as for example in the Orange Free State constitution — and this gives an added dimension to the legal knowledge of the South African lawyer.

With all these advantages, the South African lawyer has permitted himself to become a mere implementer of law, a mere black letter man. He will tell you with the competence born of sound training and deep research, what the law is on a given matter. What the law ought to be and how the legal profession can contribute to this end is unfortunately an aspect which he has permitted to slide outside his area of interest.

The irony that the South African lawyer's wide exposure to so many systems has not produced a more liberal strain of lawyer is heightened when one considers that the Roman-Dutch legal system is one of the most liberal and egalitarian one can find.

Johannes Voet, widely regarded as the most authoritative of the Roman-Dutch treatise writers, sets out a definition of the law in terms of content and form, from the standpoint of the Roman-Dutch system:

> "The law ought to be just and resonable both in regard to the subject matter, directing what is honourable and forbidding what is base; and as to its form, preserving equality and binding citizens equally".[41]

One feels constrained to the conclusion that if the South African legal profession had been more concerned with its social responsibilities as a profession, many of the aberrations upon the statute book could have been avoided. A concerted stand on basic principles fundamental to the liberal traditions of the Roman-Dutch law would have created in successive administrations a greater reluctance to trample elementary legal protections underfoot.

There are many members of the South African bar who are of liberal views, straining to correct the iniquities of their legal system, but powerless in the face of uncontrollable political forces. Some lawyers — unfortunately only a small minority — give of their time and expertise for the defence of citizens persecuted under the Pass Laws, the Terrorism Act and other legislation, but the author's conversations with such bodies as Dependants' Conference have indicated that their numbers are all too few.

While eminent barristers such as Kentridge in Johannesburg and Dison in Cape Town (Kentridge represented the Biko family at the inquest and Dison's memorable cases include the recent Cape bus case) and eminent legal academics like Mathews, Dugard, Van der Vyver and Van Niekerk, manifest a concern with the cause of the oppressed which would do credit to lawyers anywhere, it is not in every case that they can appear, however deep their concern. There may be in South Africa a few dozen like them, but there the counting stops.

Nor must we forget that the South African bar did in fact produce a man of the calibre of Bram Fischer, one-time President of the Johannesburg bar, to whom reference has been made at more than one point in this narrative. The power and prestige of the Afrikaner establishment which a son of the Orange Free State Judge President and the grandson of a Prime Minister of the Orange River Colony could readily command were discarded for the term of life imprisonment under which he ended his days.

But the Bram Fischers are few indeed. So are the Kentridges and Disons. The younger members of the bar must show more concern, if the human rights of black people are in any way to be ameliorated.

The humanitarian-oriented work awaiting urgent attention by the South African legal profession is varied and truly enormous. Legal aid clinics need to be manned, organisations such as Black Sash and Dependants' Conference need to have a roster of persons ready and willing to appear for them at short notice, intensive research and writing are required regarding the operation of South African law. In black settlements such as Langa, Crossroads, and Alexandra nearly every household has unserviced legal problems — all this and more needs concentrated attention from members of the legal profession. With all respect to a truly learned profession, it has, in the eyes of a foreign observer, signally failed to pull its weight in the humanitarian field.

Another level at which members of the legal profession can give their support, is in presenting a front of general disapproval of laws which run counter to basic human rights. What these basic human rights are is not any longer a matter of vague speculation. These rights have, in many jurisdictions, been precisely formulated and captured in constitutional documents such as the nineteen Fundamental Human and Civil Rights enumerated by the German constitution. Perhaps one need go no further than the Universal Declaration of Human Rights, practically every section of which stands completely negated by the South African statute book, as we have seen.

Professor Lon Fuller has said of the persecutions of the Nazi regime in Germany that the exploitation of legal forms started cautiously and became bolder as power was consolidated. "The first attacks on the established order were on ramparts which if they were manned by anyone,

were manned by lawyers and judges. These ramparts fell
almost without a struggle".[42]

The same can be said of the South African legal
system. There was an entrenched respect for and protection of human rights ingrained in the Roman-Dutch legal
tradition which South African lawyers permitted to be
eroded without adequate resistance. The battle is now
harder since the ramparts have already fallen, but a general
conviction on the part of the profession that the legal system
it operates cannot possibly be maintained in its present form
can lead to corrections even of an entrenched system.

As Professor Van Niekerk points out,[43] this is due in
large measure to the acceptance in South Africa today as in
Germany in the early thirties, of unbridled positivism as the
dominant doctrine of the legal profession. This view
proclaims that it is not part of the lawyer's duty to reform
the law in order to make it accord with justice, but that
such reform is a matter for the duly constituted political
authority.

The author learnt with some astonishment that in
South Africa even teachers of constitutional law are able
to take their students through their entire course in
constitutional law without reference to some of the glaring
denigrations of human rights on the South African statute
book. For example, there are courses in constitutional law
which skirt around the Terrorism Act and the provisions
for preventive detention.

There are indeed eminent South African teachers of
law such as those already mentioned, who in their books
have drawn attention to many of these features in a manner
which makes them completely intelligible both to the legal
profession and to the lay public. These teachers have introduced into their university courses careful references to
provisions of this nature and have set in motion a movement
which other teachers of constitutional law are taking up, and
are drawing students' attention to South African realities
rather than to abstract pronouncements regarding separation of powers and Westminster-style conventions.

Special mention is necessary of Professor Barend Van
Niekerk who on two occasions was charged with contempt of
court. On the first occasion his alleged offence was that he
had conducted an investigation into racially discriminatory
aspects of capital punishment in South Africa — a piece of
research which revealed a disproportionate number of
sentences of black accused persons. The second charge of
contempt related to an attempt by him to urge the South
African judiciary to exclude from evidence statements

obtained from detainees while they were in indefinite solitary confinement. The first case ended in an acquittal but he was convicted in the second.

What is noteworthy in both instances is that the prosecutions were instigated by members of the country's all-white judiciary.

It is necessary that on occasions like this it is not only the academic profession but the members of the practising bar as well who should stand for free research. By the standards of other countries with free judiciaries, Professor Van Niekerk's work would pass without question as legitimate academic research.

Professor Van Niekerk records his appreciation of support given to him in these prosecutions by some outstanding members of the bar. He mentions among others, John Dugard, Tony Mathews and Sydney Kentridge and observes, "I have not been sparing in the past of criticism of the legal profession which comprises the people who should be ready to man the ramparts in the defence of those ideas about which I shall be speaking to you today, but let me say, as I have said before, that if it had not been for lawyers and fighters for justice such as these men, those few tatters of justice still blowing in the South African wind today would long have disappeared into the arid atmosphere of our land".[44]

Sydney Kentridge sums up the South African lawyer well when he says "But the question which I want to put, without expecting an answer is: 'What are we, as counsel, doing in these courts — are we really defending the rule of law or what remains of it or as some persons, both abroad and in South Africa have said of us, are we merely participating in a charade, are we helping to give a spurious air of respectability and fairness to a procedure which is fundamentally unfair?' ".

Each South African lawyer who examines his conscience can give an answer.

There is much responsibility for reform lying upon the shoulders of South Africa's legal profession — the direct inheritors of the rich humanistic legal tradition of Grotius and Voet.

FOOTNOTES

1. In 1977 the number of arrests under the pass laws was 173,571. In 1978 it was 278,887. The 1979 figures are not yet available.
2. Hahlo and Kahn, *South Africa: The Development of Its Laws and Constitution*, p.794.
3. *South Africa and the Rule of Law*, International Commission of Jurists' Publications, Geneva, p.28.
4. Prior to 1978 the courts had held that an African ought to be

afforded a reasonable opportunity to fetch his reference book, and that such reasonable opportunity might even mean travelling thirty miles to fetch it. By s.13(a) of Act 102 of 1978, it was provided that such reasonable opportunity was limited to travelling a distance of five kilometers.

5.   Mercifully this system has now been abolished.
6.   *Human Rights and the South African Legal Order,* Princeton Univ. Press, 1978, p.76.
7.   For a detailed discussion of this provision see Marion L. Dixon, *Do Blacks Have a Right to Family Life,* Univ. of the Witwatersrand, Occasional Papers 1, 1979.
8.   See *Soweto Speaks,* p.38. See also the account at pp.38 and 39 of the various dishonesties that have to be resorted to in order to obtain and keep one's pass.
9.   Dugard, *Human Rights and the South African Legal Order,* p.78.
10.   Dugard, *op.cit.* p.82, citing House of Assembly Debates, vol. 64, col. 513.
11.   *Minister of the Interior* v *Lockhat* (1961) (2) SA 587 (AD).
12.   *The Age,* Melbourne, based on a news report dated May 25, from Johannesburg.
13.   *Newsweek,* October 29, 1979, p.18.
14.   Hansard, 1967, Jun 2, col. 7118.
15.   Second L.C. Steyn Memorial Lecture on 25 April, 1979.
16.   Mathews, *Law Order and Liberty in South Africa,* p.76.
17.   Mathews, *op.cit.* p.77.
18.   (1954) 1 S.A. 123 (AD).
19.   *Kloppenberg* v *The Minister of Justice* (1964) 4 S.A. 31(n).
20.   Mathews, *op.cit.* p.83.
21.   Mathews. *op.cit.* p.84. Indeed the ban is theoretically retrospective as well and would, as Mathews points out, apply even to a recording of his childhood prattle.
22.   See *S.* v. *Joseph* (1964) (1) S.A. 659 (T); Mathews, *op.cit.* p.94.
23.   All these examples come from pp. 102-4 of Mathews, *op.cit.*
24.   See pp.152-55.
25.   Mathews, *op.cit.* p.70.
26.   S.1(3) (c); Mathews, *op.cit.* p.72.
27.   S.6 of the Suppression of Communism Act.
28.   S.11(e) (bis) read with s.11 (2).
29.   See Mathews, *op.cit.* p.76, fn. 31.
30.   *Minister of Posts and Telegraphs* v. *Rasool* (1934) A.D. 167.
31.   (1954) 347 US 483.
32.   See pp.16-17, 140-42.
33.   See pp.152-55.
34.   Sections 1 and 5 of the Population Registration Act, 1950.
35.   Goodrich and Hambro, *Charter of the United Nations,* 2nd ed. 1949, p.88.
36.   A. Sachs, *Justice in South Africa,* 1973, Sussex Univ. Press, p.124.
37.   (1934) S.A. Reports - Appellate Division, 167.
38.   A. Sachs, *op.cit.* p.231.
39.   (1964) (1) S.A. 659 (T).
40.   *Zgili* v. *McLeod* (1904) 21 SC 150 at 152.
41.   *Commentary on the Pandects,* 1.3.5.
42.   L. Fuller, *Positivism and Fidelity to Law: A Reply to Professor Hart.* (1958) 71 Harvard Law Review 630.
43.   "The Mirage of Liberty" (1973) 3 *Human Rights,* p.283.
44.   (1973) 3 *Human Rights,* 283-285.

CHAPTER 7

Signs of Change

Attitudinal Changes

South Africa is in the throes of change. It may not be a real, substantial change in even the ground rules of apartheid, but there is a wave of rethinking and soul searching from the Prime Minister downwards. Not all South Africans are engaged in the process, nor even the majority. But a significant number of whites, including those in positions of responsibility, and a considerable proportion of the student population are troubled. The guilt complex urges them to yield at least some of their privilege. The fear complex holds many back, for they know not what black rule will hold in store for them.

Still, there is movement in attitudes such as has never occurred before. The author has been told more than once by close associates of persons in high authority, that many of the latter are today not the persons they were ten years ago. Their thought processes are entirely different. Of the Rector of one university, a professor said he could not imagine that the man in the Rector's chair today was the same man that sat there ten years ago. Of course, persons in such positions are slow to admit that for so long they practised policies which have now been proved to be unworkable and it may need a new generation of office holders to admit the error without reservation.

If it is indeed the position that there is in significant quarters a significant change in attitudes, this is the period when that change can be given momentum by the pressure of outside opinion. If the outside world should fail in this duty now it may well be failing in making use of the last opportunity that it has or ever will have. The current phase of movement towards liberalism may not last, and may well be followed by a period of reaction and hardening of attitudes. This is what the extreme right is attempting to achieve, and unless those who are on the side of change receive moral support and encouragement from the outside world they may well falter in their resolve.

The Present Prime Minister

Symptomatic of the tug between the forces of change and reaction, at the time of writing, is the apparent conflict between the Prime Minister, Mr. Botha, and the right wing of his party led by Dr. Treurnicht. The former tours the country saying that South Africa must change or perish — a position no Prime Minister had ever taken up before. On the other hand Dr. Treurnicht, still a member of the same party, says that it is madness to interfere with the traditional basis on which South African society has been organised and that the present order must be entrenched, not changed. The outcome of this conflict will determine the future course of South African history.

There is some evidence at the time of going to press that the Prime Minister's position seems now to be somewhat different to what it was thought to be some months ago when the author was in South Africa. In February 1980, he told a new session of Parliament in Cape Town that he would not deviate from the basic principles of separate development. This has been read by many observers as an abandonment of the Prime Minister's *verligte* policies under pressure of the *verkrampte* backlash and as a shattering of the hopes which he had raised both at home and overseas.' If the Mixed Marriages Act, the Group Areas Act and the Homelands policy are to continue, apartheid continues. The high hopes the Prime Minister once engendered ought not to be permitted thus to wither away and die. Should that happen all hope of peaceful change in South Africa will recede forever.

Coloured and black youth are in little mood for dialogue, and see little substance in Prime Ministerial pronouncements which are unaccompanied by Prime Ministerial action. They see such change as he has promised as being cosmetic and lacking in value and significance. They are waiting for an expression of willingness to change at least one of the major planks on which the social and legal iniquities of South Africa rest. Thus far not one has been promised. What little the Prime Minister is speaking of has come too late, and the patience of the coloured and black communities is near exhaustion.

If the Prime Minister is to keep moving along the lines of his bold pronouncements in the latter part of 1979 he needs support in the sense of driving home to the white South African public the urgency of the need for reform. Without such support his efforts may fold up under pressure.

Even if the hope seems remote, action to this end is called for now.   Else, let those who ardently profess a concern for human rights sit back to the certainty of a spectacle of carnage unmatched in recent African history.

Some Practical Considerations

Having made these reservations regarding the Prime Minister and his policies, it is necessary also to place in proper perspective the phenomenon of a South African Prime Minister who visits Soweto, confers with black leaders, castigates his extreme right wing and urgently presses for change.

Detractors of the Prime Minister and his efforts need to take account of the enormous weight of settled tradition and prejudice which even his moderate policies will need to counter.   The Augean stables cannot be cleansed in the twinkling of an eye.   The prejudice of centuries cannot be negatived by a stroke of the legislative pen.   The politician needs always to be looking over his shoulder at the attitudes of his power base.   Granted a realisation of these factors, the Prime Ministerial attitude is the most potent force for reform from within the establishment that has yet appeared in South African history.   It would be unwise in a practical world to discount it as amounting to nothing.

It should be remembered also that the Prime Minister is a pragmatic politician of great skill and that as a former Minister of Defence, he is more than ordinarily sensitive to South Africa's military difficulties.   With such a 'heavy-weight' pressing for change, the forces demanding change have a potential ally of great power if he can only be persuaded to move a little further.

The Prime Minister's attitudes are all the more remarkable having regard to the fact that when the Prime Minister took office he was commonly regarded as *verkrampte*.

Some of Mr. Botha's pronouncements bear repetition in this context.

"White South Africans must adapt or die".

"I will not tolerate any laws on the statute book
that insult people".

"You either accept my policy or look for another
leader".

"If you reject me, I will go with a conscience with
which I can live because I am not prepared to live
a lie for the sake of popularity".[2]

It has been contended in this work that white South
African opinion on the question of apartheid is in the process
of change. The proportion of whites opposing it has risen
from one-fifth to one-third and will probably soon pass the
half way mark, if it has not already done so.[3] The government
party is to the right of its electorate on this issue, and when
anti-apartheid opinion moves above the half way mark as it
surely will, the government may well need to make a dramatic reversal in its attitudes. It may well be that the astute
politician in the Prime Minister has seen this in advance and
is preparing the ground for that change. Whatever the
reasons for his attitudes, the attitudes themselves are a
phenomenon of which proponents of change need to take
the fullest advantage. To write him off, as some of them
tend to do, would in the author's view be gravely damaging
to the cause of change.

Current Initiatives and Trends

In 1979 Dr. Piet Koornhof, Minister for Co-operation
and Development, declared that "apartheid is dead". The
statement was no doubt intended to be restricted to the
incidents of petty apartheid, for as everyone in South Africa
knows, grand apartheid is alive and well. There was a flicker
of hope that one of the pillars of grand apartheid was being
assailed, when the Prime Minister announced that the
Immorality Act would be reconsidered. However, since the
announcement, the adverse reaction from the supporters of
apartheid has been so severe that this proposed reconsideration has been all but abandoned.

Let us now examine some current trends.

1. Labour

The government has announced its intention to
implement the Riekert Commission's recommendations in
the sphere of labour, which involve a removal of wage and
job discrimination, the right to form mixed trade unions,

and the right of blacks to form their own trade unions. This is perhaps of some importance, for, hitherto, the blacks did not have the rights to form their own trade unions and faced a great deal of wage and job discrimination. Critics of the Riekert Commission point out that the Commission's report does not in fact attack some of the most obnoxious features of apartheid. For example it retains the 72 hour limit during which a black person may remain in an urban area without permission. It also retains penalties for illegally employed workers while imposing increased penalties on employers who illegally employ black workers. In other words it still functions within the framework of a society which is essentially discriminatory. Indeed many of the recommendations of the Commission may have the effect of streamlining the pass laws and subjecting the coloured and Asian communities to greater controls than in the past. While it is accepted that the report may result in greatly increasing the quality of life for qualified urban black people, the report reinforces the system of the homelands and the black states. There is no planning in regard to their employment, and the report in the words of the commission itself will in no way interfere with controls over the influx of black peoples into the urban areas.

Another interesting aspect of the report is that if implemented it will increase the cleavage between the urban blacks and blacks in the homelands, by giving increased privileges to the former. In the words of a commentator in the Black Sash,[4] the report, "is a very skilled, very clever and highly sophisticated recipe for national disaster. No country can jettison three-quarters of its population and survive".

2. *Sports Policy*

There have been frequent announcements of government intention to effect change in sports policy, and change has been effected to the extent that there is now no governing policy in regard to separation in sport. The question of separation or integration is left to the discretion of the educational or sporting bodies involved. The extent to which this has in fact resulted in relaxation is discussed elsewhere.[5]

3. *Constitutional Reform*

The government has announced constitutional proposals involving a division of power with the coloured and

Indian communities. It has also stated its intention to accommodate the urban blacks within that dispensation. This is a far cry from Prime Minister R.F. Botha's remark in 1977 that his government would never in one hundred years agree to share power with coloureds, Asians or blacks.

It is interesting that one of the proposals is a three tiered Parliament for the white, the coloured, and the Asian communities. But even this so called new dispensation leaves the urban blacks completely out of the real business of power sharing. The constitutional proposals have been thrown open for discussion and have run into so much opposition that even the government itself does not seriously intend to leave the original proposals unchanged. The all-white Schlebusch Commission has been hearing evidence from many individuals and organisations regarding the constitutional changes needed. The Commission suffers from the cardinal deficiency of its all-white composition. There is no doubt that there can be no meaningful proposals in a country with a majority of black residents unless there is a proposal which involves them in some form of real political rights, and unless they are represented on the body that investigates change.

4. *The President's Council*

In these constitutional proposals one of the provisions is the creation of a 55-man President's Council comprising representatives of the white, Indian, and coloured communities. Although, as we have noted, the main proposals have run into so much opposition that the government itself has kept them on ice, there has been a move by the government in February 1980 to activate the President's Council while leaving the rest of the proposals dormant. It is also proposed that this council be given a mandate to discuss the constitutional future. This step, widely reported in the Afrikaans press, demonstrates a realisation that for the proper discussion of constitutional change, non-white leaders must be involved in negotiation.

It will be seen however that the proposal still leaves the blacks out of the discussions and out of any form of power sharing.

5. *Urban Blacks*

The government has initiated a series of consultative

committees to examine legislation regarding urban blacks and to give more detailed attention to the problem of their constitutional status. What will emerge from this we do not know as yet, but there are at present no signs of any acknowledgement of the need for real power sharing.

6. *Petty Apartheid*

It is true that there have been slight relaxations of petty apartheid. It is to be remembered however that the real issue in South Africa is no longer petty apartheid. The time when this created so much irritation as to be a principal issue in itself has passed. The reformists and the blacks in South Africa are now focussing attention on grand apartheid, and the annoyances of petty apartheid are being treated as comparatively insignificant appurtenances of the major problem. Consequently, the removal of petty apartheid, even if it should be achieved, has in the opinion of many come too late. It is to be noted also that the removal of petty apartheid is not being uniformly attempted across the country, but that it functions in varying degrees in different areas. For example, the relaxation in Cape Town which now permits mixed bus travel, will not for some time reach a like level in Johannesburg or Pretoria. It is true however that there has been a removal of such sources of minor irritation as separate lifts, separate post office entrances, separate customs queues, separate police stations, and in certain areas, separate public transport. On the other hand it is irritatingly retained in certain areas as for example in Johannesburg airport where immediately after passing customs, the tourist encounters the signs of apartheid indicating restaurants and toilets for whites only.

7. *Prosecutions for Illegal Employment*

The government has announced a nationwide moratorium on prosecutions of black persons in illegal employment. The moratorium is to operate except in the Cape Peninsula area, which is a coloured preferential area. Although such announcements have been made, however, there has been an increase in the punishments for illegal employment and employers employing persons illegally are now liable to a fine of R.500. This is an extremely deterrent penalty and makes it very difficult for employers to shut their eyes to the statutory prohibitions.

8. *International Hotels*

Some hotels have been given international licenses which entitle them to entertain guests of all racial groups. Hotels not enjoying this status are denied the right to entertain across the colour line or must at least provide separate accommodation for racial groups. Consequently many hotels and restaurants desiring to open their doors to people of all racial groups find it impossible to do so. In any event the law requires that if a member of the public should complain at the mixing of racial groups the hotel must take action on pain of losing its licence.

9. *Security Legislation*

A Commission has been appointed to investigate security legislation. This was in consequence of the very strong case made, especially by the academic community and the Human Rights Commission, that such an investigation was urgently required. The Draconian provisions of this legislation were originally conceived of as being temporary, but have now assumed a semi-permanent nature. They have been on the statute book for fifteen years and the public has become accustomed to them. It is hoped that the Commission will make some far reaching recommendations, but as yet it is too early to make any predictions.

10. *Land in Urban Areas*

A ninety-nine year leasehold tenure of land has been promised to blacks in urban areas. This is the first time there has been any recognition that blacks could have any form of tenure within the urban areas. However the actual operation of this relaxation remains to be watched. It is thought that the persons who will qualify for this ninety-nine year old leasehold are so extremely small as a group as to make no significant dent on the prevailing rule preventing any black in an urban area from enjoying any form of tenure. Although this has been hailed as a crack in the scheme of grand apartheid, its operation in all probability will be minimal.

11. *Crossroads*

The government recognition of the presence of thirty

thousand black squatters in the Crossroads settlement is no doubt a step forward in the recognition of the problems of the urban blacks.   Thirty thousand black squatters illegally present in an urban area are an infringement of the scheme of grand apartheid.   The moment a government minister gives recognition to the legality of their presence he is to an extent admitting that the scheme of grand apartheid has failed.   Consequently, what has happened in Crossroads is perhaps of major significance[6].

12. *The Quality of Life*

There is a commitment to improve the quality of life in the black communities.   For example, massive housing schemes and schemes of electrification have been mooted.   The Urban Foundation is working hard at the idea of upliftment and over R.100 million is committed to such projects as the electrification of Soweto.

All these are commendable attempts to remedy a situation of tremendous privation but they operate within the framework of apartheid.   Their detractors point out also that the money committed to these schemes is a mere fraction of the money committed to the maintenance of the apparatus of apartheid.   Further, South Africa now enjoys a sudden bonanza of around R.12,000 million as a result of the sharp upward movement in the price of gold.   It is interesting to see how much of this will be devoted to black upliftment and how much will find its way into the pockets of the country's white minority.   Already it is reported that whites are placing record orders for swimming pools and luxury cars, while black South Africans are waiting for a few cents to be taken off the price of bread.   Blacks question the sincerity of the moves for their upliftment.   The electrification of Soweto can, for instance, be actuated by a genuine desire for their upliftment.   On the other hand it is said that it can be an attempt to create a vast market in the black areas for electrical goods.   Over R.100 million has been spent recently on a new hospital for whites in Johannesburg.   Not far away is an under-equipped hospital for non-Europeans.   Adjoining the brand new hospital stands the still more than adequate white hospital which it superseded.   The old white hospital stands locked and empty.

While the movement to improve the quality of life has started, it needs a much more extensive commitment of government resources if its genuineness is to be accepted by the blacks.

13. *Education*

There has been an announcement that Bantu education will be compulsory up to the age of twelve years. This will enable more African children to go in for education and is certainly a slight improvement upon policies which had deliberately aimed at keeping blacks away from education. Allied to this there is also the announcement that Bantus may choose their language of instruction. It will be remembered that the Soweto riots were sparked off by the attempt to impose Afrikaans as a medium of instruction upon the Bantus who resented it as the language of their rulers. The ability to choose their language of instruction is a recognition that Afrikanerdom is not to be foisted upon the blacks.

14. *Judicial Attitudes*

Reference has been made elsewhere in these pages to some recent judicial pronouncements indicative of an attitude of greater judicial concern with some of the social problems of apartheid. Perhaps more frequently than before one encounters strong judicial criticisms of apartheid and efforts, where possible, to lean in favour of its victims rather than to enforce the harsh letter of the law.

Perhaps symptomatic of this trend is a decision in February 1980 by Judge President Watermeyer of the Cape Provincial Division. The court acquitted the Rev. David Russell and three others on charges under the Publications Act. The charges related to the production of two allegedly undesirable publications, "The Role of the Riot Police in the Burnings and Killings, Nyanga, Cape Town, Christmas 1976". Referring to a passage headed, "The cause of the unrest is the sin of racial discrimination", the judge said: "There are many people in this country both black and white who feel that the sentiments expressed in 'The Message' are true and that it is highly desirable that they should be openly debated and discussed". He held further that the language in the document was moderate and though it was basically a criticism of government policy its stated aim was peaceful reconciliation between the races. He held that parliament did not intend the production of such a document to constitute an offence. The judge also held that the state had failed to prove that the accused had a guilty intent as required by law.

The tone and temper of the judgement show a degree

of judicial self assertion in the cause of justice which has not been conspicuous in the recent past. It may well be that such independent and bold judicial attitudes are the precursors of a more independent judicial stance in the future.

15. *The Relaxation of Tension*

In the early months of the Prime Minister's rule he was able to achieve, according to many observers, a marked relaxation of internal tensions in South Africa. For example in 1979 there were far fewer bannings than in 1978. The number of terrorism trials was down by over a half from 1978. New black consciousness organisations were beginning to appear for the first time since the clamp-down in October 1977. Apartheid and its continuance, hitherto scarcely permitted as topics for discussion, became the subject of open debate. The very circumstance of the author's invitation to South Africa and the latitude permitted him in criticising the establishment were symptomatic of these trends.

It was significant also that the Prime Minister was able on an independent opinion poll to obtain fifty seven per cent support among the urban blacks for the view that he was doing a good job as Prime Minister --- a response unprecedented for any Afrikaner Prime Minister. Dr. Motlana, the Sowetan leader, conceded, while criticising many of the Prime Minister's moves as cosmetic, that the Prime Minister had brought about a significant change in white attitudes.[7]

Since then however there seems to have been a gradual reversion to the old tensions, in the wake of a belief that the Prime Minister is abandoning his liberal policies. Successive defeats in by-elections showed that his *verligte* policies were losing him support both from the extreme right of his party and from the left. Tension can still be eased if Mr. Botha can pursue his liberalism without wavering or faltering in the face of the reaction. He will if he does, gather strength from other elements, now withholding support because they doubt his liberalism. If he can build up some modicum of black support he would give himself a greater source of strength than any South African Prime Minister has ever enjoyed.

In any event, the process of change once begun is difficult to halt. Once initiated by a South African Prime Minister it may be difficult for his successors to ignore such trends. They may well maintain their momentum.

16. *Namibia*

It is a fact of great significance that the very South African government that enforces apartheid at home has committed itself to supporting a one-man-one-vote policy in Namibia and to a relaxation of white privilege to the extent that it is an offence to indulge in any form of racial discrimination. This is the strongest possible evidence that the ideological justification of apartheid has disappeared even within the ranks of the South African government. No longer is it possible for that government to claim with any appearance of sincerity or consistency that it believes apartheid operates to the benefit of either blacks or whites.

17. *The Army*

All races are reportedly integrated in the South African army. They eat together, sleep together and fight together and there are occasional coloured officers in command of white troops. It is true the non-white component, especially in command positions, is minimal, but when a most important agency of the government rejects apartheid within its own ranks this must make an impact upon the thinking of the government. This is of special significance in the light of the government's dependence upon the army and the army's dependence upon its black component in the event of any major civil unrest. The South African army is reportedly more liberal than the South African police and in the event of the civilian government being unable to hold South Africa together the army could play a role of vital importance. 'Liberal' attitudes in the army are therefore of special significance.

Some Qualifications and Reservations

Despite the significant nature of some of the reforms and attitudes mentioned, some further qualifications must be made, when assessing their value and impact.

In the first place there is always, in South Africa, a marked gap between the promulgation of official policy and its implementation. The gap is not merely one in time. There is a gap in purposefulness as well, between the Minister and his minions. The Minister may sincerely desire reform in some area. Those who implement his policies,

from the high official down to the humblest clerk or un-
informed underling, may think differently and quite often
retard or reverse his policy. The victims of these attitudes
are the blacks, who lack the ability to complain. The
Minister often continues to be unaware that his proclaimed
policies are being defeated by subordinates' attitudes. An
excellent example of this was provided to the author by a
resident of Crossroads who complained that although the
Minister had issued her a permit to live in Crossroads for six
months, this permit was not recognised by a patrolling
official. When she went out of Crossroads in search of employment, and her papers were demanded by this official,
the Minister's permit was treated with contempt and she
was ordered back to Crossroads. In such instances even if
a complaint should be lodged with a higher authority, it
will in all probability be treated with scant regard, being a
complaint by a black citizen against a white official. Consequently, however liberal the pronouncements from on high,
they must percolate through many layers of officialdom
before reaching the public. That percolation does not
always take place.

Secondly, Prime Ministerial pronouncements sometimes meet opposition even at Cabinet level, as in the case
of the Prime Minister's pronouncements regarding the Mixed
Marriage Act, which met with sharp opposition in the
Cabinet from the Minister of Police and Prisons.[8] Not only
is there such conflict in the cabinet. The *verkrampte* section
of the ruling Nationalist Party as well, is in constant opposition to these policies. The backlash from the Afrikaner
heartland would kill any leader who attempts wholesale
reform too precipitately.

Thirdly, while one gives the Prime Minister credit
for some of his announced policies and changes, there is
often an ambivalence in his attitudes that takes away some
measure of the enthusiasm his reforms may attract. For
example he is still wedded to the Homelands Policy and has
shown no intention of abolishing the Pass Laws. The former
is the bedrock of the policy of apartheid, the latter is its
right arm. As long as these two remain, so does apartheid.

The Human Rights Conference

There are many ironies in talking about human rights
in South Africa. In the first place we have the phenomenon,
perhaps unique in legal history, of the co-existence of a
humanistic legal system with the constant negation of the

basic principles of the rule of law. Any citizen, however humble, can assert certain rights — for example a contractual right — against even a Cabinet Minister and take the case all the way up to the highest tribunal of appeal. He has the assurance that the judges will carefully and conscientiously apply to his claim the principles of the general law. That same citizen can however be incarcerated without charge or trial indefinitely at the pleasure of the same Minister, with no recourse to the courts. That same citizen, if he is not white, has no part whatever in the making of the laws to which he is expected to render obedience, no landowning rights in areas in which he is expected to live, no equal participation in the economy to which he is expected to contribute. The Roman-Dutch legal system, meticulously crafted on principles of justice and equality, is carefully administered within the framework of a system which negates these very concepts. Such anomalies often make a mockery of any talk of human rights in South Africa.

A human rights conference in South Africa is an even greater oddity. The people who should be discussing it, those who are most concerned both idealistically and personally, are those who are in jail or exile or under banning orders which prevent them from expressing or publishing their views.

Yet a meaningful human rights conference was in fact held in South Africa in 1979 and deserved far wider publicity than it in fact received. This was the First International Conference on Human Rights in South Africa, held at the University of Cape Town from 22-26 January, 1979. The Conference resulted from the initiative of Professor J.D. Van der Vyver of the University of the Witwatersrand. Participants were brought in from outside South Africa, and some of the outstanding South African law professors in the field of criminal law and constitutional law such as Professor John Dugard and Professor A.S. Mathews participated. The Faculties of Law of the Universities of Cape Town, Witwatersrand, Durban-Westville, Natal and Fort Hare were among the funding authorities. The Ford Foundation and the Carnegie Corporation of New York jointly shared the travelling expenses of participants from outside South Africa, while the other expenses of the conference were met from funds raised locally.

The details of the organisation of this conference are not without interest as indicating the difficulties to be surmounted by persons working for change and the way in which determined action can produce results even in the face of initial government opposition. The relevant facts are

extracted from the Convenor's report on the Conference,
dated 18 June 1979.

Some of the overseas participants were well known for
their expression of views conflicting with those of the South
African government. This necessitated negotiations between
the Steering Committee and the Departments of Foreign
Affairs and the Interior. Negotiations with the latter department ran into difficulties. The Dean of the UCT Faculty
of law was requested by the Minister to "reconsider the
advisability of holding . . . the conference at this point in
time". Professor Van der Vyver argued strongly that, if
faced with a firm attitude by the Steering Committee, the
government would eventually grant all the necessary visas.
The Steering Committee, accepting this view after a protracted debate, authorised the covenor to push ahead with
the organisation and commence the advance publicity for the
conference. The Steering Committee then wrote to the
Minister indicating that postponement was not acceptable,
and that the Committee had decided to proceed as planned.

In the meantime there was political turmoil in South
Africa over the resignation of the Prime Minister and the first
revelation of the information scandal. Whether or not
induced by these events, the Minister replied that "after
careful consideration of all the facts at my disposal and
having special regard to the contents of your letter. . . I
have approved in principle that overseas speakers may be
invited to the conference". Despite this letter there were
various administrative difficulties which, with patience and
determination, were overcome and the conference became a
reality.

The conference represented a milestone in South
African human rights awareness. Delegates to the conference included Members of Parliament, representatives of the
Namibia National Front, South African police legal advisers,
the South African Council of Churches, black trade union
representatives, black journalists, academics from the black
universities and judges of the Supreme Court. If there was a
lack of adequate representation it was from the ranks of the
radical blacks and the conservatives. Still it was rare in
South African history for such a collection of people from
diverse backgrounds to discuss openly and freely the
contentious human rights problems of the country.

The conference is open to the criticism, which indeed
it has already faced, that it has failed to consider the underlying socio-economic base on which rest the human rights
denials in South Africa. Socialist and Marxist criticisms have
highlighted this aspect. Yet there is value in any discussion

that raises the community's human rights awareness. There was widespread coverage in the national press (and also some coverage in the international, but not in the English press). It has already perhaps produced results, as for example in its possible influence on the very important Steyn Memorial Lecture of Dr. D.P. de Villiers,[9] wherein he called for the amendment of current security legislation, and on debates among academics and parliamentarians.

The outspokenness of the participants at the conference will come as a surprise to non South Africans.

Professor Van der Vyver for example accused the government of resorting to "executive anarchy" in a way that has made South Africa "a disgrace to Western civilisation". Professor Hamilton, a black U.S. political scientist, spoke of the absurdity of the South African contention that blacks should be trained for citizenship. "How could you train a person for citizenship when he still remained a slave?" he asked. A member of the Side Bar in Johannesburg, Mr. Budlender, pointed to the inhuman system of recruitment of labour where the recruit became a commodity to be examined like goods bought over the counter. The recruit, according to a booklet of instructions to employers, should be ordered to run, so that unfit and sick ones and TB cases could be ruled out and applicants should be discarded if they are short of the necessary limbs. Dehumanisation was thus irrevocably linked with the labour system of South Africa. A judge of the Supreme Court, Mr. Justice M.M. Corbett, spoke of the value of giving a US style Bill of Rights a trial in South Africa.

Despite its limitations the conference is therefore significant and a possible precursor to others. It represents something more than merely chipping away at a great rock. It also helps undermine the foundations on which South African injustice rests.

The South African Church Leadership (SACLA) Conference

Reference has been made elsewhere in these pages to the great hold that the church has upon the people of South Africa both white and black. Despite the fact that the Dutch Reformed Church has given doctrinal support to the practice of apartheid, this loyalty to Christianity on the party of the black population is a remarkable feature of the South African scene.

A recent demonstration of the power of the church and of Christian doctrine in South Africa was the SACLA conference held in July, 1979, which drew several thousand participants from all racial groups. It was described as an effort to bring the healing grace of God to bear upon the fragmentation of South African Christians of all races and denominations and was remarkable in that no sponsoring body lay behind it.

The conference faced the reality of divisions in South Africa and the fact that there was violent disagreement regarding the manner in which South African problems could be solved. It sought to generate Christian fellowship and broke through major problems of lack of communication caused by lack of facilities, especially in the black areas.

The organisers of the conference also needed to fight the suspicion of many blacks who saw in this just another of the many attempts made from time to time to generate dialogue without that basis of sincerity on which dialogue can be built.

In a week of talk, prayer and experience, the several thousands of assembled delegates both black and white, worked off their tensions and sought to reach some kind of consensus. There were walk-outs, demonstrations and minor signs of violence such as slashing of tyres in the car park. Yet as Professor David Bosch, the Planning Chairman, told the conference, the conference was in fact nursed back to life despite attacks from left, right and from within the churches.

The Minister for Co-operation and Development, Dr. Piet Koornhof, was one of the speakers and so was Chief Butelezi. It was on a note of accord and unison that the conference ended, with these leaders and many others embracing each other in friendship and in a determination to achieve a change in the South African landscape.

The conference of course condemned apartheid and provided another base of common agreement for a non-violent resolution of South African problems.

Archbishop Burnett of Cape Town probably summed up the feeling of the meeting when he said that "the structural tensions in South African society are so deep that only an unusual intervention by God can head off its violent collapse". It was to this end that SACLA workers were directing their energies.

The author met many participants nearly two months after the event and was greatly impressed by the enthusiasms they continued to show for implementing the message and spirit of the Conference. Some of them were already implementing these principles in their offices, factories and social lives. Regular social meetings across the colour line were organised on a continuing basis to break down the partitions the Group Areas Act had engendered. Crusading missions to convert others were under way. The ripples of SACLA were continuing to spread. It is to be hoped that SACLA has triggered off a wave of fellowship and determination to reform the system which can be productive of significant benefits.

The Urban Foundation

In 1976, after the Soweto riots, a body of businessmen decided to establish a foundation for the upliftment of the condition of South Africa's black population. The idea was born in the mind of a lawyer, Richard Rosenthal, and spread from him to others, especially in the business world, who took kindly to the idea and were prepared to put considerable funds into it. Oppenheimer and Rupert, two influential businessmen, one English and one Afrikaner, jointly hosted an initial conference called "The Businessman's Conference on the Quality of Life in Urban Communities" and the Foundation resulted from this. The Charter of the Foundation declares that its object is to improve the quality of life in urban communities on a non-political, non-racial and non-sexual basis.

The motivation of those sponsoring and assisting the Foundation differs from one contributor to another. Some of them may be motivated by considerations of self-interest, some of them by idealism, some of them by a combination of both. White capital has demonstrated through its support of this organisation, its sudden realisation that unless it is responsive to social need, it will soon find itself dispossessed.

A justice of the Cape Provincial Division of the Supreme Court, Mr. Justice Steyn, has come down from the bench to chair the Foundation. He has already devoted two years of time to this work and has been released from his judicial duties for a further two years for this purpose. Under Steyn's leadership, the Foundation has played a unique role largely unknown and often unacknowledged, in bringing about a real upliftment of the condition of blacks. The Foundation represents a major effort to bring South Africa to a social revolution by non-violent means.

The Foundation has collected several million rand from the general public and, in addition, received substantial loans of close to R.100 million from overseas sympathisers. One of the roles it plays is to stimulate government intervention, for where the Foundation does some notable piece of work, the government does not wish to be left behind and itself either assists or matches the work done. For example, when the Foundation planned an essential rail link from Mitchells Plain to a black township, the government which at first said it had no money for this project, later found that it had.

The Foundation has been working with sensitivity, giving assistance without any appearance of patronage, and has attempted to enlist black participation as well, in its work. It is an important social factor which has acquired considerable political significance in South Africa. Through it and similar institutions, there is commencing a catalytical action which can cause a reaction in the form of changed governmental attitudes.

Organisations such as the Urban Foundation, valuable though they be, give rise to an important ideological argument. Its critics would say that raising the status and lifestyle of the urban blacks, without giving them political rights, is a government ploy. Prosperous petit-bourgeois blacks are less likely to resort to Soweto style riots and will have a stake in the system, which they will not want to lose. Moreover, South African industry will be able to sell many thousands of television sets, washing machines and other electrical appliances in an electrified rather than a coal-burning Soweto.

Conceding these factors, there remains the argument that the upliftment of the black population to a level of satisfaction of basic needs cannot any longer be delayed on any front. If some amelioration of their condition is possible, that cannot be delayed indefinitely, for one does not know when the major problem of devolution of power will be solved, and one cannot on this account abstain in the interim from all beneficial action.

The World Heavyweight Fight

It may seem strange in a serious socio-political discussion to attach much weight to the conditions in which a boxing championship takes place. Yet the staging of the World Boxing Association heavyweight title fight in Pretoria in October 1979 was an event of great political significance.

South Africa has always zealously avoided exposing its people to situations of confrontation between the races or their representatives. One notices this particularly in the state-operated television programmes. Never is a black man shown on terms of equality with a white, and least so in a situation where he matches himself on equal terms with a white competitor. Many American television films are for this reason deemed unsuitable for presentation to South African audiences, for they depict the black acting on terms of equality with the white.

The fight in question was therefore a revolutionary new departure, for here was a black contender from America, Big John Tate, contending for the title with Afrikaner Gerrie Coetzee in the midst of thousands of blacks and whites in Pretoria, the heart of Afrikanerdom. It was not without a strunggle that U.S. fight promoter, Bob Arum, achieved this result. He needed to interview the South African Minister of Sport, Punt Janson, for permission, and is reported to have said to him, "This country either has to take a stand and get in step with the rest of the world or forget international competition". The confrontation produced a declaration from the Minister that it was "the policy of the government of South Africa to allow sporting bodies to give equal opportunity to sportsmen and spectators of all races, including open access, where requested, to sporting events".

This change of policy resulted in an internationally televised fight where millions of dollars changed hands. The appetite of public and promoters was stimulated to the extent that ten more such fights are planned for the next two years. Incidentally the bout resulted in a victory for the black contender, much to the delight of the black component of the 86,000 strong multi-racial audience.

The Centre of Inter-Group Studies

Founded at the University of Cape Town in 1968 with the aim of promoting "greater knowledge, keener appreciation and better understanding among all race groups", it involves itself in such research as the preparation of a handbook on discrimination in various fields, and the organisation of conferences around this theme.

Since its foundation the Centre moved on to a more activist role owing to the absence of legitimate channels for the ventilation of grievances by the disadvantaged racial groups. This tends to drive the discontented to violence — a tendency strengthened by racial polarisation which is the direct result of government policies. The 1976 disturbances showed quite clearly the necessity for a mediating group for conflict resolution in times of crisis.

The Centre of Inter-Group Studies and internationally known experts in the field of conflict resolution[10] discussed possible steps to overcome the obstacle of polarisation of the whole community, which had already occurred. The objective was to build up a middle or mediating group as neutral ground where opposing parties could meet. A middle group was thought to be of fundamental importance in time of crisis in a society which was already divided along racial lines.

Among the methods worked out by the Centre in attempting the role of mediator and conciliator were the arrangement of joint consultations between those in authority and those who complained against it; the identification and formulation of the concerns of the black communities; the provision of legitimate channels for non-violent protest; deputations to the authorities bringing to their notice the concerns of persons under oppression; development of plans of action; submission of evidence to Commissions of Enquiry; identification of elements of violence and an attempt to urge the police to reassess their own task and role in present South African society.

The Centre, which set out as a mediator, found itself compelled by the evidence it discovered to move into the position of advocate on behalf of black communities and the victims of alleged police brutality. It identified much evidence of violent police action — particularly the action of the riot squad which had attacked innocent bystanders who had no part in the disturbances. Many of them were innocent victims who looked upon the police as the cause of their suffering and argued that the riots were in fact caused by the riot police.

The South African system is sorely lacking in safety valves and this is an area to which the government needs to give its most urgent attention. In this context the Centre performs a vital function.

Its importance becomes even clearer when we realise that blacks, coloureds and Asians are in fact without representative organs throughout white South Africa. As regards the black population, the total absence of structures amongst them is the result of deliberate government policy. The reason adduced for such a short-sighted policy is that blacks would have their representative organisations within the Bantu homelands. The government probably saw it as an advantage to themselves that the ten million urban blacks should be leaderless and unorganised. As far as the coloureds are concerned there is a Coloured Persons Representative Council (CPRC). For the Indians the South African Indian Council has been set up. Although these bodies are meant to create the impression of participation in government by these communities, they are basically subordinate to the central government and they are closely supervised. The central government may overrule their decisions, and powers of appointment to the Council are retained by the white rulers. Consequently, at no level is there any kind of representative government of the black, coloured or Indian populations of South Africa. This is reflected even in the structure of the universities, where the universities catering to the needs of these communities are themselves under much closer surveillance and super-vision than the white universities.

In the light of these facts it seems strange indeed that South Africa has thus far avoided a major conflagration. The Centre of Inter-Group studies can contribute significantly towards siphoning off some at least of the pressure. Hope-fully, it could contribute to buying that little bit of extra time so vital to the question whether change is to be peace-ful or violent.

Workers for Change

One of the saving graces on the South African land-scape is the presence of a number of organisations dedicated to working for change in the field of race relations. Re-search, upliftment, heightening awareness and promotion of inter-racial fellowship are some of their objectives. Political action cannot in the prevailing conditions of South Africa, be actively resorted to, but their work necessarily has pol-itical repercussions. Some of them have at times come under surveillance.

The organisations working in these fields are far too numerous for separate enumeration. The reader will form some idea of their range and scope from the random list that follows:

a) The S.A. Institute of Race Relations. Now in its fiftieth year, the Institute is the most active in the field of research into race relations. The student or observer re-quiring information on matters connected with race re-lations, can do no better than consult the annual Survey of Race Relations published by the Institute, a 500-page compendium of information carefully researched and excellently presented. The Institute, despite its strongly anti-apartheid stance, receives the support of members of parliament and government officials in procuring its information. It receives assistance from the Algemeen Diokonaal Bureau of the Reformed Churches in the

Netherlands and from foreign grants. It also organises conferences on themes such as "The Road to a Just Society", which generate important research papers.

b) The Black Sash. This has already been discussed.[11]

c) The Urban Foundation. This has already been discussed.[12]

d) The Human Awareness Programme. Established in 1977, its objective is the promotion of informed public opinion and the generation among the whites of an understanding of the importance of power sharing. It assists other organisations with advice in the planning of change, especially attitudinal change.

e) Akse (Action South Africa). Professor R. Tusenius, former Director of the Graduate School of Business at Stellenbosch University founded this movement to develop a new national strategy for the removal of all statutory discrimination. The movement is also — in the author's view, unfortunately — linked with the objective of developing the free enterprise system in South Africa, thus robbing it, in the eyes of its critics, of a stance of objectivity and disinterestedness.

f) The Centre for Intergroup Studies. This has already been discussed.[13]

g) Kontak. A group of Afrikaans speaking women, concerned at the lack of contact between Afrikaans women and women of other racial groups, formed themselves into an organisation in 1976 to attempt a bridging of this gap. Their activities have brought together Afrikaans and coloured women in meetings, seminars and student groups.

h) Women for Peace is an organisation aimed at fostering inter-racial understanding, harmony and peaceful change. It aims at organising meetings and parties across the colour line. Similar organisations are Women for Peace Now in Cape Town, the Women's Movement in Durban and People for Peace in Port Elizabeth.

i) The Women's Legal Status Committee formed in 1976 aims at the elimination of the legal disabilities and the upgrading of the legal status of all South African women.

j) Mowbray Inter-Race Group. The group organisers conduct evenings for discussions. between blacks and whites of black aspirations. Whites, starved in South African society of meetings with blacks of their intellectual level, are afforded this opportunity through the work of the group.

k) Dependants' Conference. This has been discussed already.[14]

The factors set out in this chapter, even taken cumulatively, are not, in the writer's opinion, sufficient to make a substantial change in the South African situation. Yet, if stepped up, they have the potential to do so. Increasing effort must be forthcoming, and an increasing tempo maintained. Pressure and assistance from outside in the manner outlined in the next chapter will help considerably. The Zimbabwean example of concessions which were to niggardly and too late is a constant reminder that if people are to be brought to the bargaining table, they must be brought at the earliest opportunity. Every passing day sees blacks moving from the ranks of those who are prepared to talk to the ranks of those who consider discussion superfluous and ineffective. Time is running out and a new and more realistic power sharing plan needs desperately to emerge.

FOOTNOTES

1. See *Newsweek* Feb 18, 1980 p.13.
2. Many more of these sorts of utterances are reported from time to time in the international press. The four mentioned above came from *Newsweek*, Oct. 29, 1979.
3. See pp.116-7.
4. *Black Sash,* Aug. 1979 p.7.
5. See pp.95-7.
6. See pp.124-9.
7. For many of these facts see *The Times,* Friday Dec.21, 1979.
8. See p.176.
9. See pp.70, 178.
10. Among the latter were Professor A. Paul Hare, Professor of Sociology at U.C.T. and Brigadier Michael Harbottle, former Chief of Staff of the U.N. Peacekeeping force in Cyprus, who was at U.C.T. as a visiting lecturer.
11. See pp.108-9.
12. See pp.218-9.
13. See pp.220-2.
14. See pp.109-12.

CHAPTER 8

What Can Be Done?

The Attack on Apartheid

An attack on apartheid can be considered in many facets. Among these are:

    i) the military aspect
    ii) the economic aspect
    iii) the communications aspect
    iv) the moral aspect
    v) the prestige aspect
    vi) the self-interest aspect

Many of these are interrelated, and a specific piece of action such as a trade boycott can operate both economically and in regard to prestige and self-interest.

i) *The Military Aspect*
The suggestions that follow do not explore the military aspect at all. The entire tenor of this book is that the military solution is to be avoided at all costs. The other aspects are all touched on in one way or another.

ii) *The Economic Aspect*
South Africa's economy, though powerful, is heavily dependent upon foreign capital.' Foreign capital can make its influence felt through the trade boycotts and various forms of disinvestment which are discussed below.

iii) *The Communications Aspect*
It is submitted that information is the prime means available for breaking down apartheid. The flow of information from South Africa to the outside world and

within South Africa itself is far too slender, and the channels of communication too few.

That the South African system has been able to maintain itself thus far is due to this information imbalance. This prevents the building up of world opinion to the point where citizens will not be content with ambiguous attitudes of protest by their respective governments. This enables justice-loving people throughout the Western world to permit the use of their small savings and capital to bolster up the South African regime. By and large, they do not know the facts regarding the use of their money by banks, corporations and churches or the way in which it buttresses racial discrimination in South Africa. Indeed till a few years ago the churches and universities of the Western world were themselves either unaware of these facts regarding their own money, or were able to preserve a sufficient distance from them to remain morally unperturbed. Information has changed all that and can effect many changes more. One purpose the present book can serve is to redress this information imbalance and to present to the reader much that ordinarily passes unreported. Information imbalance indeed is the chief weapon currently used to paralyse moves against apartheid. Many of the suggestions that ensue are intimately linked with the problem of information.

iv) *The Moral Aspect*

South Africa, paradoxical as it may seem, is deeply sensitive to the moral argument. Its deep religiousness has already been commented on. Churches, lawyers, academics and concerned laymen must undertake the task of making the moral issues clear.

Likewise, people outside South Africa can be addressed in terms of morality, regarding their duties. There are also many grey areas in relation to some moral aspects of anti-apartheid action — e.g. is there a moral duty to disinvest? — on which the formation of moral norms must proceed apace.

v) *The Prestige Aspect*

Afrikaners are a proud nation and they do not take kindly to non-recognition by the outside world. In the realm of sport their sensitivity to international boycotts has already been demonstrated. Many other areas will be available for the use of this technique.

vi) *The Self-Interest Aspect*

As a motivating force in human action self-interest

unfortunately rates extraordinarily high. Some of the measures set out below will be effective because they coincide with the self-interest of many people inside and outside South Africa, and of the South African government itself in a variety of ways.

In the sections that ensue are outlined some practical proposals falling under one or more or all of the above heads. It is for individuals, organisations and governments seriously concerned with making a dent in the South African problem to decide which one or more of these suits their own background best. It is hoped also that these proposals will stimulate further investigation of alternative lines of action.

The various suggestions set out below can conveniently be grouped under the following heads:

A) Trade Unionism
B) Investment and Loans
C) Church Sanctions
D) Boycotts
E) Individual Action
F) Foreign Policy
G) Miscellaneous

A) *TRADE UNIONISM*

1) *Dockworkers Sanctions*
The dockworkers of the world have special power which they can apply over and above the normal pressures of international trade unionism. The South African governmental machine is extremely sensitive to serious disruptions of trade, and the dockworkers of the world acting in unison have probably more power over the South African government than any other group. This power has been exercised in the past but not consistently enough in protest against South African violations of some of the basic tenets of trade unionism.

An apt illustration of the corrections that foreign action can almost immediately introduce into the South African statute book is the attempt by American miners and dockworkers in 1974 to prevent a ship from discharging South African coal in Mobile, Alabama in 1974 on the grounds that it constituted a contravention of s.307 of the U.S. Tariff Act of 1930, which prohibits the importation of goods produced by indentured labour under the threat of penal sanctions. At that time it was an offence criminally punishable in South African law for a worker to terminate his contract of employment. The South African government's response to the threat was swift and dramatic. The entire vicious nest of indentured labour legislation dating from 1856 was repealed.[2] Certain sections of the Republican Bantu Labour Act 67 of 1964 were repealed — ss.13(6)(b)(d) and (7) which dealt with penalties for breach of contract entered into the labour agents, ss.14(d) which dealt with prohibitions on harbouring Africans who had unlawfully left their employers and section 15 which made it a criminal offence, punishable by a fine of up to R.50 or three month's imprisonment for an African contract worker employed on any mine or workplace to desert or absent himself without lawful cause from his place of employment or fail to carry out the terms of his contract or refuse to obey a lawful command of his employer or use insulting language to any person lawfully in authority over him.[3]

This was probably the outstanding instance of a thorough cleansing of a section of the South African statute book. There is no doubt that more such cleansings will follow if the dockworkers of the world take specific steps for the safeguarding of the worldwide concept of trade unionism.

2) *Fact Finding Tours*
International trade unions need to keep the South African situation under constant surveillance and to send delegations of their members, from time to time, to South Africa, in order to understand the realities of South African labour problems.

For example, members of the International Metal Workers Federation, a thirteen million strong union, sent a delegation of their members some years ago to visit various foreign plants in South Africa including the Volkswagen and the Mercedes assembly plants, as well as Ford and General Motors.

International trade union action can make known to the public the various international companies which operate in South Africa and conform to the principles and practice of apartheid. This is a way of awakening public opinion in the Western world and of bringing to the notice of shareholders of those companies, the way in which their dollar or pound produces its dividends through a denial of human rights.

3) *Support of Specific Boycotts*
The selection of specific acts of boycott in regard to trade with South Africa can also be extremely effective.

If there is a device which is being manufactured abroad for use in South Africa for a repressive purpose, as for example a computer for use by South African police, workers can agree to stop work on that particular project.   An illustration of this sort of sanction occurred in October 1968, when 2,000 workers at International Computers Limited refused to work on orders for computers that were being turned out by the company for the use of the South African police.

4) *Education of Trade Union Membership*

It is important that the rank and file of trade union membership throughout the world be educated on the extent to which there is a denial of trade union rights in South Africa. Many trade unionists know vaguely that all is not well with trade unionism in South Africa but they lack the specific information which would make them active workers for basic labour rights in South Africa. Better coverage is therefore required of developments in South Africa on the labour front.   Some of the denials of basic labour rights set out in this book could well come as a surprise to some of the most concerned trade unionists. If there can be this degree of unawareness regarding general facts, unawareness of the more specific details must be even greater.   For example, few trade unionists abroad would know of an important court case in June 1978 brought by the unregistered Transport and Allied Workers Union against Bosman Transport.   The complaint was in connection with the dismissal of eight workers alleged to have been victimised for activities which in any other industrialised country would be looked upon as legitimate trade union activities.   The employer argued that the union was an unregistered one and as such had "no statutory recognition".   This finding was upheld by Justice C.J. Eloff. He found that the trade union could not represent workers in the case as it had no interest in the "right" which was the subject matter of the case — a legal result which, whatever the statute law behind it, must surely be anathema to a trade unionist anywhere in the world. Information on this sort of current development is an urgent necessity.

5) *Solidarity Strikes*

Another possible means of action is the solidarity strike. The solidarity strike occurs in the context of a multinational corporation which conducts operations in South Africa. Its workers overseas can well indicate their solidarity with its South African workers in regard to the company's

denial to them of rights regarded by Western trade unionism
as axiomatic. Pressure thus brought to bear upon the head
office can result in relaxations of the practices prevalent in
its South African operation. An example of this was the
strike at Unilever plants in seven countries which occurred in
October 1978 and brought their factories in many countries
to a standstill. This was the first time in South African
labour history that such action had been taken against a
multinational corporation by its overseas union members.
It has much scope for development and there is little doubt
that the pressure it can exert will be compelling both upon
the corporation itself and upon the South African government.

6) *Pressure on Diplomatic Representation*
Foreign trade unions can also assert themselves by
bringing pressure to bear upon the diplomatic representation of South Africa abroad. For example, in 1978,
British Trade Union leaders called upon the South African
government to list banning orders on African Trade Unionists, through a delegation which called on the South African
ambassador in London.

7) *The Formulation and Implementation of Codes
of Conduct for Industry and Trade Unionism*

Codes of conduct in the trade union field are fairly
well recognised. We have referred already to the Sullivan
Code in the United States, the European Economic
Community Code and the Canadian Government Code.[4]
For South Africa the Urban Foundation has formulated a
code which among other items speaks of removing discrimination based on race or colour in job advancement and
fringe benefits and indeed in all aspects of employment
practice.
Another way in which the international trade union
movement can make itself felt is by publishing a code of
conduct and requiring overseas companies investing in
South Africa, to observe this code.[5] For example, the
International Confederation of Free Trade Unions, with a
membership of fifty million, has issued its own Code of
Conduct for overseas companies investing in South Africa
in a booklet distributed to member nations throughout the
industrialised world. This same union launched an action
week, in 1968, for its anti-apartheid campaigns, the objectives of which were the recognition of African Trade Unions
in South Africa, equal rights for African and white workers,

and the lifting of banning orders imposed on African unionists. Not only must such codes be promulgated. The international movement should also follow the extent of their
implementation, calling for regular reports from their South
African representatives, and publishing those reports.

That such codes can achieve results is demonstrated
by the Sullivan Code which has achieved some advances in
the fields of integrating canteens, washrooms, toilets, medical
facilities and work places. However in regard to job integration and job advancement, these codes will probably not
achieve significant results unless they are closely monitored.
The monitoring function does not belong to trade unions
alone. If a company is genuine in its claim that it adheres to
a Code, it is probably in its own interests to open its doors
to a local anti-apartheid body to satisfy itself periodically
that this is in fact so. This will enhance the company's
image. Foreign shareholders have indeed a right to insist
on such a procedure.

8) *Anti-apartheid Campaigns*

Trade unions are in a uniquely privileged position to
launch effective anti-apartheid campaigns, for they not only
command attention from their large membership but also
enjoy considerable political and economic influence over the
rest of the community. The International Confederation of
Free Trade Unions (ICFTU) with its fifty million membership pointed the way in this direction with a year long anti-
apartheid campaign in 1978 and an action week from 13-21
March. They called for the recognition of African trade
unions, equal rights for black and white workers and the
removal of banning orders imposed on trade unionists.
Other actions on the part of this powerful body were a
request to European governments to stop further multinational investment and a request that the EEC code of
conduct become legally operative in South Africa.

There are many similar steps that can be taken by
national trade unions throughout the world.

9) *Lobbying Activities*

In 1978 the American Federation of Labour called
on the Carter administration to halt all Export-Import Bank
insurance, credit and loan guarantees aimed at stimulating
the movement of capital to South Africa. It also urged the
severing of diplomatic relations between the United States
and South Africa as well as other forms of abstention from
South Africa-related activities. The *Rand Daily Mail* of
27 February 1978 reported that South African government

231

sources felt this trade union stand would encourage the United States Congress to take a harder line against apartheid.

10) *Training of African Trade Unionists*
Trade unionism has in recent decades grown into a highly specialised activity. In order to obtain for South African trade unionism the maximum possible results, it is necessary that there be, among black trade unionists, sufficient leaders with a training in advanced trade unionism as well as some understanding of the manner in which the international trade union movement operates. To this end funds should be made available for training and research both in South Africa and abroad. The Executive Council of the British Trade Union Congress has made funds available for these purposes and has also initiated a plan for the financing of trade union training in the United Kingdom for South African trade union leaders.

B) *INVESTMENT AND LOANS*

1) *Disinvestment*

Disinvestment is a difficult issue. It is undoubtedly one of the means by which pressure can be applied. If foreign ownership divests its South African stocks and ceases to buy stocks in South African companies, there is no question but that South Africa will be extremely sensitive to this kind of action. One result of the scheme is the widespread unemployment and suffering it would cause to the black community — but this has been dealt with elsewhere in these pages.[6]

Objectives of such action — the reform of South African law relating to apartheid, the correction of South African discriminatory practice as prevailing in factories, the grant of trade union rights, and the abolition of the pass laws — are unquestionably so legitimate that no reasonable argument can be advanced against them save the hardship already referred to.

If disinvestment is to be applied, in what manner should it be, and to what extent? These questions again admit of no easy answer. American students have already taken up this matter and have sought the disinvestment of all university investments in South Africa. With this pressure, universities have responded in different ways and already the University of Wisconsin, Ohio University and the

University of Massachussetts have completely divested themselves of their holdings, worth nearly ten million rand. Others such as Amhurst College have followed the path of partial disinvestment. Harvard and Columbia (with holdings of eighty million dollars in forty-four companies with assets in South Africa) announced their intention to sell or not to buy stocks in United States banks which made loans to the South African government.[7]

There is another course which, while perhaps carrying the same message, may be less drastic in its operation, and that is disinvestment over a period of time, say five years. According to such a plan the South African government would be informed that unless it showed some significant relaxation in its discriminatory laws, there would be progressive foreign disinvestment from year to year. This scheme will be easier to implement as it is more likely to have the support of investors. They will not suddenly find themselves with large withdrawn investments in their hands, for which alternative investments will take time to arrange. The loss in switching investments will therefore be considerably less. This practical factor assumes importance in the light of the fact that investors are often trustees of other people's funds. Trustees, while being anxious to remedy the South African situation, must also have an eye to the interests of their investors. Senator Paul Tsongas, American democratic senator from Massachussetts, has come out strongly in favour of this alternative.

Certainly the pressure kept up by the American students serves a valuable purpose. Similar pressure by other student bodies elsewhere can help attract attention to this problem and keep up the pressure without which the disinvestment move will soon lose momentum. There is no gainsaying the fact that foreign companies, particularly British and American, provide a large deal of moral and economic support for the South African government's policies and this fact needs to be kept constantly before the public. Quite often there would be investors in those companies who would totally disapprove of the way in which their life savings are being used to bolster up a regime which depends upon and perpetuates iniquity. As Senator Tsongas has said recently, "American companies have a part to play because some deal directly with the government, selling computers used to organise the pass law system, building coal to gasoline conversion plants and selling military vehicles to the South African police and defence forces". British companies, with their considerably greater involvement in South Africa, have an even greater role, which tends to pass unnoticed under the common misconception that American rather than British capital is the vital factor buttressing the South African regime.[8]

2) *An Information Service to Foreign Shareholders*

Companies, it is notorious, exist for profit. Still a concerned shareholding public can insist on certain basic observances in the use of their money. It is important that the shareholding public be alerted to the fact that money is being made for them by violations of human rights. Many a shareholder, properly informed, would certainly exert himself to ensure that there is nothing in the earning of his dividends which will violently trouble his conscience.

One means available is for the shareholders of these companies to be circularised by workers in the South African human rights cause, bringing to their attention the various human rights violations through which their profits are increased.

This needs inquiry into the conditions in each workplace, but is not a daunting research undertaking. It needs liaison between a South African observer who can see conditions on the spot and a worker in the country where the company has its headquarters. An accurate factual statement of the conditions in the workplace and of the legal framework against which people are recruited and employed is all that is required. In fact if their work is done in regard to one company, the same material can with slight adaptations be used to cover dozens of others. All that is needed is a nucleus of workers in London and New York, and a small team of observers on the spot in the various workplaces in South Africa.

Among the human rights violations which will no doubt come as a shock to the shareholders will be:

a) the fact that the worker's spouse is not allowed to live with him.
b) the fact that most urban workers have no guarantee of the right to residence in South Africa, even if they have worked for several years in the service of the company.
c) the fact that the right to reside in urban South Africa is gained, for those not born in an urban area, only by 10 years' continuous service with one employer or 15 years' service with more than one employer. These requirements are impossible to satisfy when

companies as a matter of policy give employees only contracts for at most a year at a time. The break between the two contracts effectively ensures that the worker will never obtain the right to live in urban South Africa. The result is that the worker becomes the virtual slave of the employer, whom he dare not displease.

d) the fact that loss of employment invariably means forcible deportation to a 'homeland' the worker may never have seen, and where there is no employment for him, and consequently a life of dire want. This whip hand the employer thus enjoys under South African law violates all principles of fairplay recognised in the free world as between employer and employee.

e) the fact that trade union rights exist in the workplace for black employees, in an attenuated form if at all.

f) the fact that strikes are often broken in South Africa by the police and that police dogs are let loose upon the strikers.

These are a few facets. Many more can be mentioned. If they do not sting the conscience of the average British or American shareholder, one would be very surprised.

3) *Limiting Loans*

Many western banks have advanced large sums of money to South Africa. For example the First National Bank of Boston had advanced between 20 and 30 million dollars to South Africa, including some loans to state organisations. The bank took a decision in 1977 to limit the term of the loans to three years instead of five. Banks whose shareholders are greatly concerned about South African problems could take similar steps regarding either the extent or the term of the loan.

Since self interest is also a strong practical reason influencing such decisions, it is to be noted that the political instability of South Africa taints heavy investment in that country with a strong element of risk. The apparent outward stability hides so many deep political undercurrents that civil unrest could occur unpredictably at any stage. Soweto sparked itself off with no apparent advance warning. Worse can occur in the future, and perhaps with equal suddenness. If foreign investors should realise more generally how much South Africa is in a powder keg situation there can well be a reduction in loan facilities as well as in investments. It is interesting to note in this context that a University of Delaware Business Environment Risk Index, ranking countries on the basis of security of private invest- ments, downgraded South Africa from eighth to nineteenth position in 1977.[9]   In the same year prominent British bankers and brokers saw South Africa as an investment risk and showed a reluctance to continue investing in the country.   They mentioned the US, Japan and Europe as preferable places for UK investment.[10]   The British Prime Minister in 1978 voiced a similar fear in saying that prudent countries would be looking for alternative sources of min- erals as South Africa was "an area of disturbance".[11]

4) *Publicising the Extent of Bank Loans to South Africa*

The Corporate Information Center of the National Council of Churches of Christ in the United States of America (NCCUSA) recently published an important docu- ment titled, *The Frankfurt Documents: Secret Bank Loans to the South African Government.*   This is a significant example of the way in which research by interested organ- isations can lay bare the covert assistance rendered by the West to apartheid.   This document showed that the European-American Banking Corporation (EABC) provided to the South African Government and to public corporations in South Africa about 20 per cent of South Africa's foreign loans for the period 1970-3.[12]

The resulting action by the World Council of Churches illustrates the manner in which action can be taken upon disclosures of this sort.

The World Council of Churches circularised the EABC and its six member banks setting out the facts, as revealed, and stating that the WCC believed that the EABC should cease such loans.   In the event of the loans continuing, the WCC expressed its resolve that none of its funds would be deposited with any member bank.

This aroused resentment on the part of the EABC. In its view the WCC was trespassing beyond its proper territory, and was making impertinent and impossible requests. Their arguments included the following:

a) the investment was useful for providing higher living standards for the blacks

b) banking was a politically neutral function

c) the WCC was providing the bank with an ulti- matum rather than proposing a matter for discussion

d) the EABC could not coerce its member banks to conduct different from their normal banking practices

e) the first duty of a bank is to preserve the interests of its shareholders.

The WCC resolved, in reply, to refrain from depositing any more funds in EABC member banks.   It also urged other Christian groups to use publicity, stockholder action and withdrawal of accounts as a means of influencing these banks to cease loans to South Africa.

The resolution sparked off much activity in diverse quarters.

In Holland anti-apartheid groups such as "Prepaid Reply" commenced lobbying campaigns at national level to influence banks and politicians. In Germany, the German Student Christian movement supported the WCC resolution. In Canada, the Canadian Taskforce on the Churches and Church Responsibility took steps to support the resolution.

Not in all quarters was there agreement with the WCC position.   For example, Bishop Oscar Sakransky of the Evangelical Church in Austria wrote to the Austrian member of the EABC that he did not support the WCC resolution.

Yet there was a massive achievement that followed the resolution. The Midland Bank in the U.K. announced in 1978 that as a matter of policy it was no longer making loans to South Africa.   The Royal Bank of Canada announced that it would not make loans judged to support apartheid or the pass law system. The Rotterdam Bank and the Algemene Bank Nederland announced that they would make no further loans to the government of South Africa or its agencies.   Citibank, Chase Manhattan Bank and the First National Bank of Chicago gave limited undertakings that they would make no further loans to South Africa.[13]

At governmental level the Dutch government and the Norwegian government in 1976 decided to end export guarantees to South Africa, probably a by product of the general interest created by the WCC campaign.

5) *Imposing Conditions on Patent Rights*

Another way in which a substantial impression can be made upon the South African situation is through pressure of foreign companies insisting that if their patents are to be used by South African companies, the South African companies should comply with certain basic requirements regarding the treatment of their workforce. Foreign patents are very valuable to South African companies and it is very much on the cards that if the use of the patent is made conditional on the observance of these rules the South African companies will make an effort to comply.

6) *Norm Creation regarding Investment in South Africa*

One of the important tasks facing all workers for the abolition of racism in South Africa is the task of norm creation. The values which society regards as axiomatic determine the behavioural patterns of individuals, institutions and governments. Those values are in constant process of formation, and an endeavour well worthy of effort is to engage in a conscious and continuing contribution to the process of norm formation.

The fields of slavery, women's rights, labour rights and environmental rights provide examples of the slow evolution of such norms and of the power of such norms once generally accepted. One of the methods by which workers for the new norms helped their evolution was to focus social attention on the problem. Another was to supply information to the public. Yet another was to keep comparing prevailing practice in their fields with other accepted norms and to highlight the discrepancies.

So also, in the case of South Africa, norm formation must go on apace. Everyone is opposed to racism but there are grey areas where norms have yet to be formed. Is it legitimate to invest in a company whose South African operations recognise apartheid in the work place? Is it legitimate to draw dividends when one knows that the labour that produces those dividends is denied basic family rights and must crowd together in dingy male dormitories for fifty weeks of the year, away from their families? Is it acceptable to deposit one's money in a bank which gives loans to the South African government, thereby helping it to continue the reign of apartheid? Is it correct to use pressure on banks to cease lending moneys to the South African government? Should a company producing materials that could aid the South African government in its policies of repression, sell those materials to the South African government?

Some would say the norms involved in these instances are clear, but those norms have not percolated through to society as a whole. On all concerned with South Africa's future — individuals, groups and institutions, both in South Africa and abroad — there falls a heavy duty to contribute actively to the process of norm formation. This means writing, research, discussion and persuasion. It involves boldness and clarity in the formulation of the norms. It calls for dedicated workers in every country. The Wilberforces of the anti-apartheid movement are all too few.

C) *CHURCH SANCTIONS*

The remarks that ensue largely concern churches other than the Dutch Reformed Church in South Africa, whose doctrinal stance favouring apartheid has been dealt with elsewhere.[14]

There is a great deal that churches both within and without South Africa can do to remedy the South African situation. It must be said in criticism of the church in general that it has not been as active as it needed to be to ensure basic human dignity in South Africa. Indeed if the churches had adopted a more correct and unequivocal Christian stance it is unlikely that the South African situation would have deteriorated to its present sorry state.

In particular the Catholic, Anglican, Methodist and Presbyterian churches can apply much pressure in South Africa to challenge the many inconsistencies that still exist. This is said against the background fact that in South Africa ninety per cent of the membership of the Catholic Church, seventy five per cent of the Anglican Church and eighty per cent of the Methodist church is black.

1) *Refusal to support apartheid laws*

The Church must recognise as a general proposition that a duty lies upon it to withhold its co-operation from the state in all those areas where, manifestly, the laws of the state fly in the face of the Church's understanding of the basic tenets of Christianity. We are here not merely in the classic controversy regarding the citizen's attitude towards a law which is manifestly unjust. Lawyers have for two thousand years closely debated the citizen's duty in such circumstances. In regard to the Church there is something more, for unlike the citizen, the Church by its very calling is closely committed to a body of principles. If it is true to its mission it cannot in conscience support the state in matters conflicting with its entire structure and commitment. Moreover the Church is acting within the context of a country deeply committed to Christianity and has a special responsibility to give leadership to its flock, for there is no doubt that the average citizen, no less than the Church, is conscience-troubled by his obligations to obey some South African laws. Furthermore the Church is the one institution that can stand up against the regime of persecution of all dissentient opinion, in which the South African citizen finds himself. Indeed it would not be overstating the argument if one were to say that it would be almost an abandonment of responsibility for the Church, with all its immunity, to keep away from these issues of conscience and leave them to be fought out by the average private citizen with all his vulnerability to arrest and imprisonment.

Some years ago the Anglican Archbishop Clayton of Cape Town gave dramatic leadership in this regard. He wrote to the Prime Minister at the time of the Native Laws Amendment Bill, that although he had tried to comply as far as possible with state law, the time had now come when he could no longer in conscience lend his co-operation to the State in regard to laws which so clearly violated the law of God. Archbishop Clayton penned these lines to the Prime Minister and collapsed dead over his desk in one of the most dramatic occurrences in recent South African history. Had he lived, the Church would perhaps have taken a stand, and the whole course of recent South African history might have been different. Clergymen who have had the moral courage to stand up for their views, such as Rev. David Russell, would not have had to incur the sacrifices and the banning orders they have sustained as individuals if Church leadership had taken a firmer stand.

It is worth noting that the Bill which Archbishop Clayton protested against was designed to make association in "church, school, hospital, club or other institution or place of entertainment" difficult if not impossible. The Bill was not proceeded with, largely because of the Archbishop's protest. Other statutes in South African history could have fared similarly if the leaders of the Church had been as resolute in their protest.

2) *Equal stipends for white and black ministers*

There was a time when churches themselves endorsed the practice of wage discrimination by making different levels of stipend available to their white and black ministers. In most instances they have realised their error and are redressing this imbalance but as far as the author's information goes complete parity has not yet been attained in all cases.

3) *Sharing power within the church*

It is necessary to open to non-whites who are adequately qualified a fairer proportion of the positions of power within the church. The proportion of this sort of power sharing is today so weighted against the blacks that one might almost look upon these church organisations as denials of the power sharing concept. It is no argument that there are insufficient members of blacks capable of filling these positions. In the sphere of clergy there are more than enough qualified blacks to choose from. Among laymen, it may well be asked what the church has been doing all these generations if it has not been able to produce sufficient blacks to take over a proportionate responsibility in the layman-oriented activities of the church. There have indeed been some recent examples of an increasing introduction of blacks into church committees and other church offices. Yet one hears the frequent complaint in South Africa that these instances are all too few.

4) *The deliberate integration of congregations*

The church has in the main been content to adopt a passive role in the crime of separation of the communities committed under the Group Areas Act. Congregations which were once reasonably mixed are so no longer, with the forcible movement of whites and non-whites into separate residential districts. The church looked on while its congregations were separated on grounds of colour. It is true there is now an element of distance that prevents people who once worshipped at a church from continuing to attend. But distance by itself is no answer to so insidious an undermining of meaningful Christian fellowship. The church must move out positively to reintegrate the communities which the act of the legislator separated. Joint services need to be organised every month at least bringing together people of different racial groups, even at the expense of providing transport for this purpose. Branches of these churches abroad must also provide the necessary encouragement and emphasise the Christian ideology which makes this imperative. An age of ecumenism is seeking to draw together Christians of different faiths. Such activity, laudable in itself, seems anomalous in the absence of an effort to bring together for common worship Christians of the same denomination who are fast losing all contact with each other through racial policies which it is most important that the churches should counter. Indeed if leadership in this regard does not come from the church one may well ask from where else one may expect it.

5) *Concern with Social Problems*

The church is also a social institution functioning in

the midst of society. It has historically assumed this role and not led the life of an order of monastic recluses. The church has hitherto taken for granted the serious discrepancy between the incomes of the average white family and of the average black. This it accepts as a fact of the social scene. On such questions it has not sufficiently expressed its Christian views or afforded the kind of moral leadership one would expect. If there is in society a matter which stings the Christian conscience, one would expect the church to speak out on it. One does not say the church has not expressed itself on these issues, but rather that to an outside observer, it does not appear to have done so adequately.

6) *Solemnisation of Marriages*

One has scarcely heard a serious protest from the clergy concerning prevention by the State of marriages across the colour line. Indeed the church seems to have fallen completely into line with state policy in this regard and a South African man and woman who desire to marry across the colour line are regularly refused the services of a priest on the grounds that the solemnisation of such a marriage is contrary to state law. The church needs to consider more closely its obligations in this regard. Fear of punishment of the clergyman for violation of an unjust law ought not, according to the highest view of the priestly function, to deter a priest from acting as he thinks right and as his conscience dictates.

If two persons have been married by a priest who is satisfied that there is nothing in church teaching preventing him from marrying them, the parties are married in the eyes of the church but, when they cohabit, are committing an offence under the Immorality Act. To this anomaly the churches in South Africa have been privy, not thus far boldly asserting that the institution of Christian marriage, rests upon certain basic principles to the violation of which they will not be parties. Should a few priests have boldly defied this law and courted prosecution it would not long have stood.

The role the international church can play in this regard is to take a firm stand on this question and thus strengthen the arm of its local church. It needs to be an item high on the list of priorities of international church congresses when they meet. A pronouncement on this matter by the highest international authority of each particular church seems long overdue — not merely as an abstract proposition but as laying down the course of duty expected of the individual priest.

Another course that can be followed is for the clergy to register their disapproval of this legislation by returning their marriage licences to the State, asserting the inconsistency of their position at having to be ministers of the Church and at the same time officiating registrars of the State, where a conflict occurs between the basic positions of Church and State.   They will then be free to solemnise the marriage on a purely religious basis, with which the State cannot interfere, leaving it to the State to sort out the implications.   They can while returning their licences make it clear to their congregations that they are prepared to solemnise marriages on a purely religious basis.   Such a step will also place pressure upon the state in the form of the need to appoint thousands of civil registrars to replace the priests who now perform this function.

7) *Conscientious Objection to Military Service*

The church has thus far been silent on the vital issue of conscientious objection.   A young white South African who is opposed to military service on grounds of conscientious objections to the support of apartheid is entitled to guidance from the church on the moral aspects of his stand. The international churches need to make a pronouncement on this issue.   Many young people in South Africa are undergoing torments of conscience on this issue with little moral guidance from the church.   The problems involved need to be aired also in the international press, for the concept of just and unjust wars has more than ordinary importance today, especially after the Vietnam war.   The international churches have no doubt given their attention to this issue in the context of that war.   They need to do so in the context of the South African situation and to give clear guidance to their local churches.

Some young conscientious objectors have taken up the position that South African society is so unjust in terms of Christian morality that they cannot in conscience defend it.[15]   If courageous young men can court punishment in this way, giving themselves moral guidance which the church should be providing, it seems indeed a weak church which, with nothing to lose, fails to provide the guidance so desperately required of it by its flock.

8) *Army Chaplaincy*

Similar issues arise in the context of priests serving as chaplains in the army.   There may well be a conscience issue regarding service in an army that supports apartheid. The issue needs consideration from the international church.

9) *Legislation interfering with Sanctity of Marriage*

The Church needs also to take a stand on legislation which interferes with the sanctity of Christian marriage.

There cannot be one standard of marital duty in regard to the white population and another regarding the coloured. Unless one is prepared to turn a blind eye to it there is on the South African statute books a great volume of legislation which has precisely the effect of preventing husband and wife from living together and of breaking up families. Many well-meaning white South Africans are party to this by being party to the implementation of such legislation. There must be a stand dictated by conscience on this issue, and the church needs to issue clear guidelines to its parishioners. If the church is bold upon this — and the international church acting collectively can afford to be bold — it will greatly strengthen the hand of the conscientious Christian. Certainly if the church pronounces the legislation to be immoral it must cause the government, which is pledged to Christian principles, some deep concern. Indeed, now that the spirit of reform is in the air, it may even enable the reformists within the government to use such church pronouncements to strengthen their arguments against the old guard who resist reform — that old guard itself being committed to Christian principles.

Furthermore, such a stand by the international church can well cause the Dutch Reformed Church itself to re-examine its conscience on this issue — and that would be a most potent instrument for change.

Legislation referred to is legislation which prevents 'migrant' workers from bringing their wives with them and requires them to live in unisex hostels, and legislation which prevents the spouse of a domestic servant from living in the area where the employed spouse works. In the latter case the domestic servant, working perhaps for years to contribute to the domestic happiness of a white family, is by law kept away from her own family to the point of estrangement. Many white employers would be happy to provide accommodation for the family if that were legally permitted.

Alternatively, there should be no legal objection to that black family making a home in the city close to the servant's place of employment. This latter suggestion may sound unacceptable to some South Africans but not to anyone else, and that shows how far South Africa has departed from the moral norms of the rest of the world.

10) *Leadership in Norm Formation*

We have referred earlier to the presence of certain grey areas where the moral duty of the citizen in relation to a South Africa related activity is not altogether clear.[16] Norms must be created in these areas, which society will increasingly accept, in the same way as norms relating to sex equality, labour rights and environmental protection have grown over the years to a level of general acceptance.

The church more than any other organisation can provide leadership in this sphere. This is one of the outstanding actions possible in the moral sector of the attack upon apartheid.

One of the many activities which need to emerge from the grey area is the loan of moneys to the South African government.   The World Council of Churches provided leadership in this regard.[17] So did the U.S. National Council of Churches when in February 1978 it called on the Bank of America, Crocker International, First National Boston and Manufacturers' Hanover Trust not to make further loans or renew existing loans to the South African government.

Organisations of the church do not, with respect, always provide the moral leadership in this area which one would expect.   It is sad to note for example that while British public conscience was so much awakened in 1977 that the Roman Catholic archdiocese of Westminster announced that it would sell all but one of its 11,211 shares in Consolidated Gold Fields, Britain's Society of Jesus decided not to follow the lead of other churches and sell its holdings.[18]

It is submitted that there is much scope here for church action and leadership. The entire gamut of activities impinging on South Africa needs to be the subject of dedicated and concerned study by church groups. Guidelines should be furnished by them from time to time, and should be acted upon by the churches themselves. If the church can move on these lines vast numbers of the general public will begin to see these issues without the present misguided feeling that they are prompted by radicalism or irresponsibility, and will therefore follow them.

Although the Dutch Reformed Church has been left out of this discussion there is no doubt that many of the issues touched upon here have a bearing upon that church as well, and there may well be some issues among those outlined, to which the members of that church would feel they must give their attention as part of their Christian commitment.

D) *BOYCOTTS*

1) *General and Particular Boycotts*

The world has for quite some time been given to speaking in terms of a general boycott of South Africa. The boycott extends in theory to all things and persons South African.   Sport, tourism, trade, cultural activities and international relations, are some of the areas mentioned as appropriate for blanket boycotts.   Likewise all South Africans are, in this loose form of thinking, equally unworthy of recognition.

In certain areas a policy of boycott has proved extremely useful, and the cardinal illustration comes from the realm of sport. But for this policy, South Africa would not probably have been shaken out of its stance of banning mixed sport or any sporting competitions between whites and non-whites. Today that has been relaxed and mixed teams can in theory play all sports in South Africa. Government sports policy does not as yet imply that integration in sports will be forced on schools, according to a statement of the Minister on 21 August 1979, but still there has been a relaxation, which resulted from the South African dislike of being excluded altogether from international competition. More international pressure will mean more relaxations until hopefully the situation is normalised.

While in such areas exclusion can operate as a telling demonstration of international power, it does not follow that blanket boycotts must therefore be the order of the day in every field of activity. More discrimination in the selection of areas of boycott will often pay better dividends, in addition to being more practical. Those who talk of blanket boycotts are often quite prepared to do business with South Africa when it suits them, and some of the great powers are among the worst offenders in this regard. Indeed even some foreign churches, publicly condemning South Africa for its policies of exploiting cheap black labour, have been content to earn dividends from that very source by heavy investment of church funds in South African enterprises — a fact which aroused shocked concern when it

was first realised a few years ago. To this day the investments of certain foreign churches in South African "sweated
labour" have not been completely divulged, though some
churches have withdrawn their investments.

Some of the succeeding subsections will examine
some areas of specific boycotts. The author believes that
blanket boycotts of South Africa are both impractical and
ineffective.

2) *The Black Reaction to Boycotts*

The day before the author left South Africa, Bishop
Desmond Tutu, highly respected for his human rights efforts,
created a storm by announcing to the World Council of
Churches in Brussels that it was the duty of Western
countries to boycott South African coal.

There was immediate condemnation of this speech
by the establishment. The condemnation was on the basis
that there would be an immediate loss of tens of thousands
of black jobs, and misery and starvation to several times
this number. There were also veiled threats by authority
to the effect that whoever called for boycotts against South
Africa was an enemy of South Africa.

It requires considerable moral and physical courage
for persons in the position of Bishop Tutu to make such a
statement, and it is necessary to examine why a black leader
should think in terms of a policy which will undoubtedly
bring so much misery to the blacks.

There are many among the blacks who believe they
have long suffered intensely but to no purpose. An additional burden of suffering may be more intense but will be
purposeful and, hopefully, short. In Bishop Tutu's words they
want their shackles removed, not made more comfortable.[19]

There is also resentment that the white population
keeps repeating the argument of suffering to the blacks as the
reason for their opposition to such a boycott. In fact it will
considerably hurt white interests as well, for although white
South Africa has great staying power, it is always very
sensitive to such trade boycotts. This sensitivity arises not
merely at the prospect of loss of finance. There is also the
increasing prospect that black starvation on a massive scale
will create a civil unrest situation which the government
will not be able to contain.

Radical blacks believe that black powers of endurance
are immense. How else, they say, could they have survived

all the ill treatment, starvation and penury which they have been through all these years. There is in fact even currently a suspected forty per cent rate of unemployment among the blacks. Still they survive. Indeed black doctors in South Africa are of the view that medically a black child subject to malnutrition shows the symptoms of disease later than a white or Indian child subjected to the same privations. The resulting philosophy then is to suffer and be done with this evil dream once and for all.

Evil dream it is, of course, as any white South African must realise if he has a nightmare of being temporarily encased in a black skin. It is a completely cramped, insecure, underprivileged, frightened existence that he would have to substitute for his spacious, leisured, privileged life, and he knows it. The black knows it too, and wants to shake off this evil for ever. That is the thinking of the black intelligentsia.

Moreover there is the fact that the willingness of the blacks to enter into dialogue is being eroded with every passing day. Action of any sort appeals to them as against talk. In this context the boycott, even though suffering is involved, has great appeal.

3) *Boycotts of Government Trade*

On the basis that the South African government will use certain technologies to further its policies of repression, some manufacturers have already mooted the idea of boycotting trade with the South African government. For example in November 1977 the Polaroid Corporation (US camera and film manufacturer) cancelled its business dealings in South Africa because its South African agents had failed to abide by a 1971 understanding not to sell material to the South African government.[20] The 1971 arrangement was the result of a clear policy decision that the company would only retain its business links with South Africa on the basis that it avoided government deals. In particular the company had in mind deals with the South African Defence Force, the Security Police and the Bantu reference bureaux. It turned out that films sold by the local agents had in fact found their way to military headquarters in Pretoria and elsewhere.

Technologies which readily come to mind as being of assistance in maintaining the apparatus of repression are computer and electronic technology, surveillance and scanning devices and recording devices of all sorts. Vehicles and equipment used by South Africa's police and military and spare parts, aircraft, naval craft and of course all forms of military technology add to the list. This is not to speak of skilled labour in these fields, which is as valuable as the commodities themselves.   The U.N. Programme of Action Against Apartheid specifically mentions this aspect when it speaks of discouraging the flow of immigration, particularly of skilled and technical personnel, to South Africa.

4) *Cultural Boycotts*

Cultural boycotts are in the writer's opinion a mistake. South Africa, more than any other country, needs exposure to foreign ideas and influences.   To close it to these influences is to provide precisely that impetus to further isolationism which will promote the *laager* mentality which characterises Afrikanerdom.   Plays, writings, films, television shows, academic exchanges — to shut out all these is counter productive, especially in view of the fact that South Africa is not a closed country as some other repressive regimes are.

Mark Bonham Carter, chairman of the British Race Relations Board, after a short visit to South Africa recently observed "Everyone seems to agree that foreign pressure is important if properly applied.   In this respect the effectiveness or otherwise of boycotts deserves more subtle analysis that it has hitherto received".   The author's observations completely endorse this view.   As Bonham Carter observes, South Africa is not unlike Eastern European society.   In dealing with the Eastern bloc it has been demonstrated that the exchange of ideas does good.   The same applies in South Africa where public discussion and the press are far more open and lively than in most socialist states.

The fresh air that flows both ways from cultural exchanges can without a doubt help alter rigid stances based on misunderstanding and distrust.   Many South African scholars, as far as could be observed on a brief visit, are critical of their own system and anxious to have moral and intellectual support for their stand.   All South African scholars are anxious to have dialogue with the rest of the world.   Some of them look upon the world as having condemned South Africa without hearing her case.   Deprive the South African scholar of cultural dialogue, and the liberals lose their fervour while the conservatives become more obdurate.

Intellectual exchanges should therefore take place and thereby open up vital lines of communication.   It is to be hoped that a climate of opinion will build up which will encourage academic visits to South Africa, not by way of acceptance of the South African system, but as efforts to carry reason and understanding into a country whose policies urgently need the maximum intellectual exposure, before which some of their obnoxious features may wilt away.

This is not to say however that foreign academic institutions cannot apply some form of pressure on South Africa. So long as South African academe continues to follow policies of racial segregation in regard to its student composition and instruction, the currency of the degrees it confers can be adversely affected in the years immediately ahead. A South African degree or diploma can in these circumstances attract the sanction of non-recognition as for example when the Royal Institute of British Architects decided to withdraw recognition from five schools of architecture in South Africa if it was not satisfied by January 1980 that their courses were open to all students, regardless of race, colour or creed.[21] Such attitudes are likely to spread and if more generally practised can have a severe effect upon South Africa, which will see in this a loss of international prestige. Many South Africans are anxious in today's unsettled conditions to make a living abroad, and lack of currency of South African degrees can hit hard.

Academic bodies outside South Africa, which confer higher degrees, may need to consider this aspect very seriously.

5) *Tourist Boycotts*

In the present state of South Africa it seems entirely wrong for the tourist traffic of the world to look upon South Africa as a venue for a joyous holiday. It is built up on too much human suffering and denials of basic human values for the international community to make a pleasure resort of it. Indeed, since tourism as an industry is international and its clientele is the world, it cannot theoretically direct its clientele to a country whose national policy constitutes a standing affront to three quarters of the human race.

The international tourist industry can bring much pressure to bear on South Africa to change its policies, for South Africa values tourism. If South Africa holds out the hand of friendship to other countries, offering them a pleasant stay in her territory, it cannot offer this only to the white world. Coloured patrons of any tourist company that offers tours to South Africa are well entitled to take up the position that they will withhold their further support from a company which is in this sense a party to an affront upon themselves.

The muscle of the international tourist industry has not thus far been at all evident as an agency pressing for a change of South African policies. If it claims to be an internationally oriented business, it is perhaps time it made the performance accord with the claim.

The conferment of the status 'honorary white' under which the nationals of some foreign countries, particularly Japan, come in as tourists is to be deprecated. Those accepting this are tacitly accepting the proposition that whiteness is superior or a ground of entitlement to privilege. It is to be hoped that Japanese tourists will take note of this aspect.

6) *Sports Boycotts*

The importance of these has already been sufficiently outlined.

7) *Other Selective Boycotts*

As and when occasions offer, selective particular boycotts can be devised, to deliver effective pressures in restricted but vital target areas. A list of these cannot be comprehensively compiled, but a few suggestions may be offered.

One piece of international action which can certainly bring pressure to bear on the South African government is the air boycott. If, even for a token period of three days or a week, all airline workers would refuse to handle planes to or from South Africa, this action will give the South African government a serious foretaste of the power of concerted international action.   One hears the opinion expressed in liberal quarters in South Africa that it is surprising this particular form of sanction has not been resorted to.

As and when incidents occur in some particular South African industry it will be possible to draw international attention to that industry in a manner sufficient to mobilise opinion against it. For example, an incident of victimisation in the South African fruit industry can result in the building up of a boycott of South African fruit exports.   An incident highlighting human rights denials in the wine industry can spark off similar action against South African wines.

The denial of facilities for South African warships or military aircraft and the refusal to handle any vessels known to be carrying South African military or paramilitary material is another possible form of action, already resorted to on some occasions.

It would indeed be useful if study groups keep up a constant surveillance programme with a view to pinpointing areas where current events demand the application of pressure. The methodologies for taking such action need also to be more carefully studied. At present the operation tends very much to be unmethodical and *ad hoc*. Lack of planning and system makes the whole effort far less effective.

E) *INDIVIDUAL ACTION*

One often encounters among individuals an attitude of resignation towards the inevitability of disaster in South Africa, with a consequent unwillingness to indulge in any individual action as futile. The belief is that short of action by states or large organisations there is no action that can produce results. It is submitted that this is misguided.

Some suggestions follow, which are by no means exhaustive, but indicate the variety of possible courses of action.

1) *Moulding opinion*

Trade unions, church organisations and governments reflect the viewpoints of the majority of individuals comprising them. The conversion of the majority to an attitude of concern is work which concerned individuals can undertake. There is little doubt that if the majority of the membership of such bodies as trade unions should be made aware from time to time of the realities of the South African situation they will be severely shaken. True it is, they know of the inequalities of South Africa in a vague and general way. They need more specific and detailed information bringing the realities to them in a manner they can relate to their own experiences. A pamphlet issued by the Black Sash movement is an example of the literature that can be circulated. There is an abundance of these in South Africa which the organisations concerned would be glad to make available.

WHO CARES?

IF...

> You lived in the homelands and were 15 years old AND---

YOU — were compelled to register as a work-seeker and had to continue to register until you were 65 years old ...

YOU — were placed in a category of employment which you did not like but were forced to remain in for the rest of your life ...

YOU — knew that your future working life would be totally controlled, with no hope of change, advancement or security ...

YOU — knew that you would always have to leave home to work because of minimal employment opportunities for you in your homeland ...

YOU — knew that you would always be separated from your family because you could not work and be with them ...

YOU — already had no hope for the future though still only a child

... wouldn't you care?

IF ...

Having registered as a 'workseeker' —

YOU — were still not allowed to seek work for yourself ... BUT ...

YOU — were forced to wait to be recruited by a recruiting agent ... OR ...

YOU — were prevented from working because:

> *. a recruiting agent never came to your tribal bureau ... or ...*
> *. you were not in the queue when the recruiting agent came because you did not know when he was coming or lived too far away ... or ...*
> *. the recruiting agent never chose you because you looked too thin, too fat, too old, too disabled ... or ...*

. *you were educated enough to want skilled work which is not available to migrant workers ... AND ...*

YOU — *were faced with the possibility of never being given a job no matter how much you wanted or needed to work ...*

... wouldn't you care?

IF ...

You were 'lucky' enough to be recruited — BUT ...

YOU — *had no choice of the place where you would work because your labour bureau only supplied labour to certain specified areas ...*

YOU — *had no choice of employer ...*

YOU — *had to sign a service contract for one year before you had even seen your employer or your job ...*

YOU — *unlike your employer, were given no copy of the contract which bound you ...*

YOU — *could be left with only R1.00 per month take-home pay because your employer was legally entitled to deduct all the rest for transport, taxation, insurance, accommodation, etc ...*

YOU — *had to be discharged from your employment at the end of your year's contract irrespective of your employer's wishes or your own ...*

... wouldn't you care?

IF ...

YOU — *had to live as an oscillating migrant for the whole of your working life — AND ...*

YOU — were never allowed to have your wife and children living with you where you worked ...

YOU — could only enjoy family life when you were not working ...

YOU — had to live in a unisex hostel while you worked ...

YOU — were subjected to a life without privacy, without comfort, without space, without heat, without security, without love ...

YOU — were constantly exposed to deficiency diseases, venereal diseases, promiscuity, homosexuality, perversions of all kinds, drunkenness, violence, theft and all the evils stemming from an unnatural existence ...

while your family was struggling in the home-lands ...

... wouldn't you care?

If you were the slave of a system you had not created ... if you had to be arbitrarily selected at a human cattle market in order to enjoy a privilege of working and earning some kind of a livelihood ... if you could never ever choose the kind of work you would like to do nor where you would like to do it nor for whom you would like to do it ... if you could never live with your family throughout your entire working life, but had to choose between being with them or supporting them ... wouldn't you care?

Churches, political organisations, local councils, schools, universities and wherever else community opinions are reflected and attitudes formed are fertile ground for such activities.   The articulate individual can interest friends, involve his minister of religion, activate his club, initiate seminars, petition his member of Parliament and grant his active support to movements aimed at bringing the South African situation before the public eye.

2) *Letter writing*

The individual's letter is a potent form of attracting attention to a public issue, and its value has been amply demonstrated in recent times through the work of Amnesty International. One of Amnesty's methods of action is to create an avalanche of letters to foreign governments, voicing the concern of the average citizen with denials of human rights by those governments. No government desires to project an unfavourable image abroad and the most apparently obdurate of governments have often responded to such pressure and released political prisoners or desisted from torturing them. The South African government, however insensitive it might appear, cannot be different and it is noteworthy that rightly or wrongly it likes to proclaim that it bases its activities upon considerations of morality. Nor, in the past, has it always been insensitive. A noteworthy demonstration of its sensitivity has been its reaction in the field of sport. If that government and its individual ministers should receive a regular avalanche of letters from abroad, these must cumulatively help in moulding its thinking. This is especially true today, when the need for urgent change is accepted by the government and its members, and they are in fact looking for support for their policy of change. Even in the most cynical view of things and accepting that it is power alone that concerns a politician, there are power considerations that arise from a constant delivery of foreign letters.

In one's own country, letters to one's own government and one's M.P. can be productive of results.

3) *Formulating Action Projects*

Consciousness-raising as reflected in the previous proposals must be accompanied by positive suggestions for action. The individual, either singly or through the formation of study groups, can analyse the ways in which some particular pressure can be made effective. It may be that he works in an organisation producing electronic goods or other defence-related equipment for the South African government. It may be that he is an active member of a church organisation, or a trade union, and that these organisations have contact with South Africa. At many workplaces, there will in all probability be some existing or potential point of contact with South Africa. These need to be explored.

4) *Education*

Current school curriculum planning rarely provides for anything beyond a passing mention of South Africa. The South African situation is a particularly rewarding study as one of the best possible illustrations in world history of a society built upon a negation of principles which mankind has taken many centuries to evolve and which are now regarded as axiomatic. Specifically, in civics, history, world affairs, politics, economics and every socially related study, South Africa can be brought in by way of illustration. Unfortunately, not all teachers are aware of the excellence of the material available in the context of South Africa for the illustration of the converse or negative of the principles which they teach. There is much to be done in promoting teacher awareness of the South African scene.

The individual who has devoted time and study to South Africa as an area of special concern must reach out to teachers. If he has undertaken a visit to South Africa he can arrange to give them lectures on his personal experiences. Speaking opportunities in teacher training institutions are not difficult to obtain. Nor is it difficult to arrange opportunities for speaking to the students in the schools themselves. The mere presentation of the unvarnished facts is sufficient to create interest and to generate a feeling amongst the audience that something needs to be done. Nor is it likely that the information will be superfluous or stale. The South African scene is in such constant change and flux that there will always be something fresh for the recently returned traveller to communicate.

Likewise, speaking opportunities are not lacking in service-oriented organisations such as Lions, Apex and Rotary. It is adequate if the presentation is a merely factual one, for the facts are often too eloquent for comment.

As part of this general educational campaign, the worker will no doubt familiarise himself with available books, articles and films on South Africa. There are many books that can be recommended for simple and easy reading and films that can be obtained for screening from organisations that have interested themselves in South Africa.

When possible, media talks and interviews should also be arranged. A steady supply of articles and information to the print media will also be helpful. If it can be arranged, a regular weekly South Africa feature or column will not be without interest.

5) *Fact Finding Travel*

Much has been said already in disparagement of holiday tourism in South Africa. Reference has also been made to the value of fact-finding travel in that country. Of the hundreds of thousands of persons who often give themselves a holiday on a palm-fringed tropical coast or the Riviera, if one in a thousand should decide instead to take a fact-finding tour in South Africa he will find his time more stimulatingly spent. For the individual interested in the humanitarian cause no better prescription can be offered for foreign travel. The cumulative results of such direct observation must make a profound impression upon their respective communities when they return.

6) *Liaising with Local Organisations*

Whether on the spot in South Africa or otherwise, the individual has much useful activity open to him in assisting service-oriented groups in South Africa who are already working devotedly for the emancipation of the underprivileged. It is possible by correspondence to establish contact with these groups — e.g. Black Sash, 37 Harvard Buildings, Joubert Street, Johannesburg, Dependants Conference, 1 Long Street, Mowbray SA 7700 — and to obtain from them the latest literature on the aspects of the South African scene they handle. Black Sash puts out an excellent monthly journal containing much relevant information and the South African Institute of Race Relations produces each year an information packed Survey of Race Relations in South Africa.

These organisations welcome assistance and encouragement in this work which is undoubtedly productive of much immediate alleviation of suffering. Whatever view one takes regarding the possibility or otherwise of a major settlement of the South African problem, there cannot be the shadow of a doubt that until such uncertain events should occur, there is much human misery that can be relieved. Assistance is needed to this end, which the individual can give both by himself and by interesting others in the cause.

Hopefully, this work will produce the effect also of making the process of peaceful power transfer more feasible.

7) *Investment Research*

Investment in South Africa sometimes proceeds as we have seen, from the most unlikely quarters. Foreign churches and universities are among these. These investments are often unknown to the public and take much research to reveal.   Some churches and universities have revealed these investments, others have not.   Their membership needs to know of these investments if in fact they are in sweated labour industries.   The problem of disinvestment then arises, which we have discussed elsewhere.

The same type of research can also be of great value in regard to the shareholdings of benefit funds, trust and indeed of all company undertakings.   The shareholders are often quite unaware of their investments.   Even if they are, these can be concealed under the multitude of corporate names which afford great corporations a veil of secrecy.   Investment portfolios, likewise, often contain a substantial assortment of South African holdings.   These need to be researched as far as information is available.

8) *Stockholders Questions and Votes*

Churches, universities and companies investing in South Africa need to be kept in a state of constant alertness regarding their investments.   The individual who has armed himself with the facts is very difficult to resist when he questions those in charge of these investments either by questions addressed through the post or by oral questions at meetings.

It is important that this questioning be responsible, and that it emanate not merely from those with a reputation for radicalism.   The wider the spectrum of membership from which the questioners are drawn the more telling will be their effect.   When bishops joined the ranks of questioners at stockholders' meetings they made a tremendous impact.

Even if the questioner should meet with a negative reply, the very fact that a responsible and informed question has been asked will be of value.   In their cumulative effect they can help improve conditions in the workplace, resistance to apartheid laws, greater recognition of trade union rights and reduction of wage differentials, to mention but a few.

Mobilising the shareholders' vote is another important aspect.   Shareholders often shut their minds to their moral responsibilities, taking cover behind inadequate government policies.   A good example of this was Kodak's annual meeting in April 1978, when a motion by some shareholders to curb further sales to the South African government was defeated by one hundred and three million votes to five million.   The Chairman observed that he saw no reason to go beyond existing United States regulations on trade with South Africa.[22]

9) *The Formulation of New Ideas*

An important form of individual contribution is the formulation of new ideas for the upliftment of the under-privileged.

In 1971 Mrs. Sue Gordon organised a series of meetings in various Johannesburg suburbs at which prominent African speakers addressed groups of white housewives. From this began the Domestic Workers and Employers' Project (DWEP), whose main aim was to bring to the minds of white employers the human problems of their domestic workers. The project spread to other centres and soon Church and other women's groups enthusiastically co-operated in the campaign. In consequence there were also set up Centres of Concern where courses in literacy were offered. In addition, 50,000 copies of a five-language leaflet were distributed to workers and a booklet was prepared for employers which sold by the thousand and in fact became a best seller.

Centres of Concern are starting a variety of new activities and performing useful services in numerous spheres which but for the initiative of the DWEP may not even have been visualised.

Likewise, the Urban Foundation, now disbursing millions of dollars in the cause of black upliftment, was a project that originated in the minds of concerned individuals. Once such an idea is mooted and attracts attention there are many who will help it along actively with time and money. Just as Amnesty International became a world force after it was conceived in the mind of an individual there is enormous scope for the initiation of new ventures in South Africa.

There are numerous other projects in limited areas which are awaiting formulation and implementation if only the concerned individuals can be found who will formulate them and transform them into action. A lawyer could open a legal aid clinic in a settlement like Crossroads which desparately needs not one but ten such clinics. A Chess Club could open its doors to members of all groups. A foreign town could accept an African settlement as a twin town as Rotary often does. Mixed committees could be set up like the committee of "European and non-European" dealing with child welfare, the blind and the deaf. Groups could be formed to give special attention to specific aspects of the black situation, such as the gross inadequacy of educational facilities, wage differentials, or the housing shortage. Visiting schemes could be organised for foreign scholars to spend some time in South Africa and especially in the black townships and the homelands. University bursary schemes for Africans could be inaugurated. Mixed projects could be organised in various activities such as music, dance, writing, pottery or painting, especially among the youth.

Three further illustrations of the work of individuals may be cited by way of illustration. In the 1960's, Miss Justine Pike, the Secretary of the Race Relations Institute, conducted a number of courses on administration in order to enable representatives of African voluntary societies to discharge more efficiently the functions of office bearers. The course of instruction included basic bookkeeping and related matters. The Cottesloe Conference was organised in 1960 by Fred van Wyk in order to focus attention on the Church's responsibility in the aftermath of Sharpeville and, many years earlier, Mrs. Edith Jones persevered and finally succeeded in obtaining full training for black nurses after lengthy negotiations.

At every level there are many areas of concern awaiting the individual who is prepared to dedicate the necessary thought and effort. Indeed the problem is not a dearth of possible areas of activity, but the very multiplicity of them.

F) *FOREIGN POLICY*

1) *A Rethinking of Western Foreign Policy*

One of the main obstacles thus far to a resolution of the South African problem has been the support, direct and indirect, given to the South African government by the Western powers — particularly the United States and the United Kingdom. This has given the South African government confidence in its ability to weather the storms before it and a feeling of buoyancy.

Whatever its policies it believes it will receive the necessary support from them in a crunch situation. This feeling exists despite the many pronouncements the governments of the Western world make from time to time in condemnation of apartheid.

Western propping up of South Africa results not merely from the fact that the Western world has heavy capital investments in South Africa. It results also from the way in which the great powers have been manoeuvring in recent years for a foothold on the African continent. In the tussle between Soviet Russia and the United States for influence in Africa over the last decade Soviet Russia has focussed its attention and support on liberation movements while the United States directly or tacitly gave its backing to the former governments of Angola, Mozambique and Zimbabwe. In those cases its support continued long after any moral basis for it had ceased, and the United States changed its stance, if at all, when it was far too late. It had by then become identified in the African mind with capitalism and colonialism, while Russia had become identified with liberalism and freedom.

The United States having lost itself the opportunity to identify with African freedom or liberalism in those countries is continuing to make the same mistake in South Africa. Its foreign and military policy in regard to the African continent is still focussed on Pretoria and all black Africa knows this. Consequently, in the ideological war between America and the Soviets, the Soviets are gaining day by day. Since every African movement for freedom from colonialism has received support from Russia, South African freedom fighters themselves look for support, ironically, not to the country where the freedom of the individual is enshrined but to the country where it is suppressed.

It is submitted that United States policy makers need to take note of the fact that a continuance of her current policies can spell the loss of her last remaining foothold on the Continent. It is not too late for an unequivocal American stance against racial discrimination in South Africa. The United States cannot afford to lose sight of the argument one often hears in South Africa that the Russians have no financial stake in the maintenance of the present South African regime while America has. If America is to counter this it needs a very special effort to restore its credibility in South Africa. Else the day black rule is achieved within the context of current American foreign policy, America would have lost its last remaining foothold on the Continent.

It is more in desperation than out of ideological conviction that African liberation movements have been turning to Russia. America would ideologically have been their first and natural ally. This advantage has thus far been tossed aside by American policy makers. It is not too late for a re-examination of America's commitment to the cause of freedom in Africa.

Similar considerations apply to other Western nations, especially the United Kingdom.

2) *The Clark Proposals*

Senator Clark, whose report to the Senate on US corporate investment in South Africa has already been mentioned,[23] set out in his report a number of policy recommendations to pressure US firms in South Africa to work for the promotion of change.

These included:

- No resources of the US government should be used to promote foreign investment in or loans to SA;
- Export-Import Bank Insurance and loan guarantees should cease;
- The US commercial attache should be permanently withdrawn;
- Visits to SA by officials of the Department of Commerce should cease;
- Activities of US agencies which may indirectly promote SA investments should be reviewed and limited where appropriate;
- Economic data and counselling should no longer be supplied to potential investors by the US government;
- Tax credits should be denied to US companies paying SA taxes if those companies failed to act in ways consistent with American policy towards SA (i.e. if they invested in SA government projects, the homelands or in border areas);
- The US government should refrain from endorsing any private organisations which promote US corporate investment in SA without adhering to the investment guidelines.[24]

The proposals, not amounting to a trade boycott or to disinvestment, have not yet reached a stage anywhere near significant implementation. Most significant of the measures thus far is the Export-Import Bank Authorisation Act banning all government financial backing for exports to South Africa unless the importer has endorsed and commenced implementing the Sullivan code. There is also a total ban on sales to the South African government or its agencies until the President has determined that there has been sufficient progress towards the elimination of apartheid. There is much more to be done along these lines.

3) *Nuclear Technology*

In February 1980 the United Nations Centre Against Apartheid named eleven countries as "collaborators" in

South Africa's nuclear enterprise – Belgium, Britain, Canada, France, Iran, Israel, Japan, The Netherlands, Switzerland, the United States and West Germany.

The statement was made in the context of information released by the United States suggesting that South Africa may have carried out a nuclear weapons test in the South Atlantic in September 1979. The South African government denied any such test.

Whether the allegations against the eleven countries are true or not, there is material in the report sufficient to put the citizens of ten of those countries upon inquiry regarding the collaboration of their freely elected governments in South Africa's policies of repression. The field of nuclear assistance is the most extreme of all forms of assistance that can be given and if there is substance in the allegation there is a grave indictment here of all the countries named.

This is an issue that has been causing concern for some time. In 1975 the All-Africa Conference of Churches (AACC), on the basis of published documentation concerning nuclear collaboration between German firms and the South African government, addressed the Evangelische Kirche in Deutschland (EKD) asking that it exert pressure on the German government to cease this collaboration. Bishop Class, Chairman of the EKD issued a sharp reply denying the charges but later German church leaders met with African Church leaders at the Nairobi assembly in December 1975 and issued a document stating that further investigations into the charges would be made.[25] The Nairobi assembly called upon its member churches in France, Germany, The Netherlands, Switzerland, and the United States as countries where firms doing nuclear business with South Africa had their headquarters, to make public to their constituents the political and military implications of nuclear collaboration with South Africa.[26] Other protests in this field were by the Netherlands Council of Churches in 1976 and by the Council of the French Protestant Federation protesting against Dutch and French collaboration respectively.

The issue demonstrated the importance of an information system for the churches, for without a base of information initially made available by other sources, the churches could not have acted.

It is interesting also that the U.N. report mentioned earlier referred also to the wider involvement of which nuclear involvement is only a part, in these terms: "South Africa has long been a happy hunting ground for investors from Western Europe or North America and, to a large extent, uranium mining and the nuclear industry are simply part of the pattern".

The report went on to note: "The regime is moving steadily towards an impressively rounded capacity, especially in the field of the treatment of uranium. This emphasises the urgency of international action".

G. *MISCELLANEOUS HEADS OF ACTION*

1) *The Bar*

Two non-governmental organisations which are deeply concerned with justice and fairplay are the church and the bar.

Just as there is a great deal the international church can do, so also there is much action awaiting the international legal profession. Lawyers throughout the world are dedicated to the furtherance of justice and the stamping out of iniquity. It is true — and unfortunate — that in affluent legal professions throughout the world there are many influential lawyers whose prime concern is their own professional and financial advancement and the upholding of property and privilege. Yet, no lawyer, when faced squarely with the issue, can relegate concern for social and human problems to a low ranking in his scheme of priorities. There are also many whose sense of justice is so acute that if they really knew the full depths of South Africa's denigration of human rights, they would make it one of their principal endeavours to redress these iniquities. The cumulative power of the world's legal professions is great. They may not themselves have political power, but they are the prime advisers of those who wield political power — as well as industrial power, media power and trade union power. There is no single issue on which the lawyers of the world can unite with greater readiness than the South African question. Yet there has been so little action on this matter so deeply concerning human justice, by those whose prime

concern is human justice, that one is strangely surprised.
There is much to be said for the view that every bar
in the world needs to set up a committee on apartheid, to
study the problem, communicate information to its fellow
members as well as the public, and devise ways and means
by which human dignity can be restored in South Africa. It
is true each legal profession has many problems peculiar to
its own country with which it must concern itself. Yet
apartheid is a blot upon the international face of justice
which is a standing affront to every principle on which its
own legal system is based. If it fails to take note of it, it
is showing less than the minimum of concern for the concept
of justice which is the very justification for the existence
of the profession. Failing in this duty, no bar can claim it
has demonstrated a broad-based concern for the concept of
justice.

2) *Use of Foreign Legal Systems to Counter Apartheid*

In the United States a small group of lawyers, The
Lawyers' Committee for Civil Rights Under Law, helped
various groups to institute a variety of law suits designed
to force the United States government as well as United
States citizens to reduce their economic ties with South
Africa.[27]   On the basis of a violation of certain sections [28]
of the New York Human Rights Law the New York *Times*
was ordered by the New York City Human Rights Commission to desist from publishing commercial advertisements
for employment positions in South Africa, on the grounds of
express discrimination towards New York residents. The
decision was reversed on appeal to the Supreme Court.
The Court reached its decision on the basis that the economic sanction involved was more appropriately handled by
the federal government and that there was an absence of
interest on the part of the New York *Times* to discriminate
about the use of the word, 'race'.[29]
The case indicates, however, a powerful and little
used sanction that can be resorted to under established legal
machinery. Other cases have used United States Federal Law
(e.g. the Federal Aviation Act) in order to force a reconsideration by the United States of its South African policies.
These possibilities are not restricted to the United States.
Wherever there is human rights legislation or machinery, this

can be done. For example, it has been suggested[30]that the European Convention of Human Rights can be similarly used as a means for combating apartheid. Thus if South Africa uses European media for advertising for tourists or employment, it is arguable that these advertisements are a violation of the human rights provisions of the Convention, and States may then be obliged by the Convention to eliminate South African advertising.   The suggestion is that although the articles of the convention are not binding on third parties, the nationals bound by the convention cannot be permitted to violate rights enumerated in the convention.

This argument is worthy of investigation by foreign lawyers as providing a new legal tool by which apartheid can be fought from outside South Africa. This may foreshadow the way to a new and more creative use of regional and multinational conventions.

3) *Scholarship Schemes*

One of South Africa's great problems is the black leadership problem.   The real leadership of the black community lies languishing on Robben Island, picked up and deposited there as the first spark of leadership potential shows.

How long these talented people will remain languishing one does not know, but in any event it is necessary to build up the next layer of black leadership.   This is especially important, having regard to the effective denial to talented young blacks of the best education South Africa can offer and by the closure of the white universities to them save in exceptional circumstances.

A useful step in this direction will be to render assistance to as many talented young blacks as possible who wish to go abroad for education or training.   The South African government permits a certain percentage of young people to obtain passports to travel abroad. If a hundred young persons can be assisted in this way, this will make a significant contribution which must produce its effects in five to ten years' time.

At present such people cannot apply for a passport unless they can prove they have obtained a scholarship. The number of those capable of benefiting from such a course and eager to go is constantly increasing. Sending a hundred such people abroad is likely to cost approximately 2000 dollars per head in passage money, i.e. 200,000 dollars. Maintaining them at the rate of 3,000 dollars per year will cost 300,000 dollars — a total of half a million dollars which in comparison with the magnitude of the problem is a mere bagatelle. Some of the rich industrialised countries professedly deeply interested in the South African problem, can each put up such a sum of money with scarcely any difficulty.

4) *Coalitions between blacks and whites*

There is much scope for joint action between the communities for the elimination of racial discrimination. An increasing number of whites realise that the age of apartheid is over and that Afrikaner nationalism cannot maintain its ascendancy for ever. Among the young especially, this feeling is shared by a large number of university undergraduates in all-white universities — Afrikaner and English. Coalitions between the more liberal whites and blacks for the elimination of race as a basis of South African society must yield results.

The present tendency towards isolationism of the different university communities must end. The author, at every university at which he spoke, stressed this idea, which was greeted with approval by the student bodies in the white universities. In the non-white universities however this thought aroused a reaction of scepticism regarding the readiness of white students to participate with any sincerity. It takes some effort on the part of white students to break down this initial resistance but sincerity and perseverance must prevail. If white students do seriously reach out to their non-white counterparts, they will be accepted, and together the student bodies will become a voice which the government must heed.

5)*Preparing the ground for Constitutional Change*

There is no doubt that a sharing of power will occur in South Africa. The question is not whether but when this will be a reality.

Since its inevitability must be accepted, it is wise to

prepare for it, for if it does not come with conciliation it will come with compulsion. Preparation means softening resistance among the whites to the one-man-one-vote formula which is now anathema to many among them.

One means of achieving these results is the preparation of many alternative suggestions which, while recognising the inevitable devolution of power, will attempt to safeguard minority rights. There is work here not only for lawyers but for lawyers and concerned members of the public, acting in joint discussions and seminars.

The whites in South Africa unlike those in other African countries have as much interest in the country as the blacks. Many of them have been there for three centuries and know no other country. They love South Africa as intensely as any black. They are too numerous to be ignored or pushed into the sea. They have too much expertise for any regime to be able to ignore them save at its own cost. Consequently it is submitted that the whites do not have so much cause for fear at the devolution of power, as the whites in other African countries. Their right to constitutional protection in the same way as other minorities will be gainsaid by none.

If there should be delay in the devolution of power the worst can happen and many white lives will be lost in the conflagration. If there is acceptance now, that "one man one vote" must come, this can be averted. The task of protection is a complex one, requiring a consideration not merely of law but of South Africa's history, and its ethnic, social and economic background. Indeed it would be wise for several alternative drafts to be ironed out in anticipation so that an indication can be given to the whites that it is possible to talk in terms of a Constitution which protects them and gives them security which they so much desire. Such a scheme needs to be elaborately worked out, having regard to the many ethnic groups involved, and to the question of their special territories. The Constitution-making problem is immense, and the more time and thought are devoted to it now, the easier the process will eventually be.

6) *Touching the Afrikaner Conscience*

The enterprise is often ridiculed of making attempts

to bring home to the Afrikaner the devastating effect on human lives of the government's current policies. It is true self-interest and the fear of reprisals stand four square in the way of change. Yet change can come if there is a change in conscience, and insufficient work has been done to reach the conscience of the Afrikaner. Every little that each person can do will add up in time to a mighty whole. To abstain from this endeavour on the ground that it is likely to be fruitless means only that the Afrikaner continues in his isolation, his conscience scarcely touched.

In 1979 novelist Elsa Joubert produced "The Wandering Years of Poppie Nongena", based upon tape recorded conversations with a black woman. It related the manner in which the pass laws prevented her from seeing her family for more than a few hours a week, her failure to qualify for a work permit and her resettlement in a homeland area which was completely strange to her, her husband's departure to Cape Town to earn a living because there was no work in the homeland, his inability owing to the migrant labour laws to take his wife with him, and the manner in which she lost a grandchild in the 1976 uprising, struck by a brick and killed while being carried on her back.

What is significant in this episode is the impact it made on the Afrikaner conscience. The Afrikaner newspapers gave it prominence and letters poured in from conscience-striken Afrikaners. Many claimed they had not known the situation was so bad till they read the book. White university campuses that had turned a blind eye on racial discriminations debated the book. Poppie became a household word throughout the country.

At all levels this kind of activity needs to be stepped up. No way else can the Afrikaner be jerked out of his vanished world into the realities of the present.

Every concerned South African citizen can contribute to this campaign. Every concerned visitor to South Africa can add his mite. Visiting journalists and academics have a special part to play.

One qualification must be made. The Afrikaner does not like to be preached at as many try to do. Understandably, he resents this and quite often counters such sermonisings with a reference to the moral wrongdoings of the country the visitor represents.

Yet the Afrikaner can be persuaded by reasoned

argument which shows an understanding of the Afrikaner
background.   The author believes he has achieved success
with a number of his students in this fashion and has persuaded them to views which they might not else have
considered.   He remembers also the strong resentment felt
by many at visitors who in a stay of two or three days make
little attempt to understand the Afrikaner but publicly
castigate him for his misdeeds, adopting a high moral stance
themselves.   Such attempts strengthen rather than soften
resistance.

The approach based on knowledge and understanding
is the path to the Afrikaner conscience.

This brief survey of suggested avenues of action is
necessarily incomplete and only a sampling of possibilities.
There are many more that interested persons and organisations can devise.   Each one of them may be inconsiderable
but in their cumulative impact they can be productive of a
change of attitude — and perhaps of heart — on the part of
the rulers of South Africa.

I have ventured the view in these pages that the government of South Africa is in matters of repression and apartheid to the right of its constituency.   For reasons stated in
the text the government is anxious to preserve the apparatus
and the status quo more zealously than a cross section of
white South African opinion would require.

I have ventured the view also that this white constituency from which the government draws its strength is
changing its views and that the proportion of those supporting apartheid is diminishing.   On surveys available earlier it
had reduced from four-fifths to two-thirds.   From two-
thirds to half is the vital transition and there is reason to
believe that the balance of pressure will significantly hasten
the day when this becomes reality.

At the time of going to press (late February, 1980)
there has appeared in the international news media a significant confirmation of these views.[31] A widely reported
countrywide survey by a market research firm commissioned
by the pro-government Afrikaans newspaper *Rapport* has
shown that seventy-five per cent of South African whites
want colour discrimination scrapped, while fifty-three per
cent are prepared to work under black people with the necessary qualifications and skills.   The survey shows also that

eighty-six per cent of English speakers want the racial barriers to go, as do sixty-six per cent of Afrikaners. The news item comments that South Africans are not as keen on apartheid as their rulers believe and that the survey provides food for thought for the Botha regime and ammunition for the opposition.

It is in the hope that the delicate balance on which apartheid presently rests is shortly to be upset and that this day can be hastened, that these suggestions have been made. It is believed and submitted that they are worthy of consideration and of trial.

FOOTNOTES

1. See pp.42-3.
2. Including the Cape of Good Hope Acts 15 of 1856, 18 of 1873, 28 of 1874, 7 of 1875, 30 of 1889, 20 of 1892; Natal Ordinances 2 of 1850, and 13 of 1852, and Laws 18 of 1862, 23 of 1865, 17 of 1882, 12 of 1885, 3 of 1891, 40 of 1894, 13 of 1896, 21 of 1907, 2 of 1908; Orange Free State Ordinance 7 of 1904; Transvaal Law 13 of 1880 and Act 27 of 1909. All these were repealed in their entirety as well as two Union Acts, 26 of 1926 and 23 of 1932.
3. See *1978 Survey of Race Relations,* pp. 336-7.
4. See pp.100-1.
5. On codes generally see pp.100-1.
6. See p.247.
7. *1978 Survey of Race Relations,* p.144.
8. For the figures see p.42.
9. *1977 Survey of Race Relations,* p.192.
10. *Op.cit.* p.188.
11. *1978 Survey of Race Relations,* p.149.
12. See Alexander Kirby, ed. *The World Council of Churches and Bank Loans to Apartheid,* Geneva 1977, for the full story of these loans and the banks' reactions to WCC enquiries.
13. For these details see Darril Hudson, "The World Council of Churches and Racism in South Africa", (1979) 34 *International Journal Race and Religion,* 475.
14. See pp.88-9.
15. See pp.103-4.
16. See pp.238-9.
17. See pp.236-7.
18. *1977 Survey of Race Relations,* p.187.
19. *Rand Daily Mail,* 21 July 1978.
20. *1977 Survey of Race Relations,* p.191.
21. *1978 Survey of Race Relations,* p.461, based upon *Rand Daily Mail,* 2 August, 1978.
22. *1978 Survey of Race Relations,* p.144.
23. See p.99
24. *1978 Survey of Race Relations,* pp.141-2.
25. Hudson, "The World Council of Churches and Racism in Southern Africa", 34 *International Journal Race and Religion,* 1979 p.495.
26. *Op.cit.,* p.496 citing Paton, ed., *Breaking Barriers,* pp.167-9.

See also Dejung and Zoller, *Nuclear Collaboration with S.A.* -- *Documentation on the Reception of the Nairobi Recommendations by Western European Churches,* (mimeograph) pp.2-3.

27. For details see *Lawyers Committee for Civil Rights Under Law,* Interim Report of the Africa Legal Assistance Project, Sept.27, 1974.

28. Sections B 1-7 .O(1)(d) and B 1-7.O(6).

29. See *New York Times Co.* v. *City of New York,* Commission on Human Rights 72 Misc. 2d. 1046, 362, N.Y.S. 2d. 321 (S.C. 1974) app'd. 374 N.Y.S. 2d.9.

30. See (1977) 12 *Texas International Law Journal* 279 at 280.

31. See *The Age,* Melbourne, February 26, 1980, p.8.

Epilogue

These are some of the thoughts that have passed through my mind after a brief visit to South Africa. They are recorded as accurately and as impartially as is within my capacity. There will no doubt be errors and inaccuracies in a work that covers so vast a canvas, but I hope these are minor. They will not change the overall message this book is intended to convey. I trust this account will carry home to the reader some at least of the impact South Africa had upon me. I hope it will cause him to take some further interest in a problem area which though perhaps far removed geographically, is as close to him as his very humanness — for it is the implicit denial of basic hummanness that lies at the heart of the South African problem.

When I visited South Africa, I was of the view that, since my opportunities for observation were in a sense unique, there was an obligation upon me to record my impressions. That initial resolve has grown beyond recognigition both during my visit and in the intervening months of reflection. I have seen more clearly with each passing day the urgency of the need to communicate with the world regarding South Africa. In my own case, despite prior reading upon the topic, my awareness has been raised to an intensity only possible through immediate contact with the problem. The millions outside South Africa who are concerned with its problems but have not had opportunities of seeing these problems from within are entitled to know South African realities of the sort set out in these pages.

I end as I began on a note of hope. As President Kruger observed, freedom will burst through in South Africa as the sun through the morning clouds. Freedom is a right of all peoples, not a privilege of the Afrikaners. As Kruger knew when he invoked it, it could not be denied to any group of people on grounds of race.

What we are now debating is not *whether* freedom will come, but *how*, for the lessons of history so vividly unfolding before our eyes in Africa are too clear for all but the most obdurate to ignore. Will the volcano of bitterness now simmering below the surface spew out its venom in an avalanche of destruction or will the concept of power-sharing be conceded with reason and goodwill? These are the only alternatives before South Africa and the world, for the relentless course of events has now closed all other avenues. Between these alternatives South Africa and the world must choose, and the time for decision is *now*.

There are many both within and without South Africa who say the midnight hour has already struck — that South African history must now be written in the blood of her people. Even at this late hour, when the danger signals are flashing all around and the forces of destruction are closing in, I fervently trust that it will still be possible, if only barely so, for men and women of goodwill the world over to stand between South Africa and impending tragedy. The path is difficult and calls for high dedication and resolve. There can be no doubt that it is worthy of unsparing effort.

I close in the words of an ancient Jewish proverb: "If mankind is not for itself who then will be? And if not now, when?"

Appendices

APPENDIX A

Farewell Lecture to the Stellenbosch Law Faculty *

Members of the Faculty and students of Stellenbosch, I am coming now to the concluding part of my stay here. It has been for me a very rewarding experience to have been in your midst. I have encountered the warmest possible hospitality from your Faculty, from the student body, from the legal profession, from the judges and from everyone whom I have met in your country and for all this I must say a heartfelt thank you.

Now, I have been told to tell you something of my reactions to your country. Of course, reactions to your country start before one arrives here, because one reads about your country in the daily press in other countries. There is often, every now and again, a feature in the daily press or over television and radio telling us something about your country. It is always very much in the news. In consequence, we all have certain ideas about your country, some of them preconceived notions which need to be corrected, some of them notions which are confirmed. I came here expecting to see certain things. I have seen much that I had expected, I have seen certain areas where matters are worse than I had expected and I would like to tell you of these reactions, subject to the qualification that my period of observation has been all too short.

I have not come here with preconceived notions. I have come here with as open a mind as possible. With the limited experience and the rather intense observation of the last few weeks I have formed

---

*This was the author's farewell lecture to the students and faculty at Stellenbosch and has been transcribed from tapes made available to the author by the Stellenbosch Faculty. The author wishes to record his appreciation of the complete freedom accorded to him to express his views without inhibition. In this the Stellenbosch Faculty more than honoured its assurance to him of complete freedom. It is here reproduced both as a tribute to the University authorities and as an indication of the scope for possible academic reawakening of the community.

certain impressions and for what they are worth I will give them to you. They are not being given to you in the sense of an outsider laying down views to you, or telling you how things ought to be, but merely as observations of a visitor who has tried to learn and observe and who desires to communicate his reactions to the people here at Stellenbosch.

In the first place, in regard to the matters that struck me as being more favourable than I had expected, there are quite a few of them. I find here lots of people who are dedicated to the cause of change, lots of people who are dedicated to the values of equality and freedom. There are many who are not content to keep these at the level of abstract idealism, but are working actively towards them. There is also a strong liberal movement among the University body too, which I am very pleased to note.

I have also met lawyers who have been devoting themselves actively to the cause of equality and freedom, very often to the sacrifice of their own interests. There are ladies here who devote themselves so wholeheartedly to reform that their lives are utterly absorbed in social service. I speak in particular of some members of the Black Sash movement whom I have met, who have made it their life's objective to work for the upliftment of the underprivileged people in this society. I have also met people who have worked in other organisations, but they are too numerous to mention. One group I met over the weekend, known as the Dependants Conference, is an organisation of people who have been working actively towards giving to prisoners and to their dependants something of human comfort. I was talking to some of these ladies over the weekend and I find that they devote themselves night and day to organising for prisoners on Robben Island at least one visit per year from a member of the family. They have worked to get down from however distant the homeland one member of each family once a year. But for this the people there on Robben Island, condemned to be there for the rest of their lives, would be progressively cut off from home and family and human contact. I learnt that these people who come once a year to meet their husbands or sons or fathers as the case may be do not have the opportunity of personal contact. They are separated by an iron grill, or glass partition and speak through telephones. Yet even that measure of limited personal contact makes a tremendous difference which keeps those people with something in the world to live for, whereas otherwise all hope might die out. I went up to the office of these workers and saw the way in which people have been brought from distances to see their kinsmen. I met a youth who had come 600 miles to see his brother, an eighteen year old prisoner, probably someone very like yourselves, who had been sentenced to a term, I was told, of 120 years of imprisonment. Since some of these sentences are to run concurrently, he has to serve a total of forty-two years of imprisonment. Now this brother had come from that far away homeland to speak to him for half an hour as his one contact with his family for the whole year. If you, with the devotion I have observed to prevail among Afrikaner families, should put yourselves in the position of those people — your own age group and your own fellow citizens — you will see what a tremendous service this means to the people to whom it is given.

There are many ways, such as this, in which people who are on the privileged side of society can work for the underprivileged and I think in a society where the differences are so acute, it is the bounden duty of everyone with a conscience to do at least that kind of work. So this is something I was pleasantly surprised to see and it is much more than I had expected. I have also visited the Athlone Office where people come with their pass law grievances and I found voluntary workers there, patiently noting the complaints of these people, trying to ring up and arrange legal representation and trying to see in what way they can be of assistance. While I was there I saw a stream of people coming in, "My husband was arrested on Wednesday, I don't know why. I don't know where he is, I don't know what has happened to him. I want to know where he is and that he is well".

A mother comes weeping: "My son was picked up on the road on Wednesday, I don't know what has happened to him, please look into the matter". A young man, almost too terrified to talk coherently, says, "I lost my passbook yesterday, I don't know what to do, it's a terrible loss, I lose my job, I lose my position here, I will be transported back to the homelands. What can you do for me?".

The ladies there — all voluntary workers, working with great devotion — make a note of these particulars, telephone lawyers, arrange legal aid and try to make some plan to pull these people out of their misery. These are some of the things I have seen which impressed me very greatly.

I also met white people working for the poor at Crossroads where there are so many hundreds and thousands of human problems crying out for attention.

I visited Crossroads last weekend in the company of a lawyer friend. I saw of course, the way in which this shanty town had been organised by the people themselves with their own informal local government organisation.

We thought we'd knock at some doors in order to see and speak to the people there and you as law students will be interested to know that within a minute of our knocking at each of those doors a legal problem surfaced. In one house we found a man who seemed to be in his forties who had been a skilled workman employed in some company for some fifteen or twenty years. While in the service of the company, he had fallen down two storeys and had seriously hurt his spine. He was almost crippled — he could just hobble along. He was certainly out of action as far as future employment was concerned. The company had told him that he would not receive any payment so long as he did not work. Now, that was a textbook case of workmen's compensation entitlement, as any lawyer would say. If any man deserved workman's compensation and had to be given it, here he was — but he had just no way of reaching through to the legal system that could have helped him, no way of reaching through to some lawyer who could lead him to the compensation that was his undoubted right.

The firm was quite happy to deny him workman's compensation and here he was, leading this life of misery, and hobbling around in his home with a legal system — an excellent legal system maybe — out there, supposedly giving remedies to people precisely in that situation. How could he meet a lawyer? He would have to go out of Crossroads, which is larger than a University campus. He would have to find his way to the city, which was eighteen miles away. He would have to make an appointment with a lawyer, and pay the lawyer's fee. Now, all this, while theoretically possible, is practically impossible. Far from leaving Crossroads and going to the City, this man could not even leave his house.

Now those are things that all of you can do. You are people who are to be the lawyers of the future. You are people who, when your time comes, will be serving society through your chosen discipline. Your chosen discipline is one of those disciplines in which it is possible to render tremendous service to the community in which you live. I say this, not merely to law students in your country, I say this to law students in all countries I have visited. You are in a uniquely privileged position of being so placed that you have the ability to translate good thoughts into good deeds, good ideas into good laws, good laws into actual remedies and reliefs.

Even if a country has an immaculate set of laws on its statute book, these laws are useless unless they reach the people for whom they are meant. You require bridges between the legal system and the people who need it, reliefs and remedies. Those bridges can only be built by lawyers and by law students and there is therefore a special responsibility upon you. I say that with all the earnestness at my command. A very special burden lies upon you, not merely to make a good living for yourselves as lawyers when your time comes, but to give of your skill and talent and experience to the community to which you belong. This community in particular has a crying need for precisely the kind of service that people like yourselves can give.

I delivered a lecture at the University of the Western Cape on Friday and I mentioned this very matter to them. The students told me — and I was delighted to hear this — that their law faculty maintained six legal clinics and one of the legal clinics was at Crossroads. Legal clinics are a potent means by which law students and lawyers can reach these desperate people who need the assistance of the law. If I may say so, I see this as one of the clearest duties of people who are to be the upholders of the law in future.

Apart from that, you will ask me what are my other favourable reactions. I have found that there is a greater deal of criticism of authority and of the government, in the press, than I had thought there would be. I know this is circumscribed and I know that there are various limitations on this in many ways, but still, what I saw was more than I had expected to see. I had not expected to see the outspoken editorials for example that I see in the daily papers here. I have also been pleasantly surprised perhaps to see the degree of academic freedom that prevails here. In this, I know there are certain limitations. It will not be the same academic freedom that prevails in other countries, but I notice that your lecturers and academics are fairly outspoken in their discussions and it is something I had not expected from outside.

I also notice as a very fine feature of society here, the religiousness, the intense religiousness, of people of all walks of life. This is something which it is pleasant to note, in a world where religious values are fast declining. The extent of the hold that religion and religious ideas have over the people here is something that strikes a visitor most forcefully. I have heard of events like the SACLA Conference where the various religious leaders of all denominations have come together in a common exchange of ideas of Christian fellowship and with the resolve to make South African society better than it is. And it is through sparks of fellowship like this and through the resulting interchange of ideas and through the resolve to do what lies in one's power to improve society, that lasting good can eventually be achieved.

I notice also active institutions like the Urban Foundation which are moving steadfastly to ameliorate the condition of people in this society who need assistance. I have also noted some efforts being made by the government to relax some at least of the petty restrictions which cause so much annoyance and so much humiliation to people in this country as well as to visitors from outside.

Well, those are all on the positive side, and those are features which one has to come here to see.

True, they all suffer from the limitation that they are acts within the system of inequality and do not seek to alter the system itself, but still they are important services which can help to change dominant attitudes. Most certainly they also relieve an immense amount of present misery. I for one consider them commendable, though I know there are many who denigrate this sort of effort.

A common attitude abroad towards South Africa and South Africans is, "Oh well, this person is from South Africa. Therefore he must be of the same views as everybody else there. We must have nothing to do with him". To give you some idea of how the rest of the world reacts, even when I was considering the invitation to come here to your University, there were many people who told me to have nothing to do with that invitation because, after all, it came from South Africa and everything South African was suspect. However, I took the view that dialogue is of the utmost importance because it is only through dialogue that you break down misunderstanding. If people at an intellectual level refuse to engage in dialogue that is a sure way in which injustice can become fixed. You have to open the windows and let the fresh air in on both sides because, after all, everybody is basically a human being with the same aspirations and largely shared feelings of right and wrong.

People entertain ideas and do things which seem wrong to others, not because they are inherently bad or wicked but because they see things differently. Consequently it is necessary to meet them in dialogue and see if they can be persuaded that their views are erroneous. I am pleased that I have had the opportunity of coming to your country, because I have been able to see so much I would not have seen, learnt so much I would not have learnt, and established a kind of dialogue and rapport which I am sure is going to be of great value.

Now, on the debit side. There is a whole range of matters deserving of criticism which I have observed here, which I must draw to your attention as the reactions of a visitor, seeing your country for the first time.

The first rude shock I had was a minor shock when I came to the airport at Johannesburg. I had been told that petty apartheid was being abolished and on arrival at Johannesburg airport, I did indeed find to my satisfaction that at the point of entry there was no differentiation in regard to colour in the passport area. All incoming passengers came in the same way. But my satisfaction was shortlived. No sooner we passed passport control and customs the colour differentiation began. I saw that even if I wanted to buy a newspaper there was a place for whites and a place for non-whites. There were white and non-white toilets and white and non-white restaurants. This was a rude shock, and the first time I had ever seen any such thing in my life. Apart from the injustice and the humiliation of the people of your own country, there is the humiliation of visitors coming to your country, or even passing through. It is a terrible black mark on South Africa, that in this day and age this blatant discrimination should continue. Today there is a mood of change in the air at least as far as concerns petty matters of that sort, and I think that enlightened and reasonable people in this country must get together and forthwith abolish that kind of petty discrimination which does so much harm. It certainly does tremendous harm to your image, and to your good relations with people abroad. Certainly to the international traveller, it is a grievous shock, at a time when the world is being told that apartheid is dead or dying. With all this annoyance, I would still class this initial incident as a petty shock.

And now for a rude shock. The first rude shock that I experienced, was when my friends at Cape Town took me on a tour of District 6. Now, there is very little to see in District 6 because it is all flattened to the ground except for a few houses that remain, but what shocked me was this. I knew of apartheid, I knew of the way people had been separated, but I never dreamt that it had been implemented with such a heavy hand. This was reminiscent to me of pictures of wartime London or bomb-scarred Berlin at the height of World War II. I remembered also the wartime practice of tearing down residential houses to create fire gaps for preventing the spread of fire from one block to another. Now that is what it reminded me of, and here in peacetime was a wartime phenomenon, imposed upon the people, not by a foreign enemy but by their own government. Its purpose was the separation of people who had been living in amity with each other for generations. And not only was it a demolition of bricks and mortar. Whoever was doing this was riding rough shod over human emotions and human associations. When you grow up in a district and live in it for fifty or seventy-five years, it becomes part of your life. You are wedded to that place. To have people, even aged ones, transported in the name of a differentiation of colour, without regard to those human emotions, struck me as being quite terrible. I have read in your Cape Town newspapers and elsewhere about the way in which elderly people were moved out — people who became gravely ill in consequence of being served with notices to leave the places where they had lived ever since their memories began. That was the first rude shock I experienced.

The second shock was the total isolation, one from another, of the component groups of your population. I am not referring here to physical isolation but mental and intellectual isolation. I have been speaking to students at all the three universities in this part of the world, that is the University of Cape Town, the University of the Western Cape, and here at Stellenbosch. At all these places I have been received with great friendship, which I much appreciate, and I have been able to exchange views with the student body and have thus been able to form some impression of their ways of thought and of their general reactions to the country's problems. It left an indelible impression on my mind that here were the elite of this country, the cream of the intelligentsia of your respective groups, the leaders of the future, all studying so close together, but all operating with scarcely any contact whatsoever. You have no inter-communication with each other, and though physically you are in the same province, mentally you are poles apart. Socially, you have no means of knowing how your counterparts live or react to social problems. There is nothing fraught with greater danger for the future of a community than that kind of isolation. Social isolation, intellectual isolation and physical isolation must be broken down. That is my view for what it is worth. This is a suggestion that I would like to leave with you — that it is incumbent on the student bodies of all three universities to reach out to each other and find ways in which they can meet and come to know each other as human beings. As the intellectual leaders of the same country, you must have something in common. You have the welfare of your country to talk about as a common topic and I think it would be the saddest thing for South Africa that this tremendous human resource, namely the intellectual power of all of you, should function in isolated compartments. As I said before, I believe in dialogue — dialogue between the people of South Africa and the outside world. I pursue that further into the plane of dialogue within South Africa and specifically between the undergraduates, without regard to race or colour. How else can you know and understand these other people in the midst of whom you are living? You should please make an effort through your student societies or other organisations you have, to meet and come to know your counterparts in those universities. It may be something simple, like a chess tournament, it may be working together, it may be a debating match — anything at all to bring yourselves in contact with these people. In fact, I may tell you that at the Western Cape they did say that they had tried to reach out to you and to the Cape Town students and that there had been a lack of enthusiasm on your part.

I would say also, that since you have been the privileged group, the burden is upon you to do this. You may meet with initial rebuffs because their point of view is, "Well, they have left us out in the cold, it is for them to communicate with us, and in any case we do not believe in patronising approaches. We do not believe in anybody coming to us without any real warmth or friendship". You will have to break through that because that is something that has unfortunately been created over the years. If you meet with one or two, or three or four, initial rebuffs, please do not mind that. The willingness to have dialogue is there, if only you can reach through and break through that reserve. Once you break through that reserve, you will find them to be fine human beings like yourselves, having the same needs, sharing the same aspirations, and you will find that you have far more in common than you thought you had. There is no purpose in keeping society within these separate compartments, one living in a gilded cocoon, the other in a state of under privilege, and neither understanding each other. If I can leave one idea with you, it is that you try to communicate as much as you can.

The indifference of the legal profession taken by and large, is another matter that struck me. You will notice that I discussed this in some other lectures too, on the relationship between law and society. Law tends to be administered as a black letter subject. "What is the law of this country?" "Open a law book and between its two covers you will find the law." That is the way lawyers used to function in previous generations. All over the world it is now accepted that that is outmoded. Lawyers need to see the law in the field. It is no doubt useful to work out what Grotius or Voet said about some fine point of Roman Dutch law. That is good enough as an intellectual excercise, but it has its limitations if you do not concern yourselves with the question of how it operates in the field.

Shall we say for the sake of argument that a poor woman who has bought a loaf of bread finds some stones in it. There will be many fine principles in the law books about conditions and warranties and fundamental terms, but that is an academic discussion, unrelated to the poor woman's problem. Within the framework of your legal system can she obtain relief against the comparatively affluent shopkeeper who sold it to her? Are there small claims tribunals or consumer protection bureaux to which she can go without all the expense of a formal lawsuit? Must she always think of legal rights in the context of expensive lawyers? Are there adequate legal aid schemes that reach her? And what is the position in the case of a justiciable dispute between a poor black woman and a white bureaucrat who had driven her from pillar to post?

You don't find the answers to these questions in your law books. You will have to observe social realities and work out the answers yourselves. One does not know how many members of your legal profession concern themselves actively with these matters, but from all that I hear, the proportion is minimal. The lure of the powerful client, the luxury fees, the glamour of professional advancement — all these are difficult for most lawyers to resist. I trust that when your time comes you will be more mindful of these matters. Remember that the law in the field operates a thousand times more often than the law in the books. The law in the books may give us the guidelines, but we need to see how this gets translated in the field in terms of the rights and duties of human beings. That is something lawyers in this day and age are becoming extremely conscious of — I don't know to what extent, 'perspective' subjects figure in your university curricula, but I would submit that in university curricula throughout the world — and especially in a country with the problems of South Africa — the so-called perspective subjects are of prime importance. The philosophy of law — what are the ends of law and what is the nature of law? — is of prime importance. So is the sociology of law. One must be able to step back from the intricacies of a legal system and view it from a distance to gain a view of how it operates in society. There seems to me to be a great neglect of these aspects in this country both in legal education and in actual professional practice.

Consequently, when I see your highly skilled legal profession here — in fact, they were kind enough to entertain me yesterday — I think how potent a force for reform they could be if they collectively acted to set right the anomalies in your legal system. I have the highest regard for their ability and their integrity and their learning, but at the same time I would suggest that the legal profession in this country — and you will be the legal profession in time to come — needs to reach out from its enclaves far more than it has done. They should undertake upon a roster system the defence in civil liberties cases and should give of their time and talent to various other socially oriented activities. As Justice Holmes said, at the turn of the century. "Today is the day of the black letter man, but tomorrow is the day of the economist and the sociologist". That tomorrow dawned long ago, but legal professions the world over have not been sufficiently conscious of it. So, please try to turn your legal skills into socially useful skills. That is an important message I leave with you — a message more important to the law student of South Africa than of any other country I know.

Now then, in regard to your laws. I would first mention the pass laws. I have seen some of the practical problems that arise. It is difficult for you to understand these when you do not meet with the possibility of arrest on the streets, the possibility of being broken into at midnight in your home, the separation of husband and wife by law, the fact that a husband has to travel a thousand kilometres to see his wife. You do not know what it is to have to work ten years or maybe fifteen years to establish your status to live in this part of the country. You do not have the ever present consciousness that if you lose your passbook, you are in dire trouble and may have to leave for ever the environment you have lived in for years.

Now these are things which you would not realise because they never apply to you. Try, please, to get under their skin and see how it feels. This is one of those features on your statute book which, when one comes here, one finds terribly difficult to understand.

There is also your security legislation which permits a person to be arrested and to be confined at the Minister's discretion without trial indefinitely. Now, so long as one is a person to whom that kind of possibility is remote, it is perhaps academic. But if you live and move in a community where there is an ever present possibility of the midnight knock, and the removal of a loved one, perhaps never to be seen again, it is a different thing altogether. It is a dark shadow under which you live your entire life. To be taken out of university or out of school at that golden stage of idealism which young people in all countries go through, and to be imprisoned for that very idealism perhaps for life and without trial or even a charge stated — that is the spectre that hangs over your compatriots and contemporaries who happen to be born with a black skin. Imagine yourselves in their position and you will realise what a blot this legislation is on the statute book of any country. That is something which I feel, with all respect, needs very great attention on the part of the legal profession to have it removed.

I was delighted to read a speech the other day by a very distinguished South African lawyer, D.P. de Villiers, calling for a reconsideration of this law. He points out that these laws were initially introduced as merely temporary measures, justified on the basis of a very dire threat that the country was then said to be facing. Whatever the justification for their introduction, they were introduced as temporary measures according to the government itself. Today, fifteen years later, we find them still on the statute book with their intensity increased. Confinement without trial or charge at the Minister's discretion was first permitted for 90 days, then 180 days, and then the period became indefinite. De Villiers asks how the legal profession can continue to remain unconcerned when this continues on the statute book, and he calls on the entire legal profession to unite and do what they can to have this legislation looked at again. I am extremely pleased to see that there has been an announcement that a committee will be appointed to look into these laws. Viewed from abroad these laws and the pass laws are probably the laws that have brought South Africa into disrepute more than any others. These are the laws that people outside of South Africa just cannot understand. There are, no doubt, countries where there are many more arrests and arbitrary imprisonments and tortures and executions than in South Africa. We read of them in the news almost every day. One often hears South Africans point to this and complain that the world points the finger of blame at South Africa alone. Now, in the first place, two wrongs don't make a right. In the second place, those countries, however ill-governed, do not, by law, discriminate between people on racial grounds and subject one racial group to a vast volume of penal legislation not applicable to the other. In the third place some of those countries have done away with all pretence of law and legality, while South Africa has a long and rich legal tradition continuously maintained and a finely trained judiciary. In the fourth place nobody in those countries seeks to justify those acts on high principles of morality or religion.

Which brings me to my next point. South Africa is a country which has a deep religious tradition. Religion has helped to contribute the concept of equality to the Western juristic inheritance, and I have been at pains to tell you over the last so many lectures how this concept has evolved for two thousand years from the time of the Greeks — through the Judaeic and the Christian tradition. This ancient tradition of respect for the inherent dignity of the human personality and of equality before the law — the tradition that every human being must have the opportunity of developing his full individuality, and the tradition of equality that follows from that concept — have been the twin pillars on which Western legal systems rest. If you have these base pillars properly laid, your superstructure can be built and altered and corrected, till you get a superstructure that is suitable. But if the pillars themselves are not properly laid, then the superstructure cannot stand secure. It must tilt and lean over and eventually collapse through instability. If you don't recognise these principles you cannot claim, I would submit with respect, to be a proper legal system. Both these basic principles are missing in the South African legal system, although South Africa is part of the Western legal tradition and the inheritor of its religious tradition and its excellent legal system, moulded by Grotius and Voet, Vanderlinden and Van der Keesel, and all that galaxy of Roman Dutch lawyers. They devoted their entire lives to these concepts, and you are the principal inheritors of their work. Lawyers in

South Africa must seriously ask themselves whether they consider that they truly honour this great tradition. I say this again to you as the lawyers of the future. I leave this thought with you — do not be satisfied with something that does not appeal to your conscience. If you feel that a law does not accord with it, work as lawyers for the correction of that law. If you correct those laws, you are not only justifying your existence as a lawyer, but fulfilling your existence as a human being. That, I think, is a very great trust which is imposed upon you lawyer members of the white community, who are the privileged group among the privileged group.

With regard to employment legislation, there are many matters of injustice which need attention. There is the fact that employment is linked up with the right to stay in an urban area. If a black employee loses his employment, he often loses his right to stay here. Consequently the employer has a double weapon which in employment law anywhere else in the world would not be tolerated — namely the threat not merely of dismissing the men but the implicit threat that through dismissal the employee automatically loses his claim to live here. He would have to go back a thousand kilometres perhaps, to a place he does not know. That is a threat which an employer ought not to wield according to any modern principles of employment legislation. It means an employee will have to cringe and be servile, whatever indignities are heaped upon him.

The Immorality Acts are another feature of your statute book which the rest of the world does not understand. The world naturally cannot understand legislation which ordains that people who may be married in the eyes of God are committing an offence in the eyes of man if they live together. For example, if there are people, maybe South Africans, who have gone abroad and got married across the colour line, and they come back here, they are presumably committing an offence here. If a priest should marry South Africans because there is no scriptural impediment to their marriage, the law will punish them for living together though their religion says that is their duty. Your police force disturbs and invades the privacy of the home in order to enforce the Immorality Acts, often bursting in at dead of night.

Also, you have situations which, to somebody coming from outside, seem so entirely strange. Yesterday at the Cape Town bar I met coloured lawyers. Now, you will ask what is strange in that? I met coloured lawyers, people qualified to practise law at the bar of their country, people responsible enough therefore to handle the matters of others of any magnitude or complexity — but not responsible enough to vote! That coloured lawyer, educated enough to handle the affairs of anybody, is kept away from all participation in the affairs of his country. On what basis? Not lack of competence or understanding, surely, but merely because of his race and colour. He has no right to live in an area where his colleagues of other communities live. If he is black and lives in a black settlement he will not even be able to invite them home to dinner without police permission. These are things a visitor finds very difficult to understand.

One thing that human beings cherish most dearly is their human dignity. Black or white, there are common longings which all persons share alike. You like to have a job, to have a secure home, to enjoy the comfort and society of wife and children, to feel the warmth of love and affection in your family circle. I am sure you love these things and you are fortunate in that you have them easily. These are things that the other sections of your community also would like to have, but they don't get them so easy. In fact the legal system of your country makes it difficult or impossible for a large segment of them to have precisely these things. I am sure you would not be party to that if you realised quite clearly the social realities that result from these laws. If you have spoken to a person who has come from a homeland and works here for fifty weeks of the year, or to the wife of such a person, as I had the opportunity to do at Crossroads, you will understand my concern. The women of Crossroads are there in protest that their husbands have to come so many hundreds of miles to work here for fifty weeks, without the right to bring their wives or children with them. The husband goes back once a year to spend two weeks with them. The children have grown up not knowing their father; wife and husband have become estranged. The man has to find twenty rand for his trip each way, that's forty rand. In other words, after buying a few presents for his wife and children, he still needs to have forty rand saved. The existing legal dispensation thus forces husband and wife to live apart. The men live in a unisex atmosphere where there are streets and streets of men only. The women back in the homelands are without their men, leading an unnatural existence which is a denial of basic human rights. The women of Crossroads sought to put this right by following their men and coming and living here. And what happens? They complain of the midnight raid, they complain of living in fear, where at the approach of authority they run away, whatever be the time of day or night.

These are the human aspects which to the eye of a legal visitor like myself result from your legal system. I would be less than frank if I did not tell you that these are some of the adverse impressions that are left upon a visitor's mind.

You will excuse me if I have been outspoken and frank. It may be that what I am saying is entirely without justification. You will use your reason and accept what I say, if it deserves to be accepted, and reject what I say if it does not deserve to be accepted. But I leave these thoughts with you in the hope that as you mature into the lawyers who will lead society in the future, you will perhaps carry into your work some little recollection of what I have told you today.

I hope you will be able, each in your own way, to translate these ideas into practice. I have outlined some of the ways in which you can do so and I do trust you will. Thank you.

APPENDIX B.

STATUTES OF THE REPUBLIC OF SOUTH AFRICA
CLASSIFIED AND ANNOTATED

TITLE: COLOURED PERSONS

TABLE OF CONTENTS

Preliminary Note

Statutes (Chronological)---

Coloured Persons Representative Council Amendment Act, No. 87 of 1970
Powers and Privileges of the Coloured Persons Representative Council Act, No. 91 of 1970
Transport Services for Coloured Persons and Indians Act, No. 27 of 1972
Coloured Persons in South-West Africa Education Act, No. 63 of 1972
Namaland Consolidated and Administration Act, No. 79 of 1972
Basters of Rehoboth Education Act, No. 85 of 1972
Nama in South-West Africa Education Act, No. 86 of 1972
Coloured Persons Representative Council Amendment Act, No. 99 of 1972
Coloured Persons Education Amendment Act, No. 53 of 1973
Members of the Coloured Persons Representative Council Pensions Act, No. 79 of 1974
Coloured Persons Representative Council Amendment Act, No. 32 of 1975
Rural Coloured Areas Amendment Act, No. 28 of 1976
Coloured Persons Education Amendment Act, No. 29 of 1976
Coloured Persons in South-West Africa Education Amendment Act, No. 30 of 1976
Basters of Rehoboth Education Amendment Act, No. 31 of 1976
Nama in South-West Africa Education Amendment Act, No. 32 of 1976
Rehoboth Self-Government Act, No. 56 of 1976
Coloured Persons Representative Council Amendment Act, No. 94 of 1976
Second Coloured Persons Education Amendment Act, No. 95 of 1976
University of the Western Cape Amendment Act, No. 127 of 1977
Rural Coloured Areas Amendment Act, No. 31 of 1978
Coloured Development Corporation Amendment Act, No. 33 of 1978
Coloured Persons Representative Council Amendment Act, No. 84 of 1978
University of the Western Cape Act, No. 88 of 1978
Coloured Persons Education Amendment Act, No. 50 of 1979
Coloured Persons Representative Council Amendment Act, No. 57 of 1979

This list of statutes dealing with one racial group, the coloureds, who are in many ways more privileged than the blacks, is reproduced to show the extent of purely racial legislation appearing on the South African statute book.

APPENDIX C.

Extracts from the Immorality Act

16   Sexual offences between white persons and coloured persons —
(1) (a) Any white female person who —
(i)   has or attempts to have unlawful carnal intercourse with a coloured male person; or
(ii)   commits or attempts to commit with a coloured male person any immoral or indecent act; or
(iii)   entices, solicits, or importunes any coloured male person to have unlawful carnal intercourse with her; or
(iv)   entices, solicits, or importunes any coloured male person to the commission of any immoral or indecent act; and

(b) Any coloured female person who —
(i)   has or attempts to have unlawful carnal intercourse with a white male person; or
(ii)   commits or attempts to commit with a white male person any immoral or indecent act; or
(iii)   entices, solicits, or importunes any white male person to have unlawful carnal intercourse with her; or
(iv)   entices, solicits, or importunes any white male person to the commission of any immoral or indecent act,

shall be guilty of an offence,

(2) (a) Any white male person who —
(i)   has or attempts to have unlawful carnal intercourse with a coloured female person; or
(ii)   commits or attempts to commit with a coloured female person any immoral or indecent act; or
(iii)   entices, solicits, or importunes any coloured female person to have unlawful carnal intercourse with him; or
(iv)   entices, solicits, or importunes any coloured female person to the commission of any immoral or indecent act; and

(b) Any coloured male person who —
(i)   has or attempts to have unlawful carnal intercourse with a white female person; or
(ii)   commits or attempts to commit with a white female person any immoral or indecent act; or
(iii)   entices, solicits, or importunes any white female person to have unlawful carnal intercourse with him; or
(iv)   entices, solicits, or importunes any white female person to the commission of any immoral or indecent act,

shall be guilty of an offence.

(3)   It shall be a sufficient defence to any charge under this section if it is proved to the satisfaction of the court that the person charged at the time of the commission of the offence had reasonable cause to believe that the person with whom he or she committed the offence was a white person if the person charged is a white person, or a coloured person if the person charged is a coloured person.

APPENDIX D.

A Race Classification Judgment

VERHOOG v. SECRETARY FOR THE INTERIOR

(Cape Provincial Division)

1967. April 30. van Zijl and van Heerden, JJ.

Population registration. — "Not in appearance obviously not a white person". — Test. — Act 30 of 1950, sec. 1(b), as substituted by Act 61 of 1962.

van Zijl, J.:   At this stage of this appeal it is necessary for the Court to make a finding in terms of sec. 1 of the Population Registration Act, 30 of 1950, in regard to the appellant's appearance.
  The Act has defined a white person as meaning a person who:
    (a) in appearance obviously is a white person and who is generally not accepted as a coloured person: or
    (b) is generally accepted as a white person and is not in appearance obviously not a white person...
In the second portion of the definition reference is made to certain other matters which do not concern us in the present enquiry and I have accordingly not quoted them.   The definition in the original Act has been amended by substituting the present definition which appeared in Act 61 of 1962.   Act 61 was signed in Afrikaans.
  The Court has had the advantage of seeing the appellant in this matter and has also heard two physiologists and anthropologists from Cape Town University who have testified as to the appearance of the appellant.   The Court must now make a finding as to whether the appellant falls in appearance under either of these definitions.
  In appearance the appellant is not obviously a white person. He cannot therefore be classified as a white person in terms of para (a) of the definition.   The enquiry then is whether the appellant is not in appearance obviously not a white person.   Now, the Afrikaans text of the Act reads:

"nie volgens voorkoms klaarblyklik nie 'n blanke is nie".

  The important word in the Afrikaans text is "klaarblyklik" and in the English text "obviously".   We have got to enquire into whether the appellant is not according to appearance "klaarblyklik nie 'n blanke nie" or according to the English text "obviously not a white person".   The compilers of *Die Afrikaanse Woordeboek* have not yet arrived at the word "klaarblyklik" but in *H.A.T. Verklarende Handwoordeboek van die Afrikaanse Taal* by Schoonees, Swanepoel Du Toit en Booysen "klaarblyklik" has been defined as "soos duidelik blyk, onteenseglik".   In the *Verklarende Afrikaanse Woordeboek* by Kritzinger, Labuschagne, Pienaar, Rademeyer and Steyn, "klaarblyklik" has been defined as "heeltemal duidelik: vanselfsprekend".   *Die Afrikaanse Woordeboek* in defining "blyklik" gives as one of its synonyms: "blykbaar", and "blykbaar" is defined as "duidelik te bespeur: wat geen twyfel oorlaat nie".
  My learned Brother and I then looked at van Dale, *Groot Woordenboek der Nederlandsche Taal,* which defines "klaarblyklik" as: "duidelik blijkend, onmiskenbaar, ongetwijfeld, ontegenzeglik".

290

The *Woordenboek der Nederlandsche Taal,* that is the big *Neder-landsche Dictionary* corresponding to the *Oxford Dictionary,* defines "klaarblyklik" as: "Geen Twijfel overlatende, overtuigend".

We also looked at the English dictionaries. The *Oxford* is far more helpful than *Webster.* The *Oxford Dictionary* gives the definition of "obviously" as being "clearly perceptible, evident, plainly manifestly". "Evidently" has been defined as: "so as to be distinctly visible or perceptible: with perfect clearness, conspicuously. Hence in active sense with powers of perceiving knowing, explaining, etc., without possibility of mistake or misunderstanding; clearly, dist-inctly". "Manifestly" has been defined as "clearly revealed to the eye, mind or judgment". In *Webster,* "manifestly" has been defined as: "capable of being readily and instantly perceived by the senses and especially by the sight; capable of being easily understood or recog-nised at once by the mind". "Plainly" has been given much the same definition.

From these definitions it is clear that the enquiry before this Court is not whether the man passing in the street would say: "this man is obviously coloured", it is an enquiry into whether this man in appearance could possibly be regarded as a white man. The enquiry is: "is hierdie persoon van voorkoms onteenseglik nie 'n blanke nie:" "is hy van voorkoms sonder twyfel nie 'n blanke nie:" "is die persoon van voorkoms omniskenbaar nie 'n blanke nie:" "can it be said without possibility of mistake that this person is in appearance not a white person". When this test is applied to the present appellant I do not think it is possible for anybody to say the appellant in appearance is "onmiskenbaar" or "onteenseglik" not a white person or that without possible mistake it can be said that the appellant is in appearance not a white person. The appellant may in appearance be so predominantly coloured that anyone seeing him would say he is a coloured person but he might still of appearance be such that if he associates with white people he could be regarded as white. If this is so then he is not in appearance obviously not a white person; "hy is nie volgens voor-koms klaarblyklik nie 'n blanke nie". The enquiry is not whether from appearance the appellant would generally be regarded as coloured. The enquiry is whether notwithstanding his coloured appearance the appellant could possibly be regarded as white, and I am satisfied it is possible that he could be so regarded.

In terms of the second definition the Court comes to the conclusion that the appellant is not in appearance obviously not a white person. The question whether he should not be classified as a white person depends upon whether he is generally accepted as a white person.

All the evidence goes to show that the appellant in this matter is generally accepted as a white person. The Court, having found that the appellant is not in appearance obviously not a white person, comes to the conclusion that the appellant is entitled to the relief claimed in regard to his reclassification.

The Court therefore orders that the decision of the Secretary and of the Board be set aside and that the appellant be reclassified as a white person. The appellant is given the costs of the proceedings in this Court.

van Heerden J., concurred.

Further Extracts from 1974 Synod Report
of the N.G.K.

Article 64.2 Points of difference.

There is, however, a difference of opinion on the role of church and state in the contracting of such marriages. According to the RES of Lunteren, church and state should not prohibit such marriages for they have no right to limit the free choice of a marriage partner. This conclusion is patently one-sided as well as an oversimplification of the facts. A marriage is in the first instance a personal and family affair, but it also has social, religious and politico-juridical significance; therefore, such a marriage does not fall entirely outside the concern of society, church and state. In the first two instances the "interference" would not be of a decisive nature — in the sense that society and the church would prohibit such racially mixed marriages. This does not mean, however, that society and the church have no interest in the contracting of such a marriage. As far as the church is concerned, it most certainly has a pastoral calling to warn against the contracting of such marriages in certain circumstances and in a particular social structure to which racially mixed marriages are foreign. This warning would be essentially pastorally motivated, in view of the unfavourable complications of such a marriage for the partners themselves, but more particularly for their progeny.

The position of the authorities in this regard is quite different. In normal circumstances it is certainly not the function of the authorities to interfere in the free choice of marriage partners. And yet it is quite possible and conceivable that the authorities would in certain circumstances prohibit the contracting of such marriages. In the stabilisation of relationships in a multiracial and multinational situation, the equilibrium may be disturbed by the contracting of racially mixed marriages and in these circumstances the preservation of "peace" in the Biblical sense would be of more importance to the authorities than the free choice of marriage partners by certain individuals. But this should at all times be seen as an extraordinary measure and this prohibition should, as a matter of course, be reviewed whenever circumstances permit it.

Article 65. Basic considerations.

In considering racially mixed marriages, one should take cognisance of the following:
Such marriages are physically possible.
Factors which impede the happiness and full development of a Christian marriage and those which would eventually destroy the God-given diversity and identity, would render such a marriage undesirable and impermissible. Such factors are manifest when there are substantial differences between the two partners in respect of religion, social structure, cultural pattern, biological descent, etc.
Such marriages are undesirable for as long as the impeding factors exist.

Article 66. Concluding remarks.

This report does not pretend to cover completely all aspects of the problems besetting South Africa.

The church has with much appreciation taken cognisance of the attitude and actions of the central, provincial and local authorities and of the relevant ministers, departments and officials of the Republic of South Africa and of other states in which the mother and daughter churches of the Dutch Reformed Church do missionary work. The church has also taken note of the massive task which has been successfully undertaken by these states, and of the progress made in the solution of the multifarious problems in our multinational country. They are assured of the church's sustained interest and intercession for the great challenges and problems of the future.

The Dutch Reformed Church is only too well aware of the serious problems in respect of inter-people, inter-racial and inter-human relationships in South Africa. It seeks to achieve the same ideals of social justice, human rights and self-determination for peoples and individuals, based on God's Word, as do other Christian churches. It is also convinced that it is imperative for the church to fulfil its prophetic calling, to be sympathetic, to give guidance according to Scripture and to intercede on behalf of man. If the Dutch Reformed Church does differ from other churches, the difference is not due to a different view of moral concepts and values, or of Christian ethics, but to a different view of the situation in South Africa and the teachings of God's Word in this regard. There is no difference in ideals and objectives, but merely disagreement on the best methods of achieving these ideals.

GLOSSARY

Afrikaans	Language of the Afrikaner. Derived from Dutch, grammatically simplified and with an admixture of African, Malay and other words.
Afrikaner	White Afrikaans-speaking South African, descended from Dutch and/or French Huguenot ancestors.
Afrikaner Broederbond	See Broederbond.
Afrikaner Bond	A party founded in Cape Colony by the Rev. S. J. du Toit in 1879 aimed at federating South Africa in one republic.
Afrikanernasie	The Afrikaner nation.
ANC	African National Congress. Founded 1912. Banned 1960.
Apartheid	Separateness (of the races).
Apartheid-baaskap	Separateness and dominance of the whites (an election slogan).
Armblanke	The poor whites. Mainly farmers moving to the cities during the depression.
Baas	Boss.
Baaskap	Domination, boss-ship (of the whites).
Bantu	A person generally accepted as a member of any indigenous race or tribe of Africa.
Bantustans	A "homeland" of the Bantu people. Part of the political dispensation worked out by the Nationalist Party for the segregation of the blacks.

Blanke	White.
Boer	Literally, farmer. In relation to the Boer war, the term was used to refer to the Afrikaner, in general. Today a derogatory term.
Boer War (1899-1902)	War between the Afrikaners and the British, resulting in the victory of the latter. Also called the English war, the Anglo-Boer war and the second war of independence.
Broederbond	The brotherhood of Afrikaners formed in 1920 and pledged to asserting Afrikaner supremacy in South Africa. Originally an open society, it later became a secret organisation of the Afrikaner elite. It is the most powerful organisation in South Africa.
Broederbonder	Member of the Broederbond.
Bushmen	Physically small aboriginal tribe, virtually annihilated by the trekboers through organised hunting parties in which adults were killed and children captured. In one such party 250 Bushmen were killed. Their remnants now live in a reserve in Namibia.
Die Burger	Influential Afrikaans paper founded in Cape Town in 1915. Its first editor was Dr. D. F. Malan who in 1948 led a purely Afrikaner party to victory at the polls.
Die Stem — "The Call"	South African anthem heavily laced with the symbolism of the trekker wagon. Of great emotional appeal to the Afrikaner rather than the English or other sections of the population.
Die Transvaaler	Afrikaans party in the Transvaal. Founded in 1937.
Dompas	The Pass and Reference Book.
Great Trek (1834-38)	See *Voortrekkers*.
Homelands	Same as the Bantustans.
Hottentots	Short, nomadic, pastoral, aboriginal people, closely allied to the Bushmen in racial characteristics and language.
Inkatha	A non-violent liberation movement committed to African solidarity and justice for all racial groups. Headed by Chief Buthelezi, and with a paid-up membership of around 200,000, it is the most powerful black movement in South Africa.
Jameson Raid	A march into the Transvaal of 600 troops, led by Dr. Jameson to support a planned uprising of the Uitlanders in 1895. It was one of the incidents leading to the Boer War.
Kaffir	Derogatory term for a black.
Kaffir op say plek	(the native in his place) — an election slogan.
Kraal	A collection of African huts. The typical setting of rural black African life.

294

Laager	The circle of ox wagons formed at night for the protection of the trekkers. Also used for a means of defence against the blacks whenever there was a skirmish. Hence — *laager* mentality an inward looking mentality.
Migrant labour	Labour from the homelands working in the cities and mines.
Nederduits Gereformeerde Kerk (NGK)	The Dutch Reformed Church.
Ossewa brandwag	(Ox wagon sentinel) — a militant anti-British group, particularly during the Boer War.
PAC	Pan African Congress organised in 1958 principally by defecting ANC members. Banned in 1960.
Pass Laws	Laws requiring blacks to carry Reference Books in all places, under pain of imprisonment.
Platteland	(prairie or rural). The Platteland seats are generally held by the National Party.
Rand	South African currency unit — approximately one dollar.
Satyagraha	(Indian). Passive resistance. Derived from *satya* (truth) and *graha* (fight) literally, fight for truth.
Shebeen	Pub or liquor shop in black township.
Stoep	Verandah
Stryddag	Day set aside to commemorate the struggles of the Afrikaners in the past.
Swart gevaar	Black danger.
Trekboere	Trekking farmers. They moved away from the Cape, and for three or four generations led a life of nomadic farming, over-grazing large extents of land and moving on to fresh pastures.
Trekkers	See *Voortrekkers*.
Tweetalig	Bilingual, i.e. Afrikaans-and English-speaking.
Uitlander	Foreigner. Especially used of the British settlers in the Transvaal.
Velt (or *veld*)	Open grass country.
Verkrampte	A term used to denote extreme conservatism and support of the existing order in South Africa.
Verligte	A term used to denote liberalism within the context of the Nationalist Party.
Volk	The nation or the people. Used by the Afrikaners in reference to themselves rather than the entire nation.
Voortrekkers	Afrikaners who went out from the Cape on the Great Trek to escape British domination.
World (formerly Bantu world)	African edited but European controlled daily paper.

Index